Hyper-Organization

Hyper-Organization

Global Organizational Expansion

Patricia Bromley & John W. Meyer

OXFORD
UNIVERSITY PRESS

Great Clarendon Street, Oxford, OX2 6DP,
United Kingdom

Oxford University Press is a department of the University of Oxford.
It furthers the University's objective of excellence in research, scholarship,
and education by publishing worldwide. Oxford is a registered trade mark of
Oxford University Press in the UK and in certain other countries

First Edition published in 2015

Impression: 1

Published in the United States of America by Oxford University Press
198 Madison Avenue, New York, NY 10016, United States of America

British Library Cataloguing in Publication Data

Data available

Library of Congress Control Number: 2015939291

ISBN 978-0-19-968985-9 (hbk.)
ISBN 978-0-19-968986-6 (pbk.)

Printed and bound by
CPI Group (UK) Ltd, Croydon, CR0 4YY

■ PREFACE

The study of organizations has become a major enterprise. University courses on the subject were rare a half-century ago. Now they are commonplace, and can be found in many fields of study: business, education, political science, sociology, psychology, economics, public administration, medicine, and public policy. These changes in academia reflect changes in the real world: organizations have expanded globally in number, complexity, and fields of activity, so there is more to study, to teach, and to assess.

For the most part, academic research "normalizes" the existence of organizations. It examines behavior in them, and aspects of their operation, but less often asks why they are there in the first place. The same is true of daily life. Mostly, we take organizations as givens, assuming they exist because they achieve some instrumental purpose. An exception occurs when people are affected by organizational expansion. A new requirement comes into place, and we are touched by it: perhaps we advocate it, but just as often we find it intrusive. As a personal example, recently our universities adopted, in the name of student privacy, the rule that we may not return our students' graded examinations in the traditional box outside our office door. They must be sheltered by us, or a responsible administrator, and returned individually to each student. At some universities, faculty must complete training sessions on these privacy laws. In another instance, syllabi expand to include matters like the rights of disabled students, or statements about ethics; some also include policies about course "greenness," or warnings about profanity. Some people champion such new rules and formalities as progress toward a more just and equitable world; others complain about "bureaucracy" and the ever-expanding administrators. Often, by turns, they do both, and both things could be true.

Although we frequently notice organizational expansion in our daily lives, and lived experience tells us that these structures are regularly inefficient or ineffective, there are few intellectual tools to help us understand why these structures exist and grow, and why they might systematically or inherently stray from their primary goals. The fundamental question of why formal organizational structures exist and grow has been marginalized in research. Organizational scholars largely take it for granted in their work, and study behavior and change within this widely accepted structure. A partial exception lies in aspects of the institutional theory tradition, from which our work derives, and in the related tradition of population ecology. In these lines of thought a core idea is that organizational structures—and by implication organizations themselves—arise from characteristics of the wider social environment, and that some of these characteristics reflect general cultural principles. So organizational structures may reflect changing social and cultural beliefs apart from functional or instrumental purposes. Thus the academic administrator who imposes the new requirement about returning examinations to our students derives authority from changes in the wider environment stressing individual privacy. Similarly, the professor who implements a "paperless" course draws on external cultural ideologies and rules about protecting the natural world. Perhaps actual or potential legal changes or formal policies lie in the background, or perhaps there is simply a professionalized concern about student rights or the planet's health that is proactively brought in by organizational participants.

Thus, the fact that organizational structures expand worldwide in many different social arenas suggests that this growth reflects great changes in the wider social and cultural environment apart from any internal processes and decisions within organizations themselves. More recent developments of institutional theory call attention, beyond analyses of the dependence of organizations on environments, to the expanding rationalization of those environments—the articulation of elaborated means–ends relationships rooted in such cultural frames as the sciences or general laws. Our administrative protector of student privacy rights is unlikely to be imposing idiosyncratic or locally developed imperatives reflecting a powerful dean or provost or president. The officer's authority reflects external changes in society—in the law, or other dimensions of the professionalized culture.

This book proceeds in two parts. In Part 1 we start with the observation that formal organization has expanded rapidly in the last half-century: in every country and every area of social activity, organizations grow in number and elaboration. Next we provide an analysis of the global cultural changes within which this explosion of organization occurs, and how they produce contemporary organization. Specifically, we discuss how cultural rationalization, which we see as involving expansion in scientific approaches, human empowerment doctrines, and education, underpins the organizational revolution. We conclude this Part with a discussion of the main vehicles that transmit culture into local settings; namely, law, accounting, and broad and extended professionalization.

In Part 2 we turn to a more conceptual endeavor. We work towards an extended definition of what is now meant, in contemporary social life and analysis, when people build or talk about "organization" and "organizing." Our analysis links the defining characteristics of organizations to the cultural underpinnings spelled out in Part 1, and discusses the consequences for the nature of organizational structures. We see the elaboration of rationalized organizational structures throughout the contemporary world as creating structures of surprisingly non-rational character, filled with externally generated internal inconsistencies.

Thus, our goal is twofold. First, we aim to provide an explanation for the existence and growth of organization, without assuming they are necessarily structured in the way that achieves set purposes most efficiently or effectively. A second, closely related, goal is to develop a definition of what it means to be an organization or to be organized in the contemporary world, and why organizing frequently involves inconsistency. To understand our efforts, readers must understand our uses of some core terms.

Organization: By "organization" we refer to a folk concept now highly institutionalized in society (which is why people can give dozens of academic courses on it). In this book, we start with a casual definition in Part 1 (Chapter 1), and then work toward an elaboration which we present in Part 2 (Chapter 5). Central components of the definition include: (a) to call a social entity an organization implies some *differentiation* of distinct component parts—departments, roles, rules. (b) These parts are set in an articulated *rationalized* relation to each other, depicted functionally as leading to clear core purposes and outcomes. There are vertical relationships of supervision, and horizontal ones of intended functional interdependence. (c) The overall entity is depicted as integrated and unified around its own articulated purposes. It is, thus, a legitimate *social actor,* choosing and producing purposive *social action,* not simply an inert frame for action.

To "organize" is to create a social entity with these properties, or to elaborate an existing entity along these dimensions. When our university "organizes" the privacy rights of students, it creates distinct offices and rules. These have hierarchical relations with formerly more autonomous professors. The offices and rules are justified by their functional contribution to the university as an integrated purposive entity—presumably aiding in effective teaching, although the exact link may be unclear, or ideological. Overall, the new arrangements slightly expand the identity of the university as a social actor: the university takes responsibility for yet one more dimension and outcome in faculty and student life.

A common reaction to any problem in the contemporary world is to say "we have to get organized." To be disorganized is usually a negative thing, promoted only by occasional artists and poets. The professor who complains about the cumbersome new method of getting examination papers back to students is clearly old school: celebrating an encrusted university—a traditional academic bureaucracy more than a responsive, responsible social actor.

In this book, we see organizations as deriving from, but distinct from, some older forms of social organization. As we see it—and as the terms are commonly used—bureaucracy is distinct from organization. Bureaucracy is rationalized and differentiated, yes, but it is not itself a unified actor in society. It is designed to be a servant of some higher sovereign: the state, the church, the owners, or perhaps a medical or academic profession. Those are the actors: the bureaucracy is their servant or tool. In contrast, a modern organization is itself a responsible and authoritative and autonomous actor: itself legally and socially liable. We use the term *sovereignty* to capture this autonomy, and the transformation of older bureaucracies into organizations involves the elaboration and exercise of much of it. Organizations can make decisions: bureaucracies can't (at least in appearances), but rather are to carry out the decisions of others. As we discuss in this book, a major trend in the world is for bureaucratic structures to become more like organized actors: to become accountable, autonomous decision-makers, responsible for their own goals and outcomes.

An organization is also distinct from an association. An association—say of professors supporting or protesting student privacy rights—may have clear purposes as a social actor. But it is unlikely to have, in any complete way, the rationalized and differentiated form assumed by an organization. But one of the most common trends in the contemporary world is for associations, new and old, to evolve in the direction of the formal organization: that is, they "get organized." Associations and charities now apply for legal status, develop mission statements, link these goals to resources and plans, and incorporate roles for management and decision-making.

Our work is on the rise of organizations in the contemporary world. We give an account of it rooted in the extraordinary waves of *cultural rationalization*. By cultural rationalization we refer to (a) the growing authority and legitimacy of scientific thinking as a basis for social action and structure in global culture, which is tied to (b) the expanded and standardized status of the empowered human persons as constructed in this culture. Both principles are transmitted through and reflected in (c) the worldwide expansion of formal schooling at all levels.

We see the expansion of this culture, and of the organizational structures created and sustained by it, as extreme: beyond the normal forces of economic interest and political power which themselves increasingly employ organizations as their media. Thus we see contemporary organizations, and many of their components, as rationalized and differentiated around relationships that make sense only rhetorically, far beyond clear functional terms. Indeed, organizations and their components are often curiously abstracted from realities. We see them as often integrated only abstractly around their identities and purposes; in reality, causal relations between elements can be transient and unclear.

For this modern expansion of organization beyond clear and visible and demonstrable functional relationships, we use the term *hyper-organization*. Sometimes, whole organizations seem to have this character—they are elaborated structures having little to do with the actual management of any activity, or the accomplishment of any clear goal. A consulting firm, offering advice on "management" or "development," might have something of this character—having a very unclear relationship to anyone's "bottom line."

Perhaps our organized guardians of student privacy rights, at least hypothetically regulating the way we return examinations to students, have something of this character. Their relation to any real activity is unclear, and their relation to any goals of the university as organization is very unclear. But similar structures are to be found in all types of organizations: the most hardened production firm now is likely to have organized offices and officers of very uncertain value in terms of the final products.

We present the definitions above as starting points. A main effort in our book is to elaborate them, and to show how large-scale social forces now construct the meanings involved in the modern conception of organization and organizing.

People today, however much they resist being foci of organizing activity, take organizations for granted. They believe in improving them, and see improved organization as the means to solve many social problems and attain many social goals. If they criticize the state organization, they imagine it can be replaced by even more private organization.

So it goes with academic thinking about organizations. Business school professors are in the business of expanding and improving purposive organizations. They are not training MBA students to be time-serving bureaucrats. The same is true, by and large, of those in more purely academic settings.

Many lines of thought and research related to organizations are critical; for example, condemning the way these structures enable elites to amass power, alienate, and dehumanize individuals, or become sub optimally inefficient and ineffective. Our point is that such criticisms tend to lead to the creation of more organization, not less, under current cultural conditions. Present-day people, and their academics, tend to believe in organizing and organizations. Attention to instrumental action in, and improvement of, organizations leads away from the focus of our efforts in this book. We try to explain, not the success or failure of particular organizational structures, but (1) *why they exist, exist worldwide, and exist in so many different arenas of social life*, and (2) *why, in becoming real social actors, they incorporate much internal conflict and inconsistency, which is difficult to see as having a clearly rational character and justification*.

Given this goal, our effort is analytic in character, not normative. We discuss a few normative issues in our concluding chapter, but these are secondary. We are interested in analyzing the major cultural shifts that create a world of organization, not assessing its virtue or value. That is the posture of this book, and the posture of its authors. Personally, we understand that organizations are created and expand to take on all sorts of tasks of radically varying value: organizations promote, and are constructed to promote, both great good and great evil. Every development in contemporary society is likely to take organizational forms. For this reason, there is no realistic way to assess the overarching morality of organizational expansion as a massive social trend because it occurs on so many dimensions, toward so many ends, in so many places around the world.

Of course, as with any of the great movements constructing the modern world, our academic and popular cultures are saturated with normative assessments. Some dominant ones stress the great virtues of rationalized organization, under the heading of "transparency." Now one can readily find analyses classifying all the countries of the world on the single dimension of transparency and its opposite. The alternative is often called corruption, and millennia of social life and culture are rhetorically swept aside under this heading. Ordinarily, any new problem or disorder discovered in the contemporary world produces great demands for more organization.

But in balance, it is also true that modern societies are filled with assertive normative claims against the rise and expansion of organization. Sometimes these are envisioned as located in the past—and sentimentalized visions of past golden ages, filled with individual craftsmen, doctors, teachers, and leaders, are routine in every field of social life. Sometimes they are seen as located in the future, sustained by new technologies of communication and cooperation. And often, they are envisioned as occurring in innovative structures in the present, for example with network arrangements replacing formally organized ones.

In this book, we do not espouse these sorts of view. We sometimes employ normatively colored language or imagery, but our purpose is to make clear the surprising and non-rational character of much contemporary organizational life, not really to normatively assess it. The pervasive character of organizational rationalization makes it all a taken-for-granted business, and we try to employ examples of striking contradictions to undercut the routine assumptions involved. We have a macro-sociological conception of the causal processes involved in the evolution of organization, but no overarching claims about the value of the enterprise, or about alternative arrangements in the past, or possible alternative social structures in the future. We want to explain, not evaluate, the "society of organizations."

ACKNOWLEDGMENTS

Many colleagues have contributed to our work, both in its long development and more immediately to the current text: we try to acknowledge much of this help in the book itself. Our work follows a line of theory and research on the ways organizations are built out of structures and discourses in their environment. It is thus indebted to foundational figures in institutional (or neo-institutional) theory, among them Nils Brunsson, Paul DiMaggio, James March, Walter Powell, Brian Rowan, and W. Richard Scott. It more directly reflects the recent contributions of a great many others working in this tradition in the United States, and colleagues in Europe such as Kristina Tamm-Hallström, Raimund Hasse, Georg Krücken, Renate Meyer, Kerstin Sahlin, and Peter Walgenbach.

The most immediate antecedents of this book are in the work of our colleagues Frank Dobbin, Gili Drori, David Frank, Hokyu Hwang, Ron Jepperson, Walter Powell, and Francisco Ramirez. These people have provided valuable comments on our ideas (and sometimes texts), as have Elizabeth Popp Berman, Wade Cole, Ann Hironaka, Wesley Longhofer, Michael Lounsbury, Renate Meyer, Charles Perrow, Hayagreeva Rao, Evan Schofer, Amanda Sharkey, David Suárez, Kiyoteru Tsutsui, Marc Ventresca, and participants in many seminars at which we have presented our work: Sciences Po and ESSEC in Paris; the Universities of California (Irvine, Berkeley), Hamburg, Vienna (Economics and Business), Virginia, Michigan, Utah, Constance, South Florida, Goettingen, Lucerne, and Tokyo; Harvard, Stanford, and Stockholm Universities; and several centers or institutes—EGOS, Scancor, Score (Stockholm), Max Planck (Cologne). Detailed comments have come from Frank Dobbin, Christof Brandtner, and a number of anonymous reviewers. Our work, as it has developed over several years, has benefitted from the ideas of many very sophisticated colleagues, and we are grateful for their help.

A variety of institutional sources provided funding for parts of our work, and we appreciate their support. For John Meyer, grants from the National Research Foundation of Korea (NRF–2011–330–B00194) and the Spencer Foundation (200600003), for Patricia Bromley, generous research funding and leave from the Master of Public Administration program, the Department of Political Science, and the College of Social and Behavioral Science at the University of Utah.

Beyond collegial and institutional assistance, we have benefitted from the personal support of many friends, close collaborators, colleagues—and our own family members. We are deeply thankful for their care and commitment.

▓ TABLE OF CONTENTS

▨ LIST OF FIGURES

While every effort was made to contact the copyright holders of material in this book, in some cases we were unable to do so. If the copyright holders contact the author or publisher, we will be pleased to rectify any omission at the earliest opportunity.

▦ LIST OF TABLES

LIST OF ABBREVIATIONS

AACSB	Association to Advance Collegiate Schools of Business
ACBSC	Accreditation Council for Business Schools and Colleges
CDP	Carbon Disclosure Project
CEO	Chief Executive Officer
CFO	Chief Financial Officer
CR	corporate responsibility
CSR	corporate social responsibility
ERG	Employee Resource Group
FASEB	Federation of American Societies for Experimental Biology
FLA	Fair Labor Association
GER	Gross Enrollment Rate
GRI	Global Reporting Initiative
IACBE	International Assembly for Collegiate Business Education
IEA	International Association for the Evaluation of Educational Achievement
IFC	International Finance Corporation
IGO	inter-governmental organization
INGO	international non-governmental organization
ISO	International Organization for Standardization
LEED	Leadership in Energy and Environmental Design
LGBT	lesbian, gay, bisexual, transgender
MBA	Master of Business Administration
MNC	multi-national corporation
MOOCs	Massive Open Online Courses
MSMEs	micro, small, and medium enterprises
NEAT	Nike Environmental Action Team
NGO	non-governmental organization
NICs	Newly Industrializing Countries
OECD	Organization for Economic Cooperation and Development
PISA	Programme for International Student Assessment
PWC	PriceWaterhouseCoopers
S&P 500	Standard and Poor's 500 Index
SERRV	Sales Exchange for Refugee Rehabilitation and Vocation

SHAPE	Safety, Health, Attitudes of Management, People Investment and Environment
TIMSS	Trends in International Mathematics and Science Study
UBASE	Project on Universal Basic and Secondary Education
UK	United Kingdom
UN	United Nations
UNCTAD	United Nations Conference on Trade and Development
UNESCO	United Nations Educational, Scientific, and Cultural Organization
US	United States

1 Organization and hyper-organization

The expansion of rationalized formal organization is an extraordinary feature of recent decades—and indeed the whole period since the end of World War II. New organizations arise at great rates. Existing structures gain in complexity, becoming "more organized." Expansion is especially characteristic of domains formerly seen as informal or unclear, like planning or human resource management. The changes occur worldwide, so that organizations now routinely appear in the most peripheral countries. They occur in the widest variety of social sectors or fields: businesses, government agencies, and entities in what is now called the non-profit sector, all take shape as what we recognize as formal organizations. Religious and recreational bodies, medical, educational, and charitable structures shift from their earlier distinct designations and arrangements (e.g., as firms or schools or hospitals) to the template of the formal organization, and rapidly acquire the trappings of this general model. A school district, university, or government agency, in becoming "an organization," will likely take on structural characteristics that would not have been there a few decades ago—formal planning, human resource management, environmental protection, and indeed management itself. In both traditional organizations and these newly structured ones, human activities across a wide range become "organized", and there are managers, planners and planning, student or client services personnel, safety and environmental protection and reporting officers, and human resources staff. These people explicitly structure matters formerly not organized: performance measurement, benchmarking, vision and ethics statements, and so on.[1]

Because organizational expansion is so extreme, reaching countries and social sectors worldwide, and covering activities so far removed from traditional functional political and economic activities, the changes transcend anything that the traditional economic and political theories can explain. In fact, the rapidly growing field of organizational studies tends to focus on the behavior of people in and around organizations—not why its object of study exists and grows so rapidly.

In our view, the changes can best be seen as reflecting a great cultural wave, or a studied preference for organization over and above any specific functional requirements, resulting in a "Cambrian explosion" of organizing.[2] Much of the typical modern organization so exceeds the basic structuring of productive activity that we can think of it as hyper-organization, by which we mean the extension of organization into realms difficult to define and measure, and difficult to assess as contributing to any clear goal. In hyper-organized contexts the ties between formal structure and specific political or production outcomes stem more from cultural rules than knowable or observable causal chains.

A striking feature of contemporary organization theory is that little of it directly examines the existence and essential features of all these organizations and the organizing work that produces them. Many scholars study individuals inside organizations, some look at social movements, and others examine network or exchange relationships, but few problematize the rise of organizations.[3] The lack of research on why organizations exist is surprising, given they reflect a relatively new model of social structure and have infiltrated nearly every aspect of contemporary life. As management guru Peter Drucker has pointed out, the word "organization" as we understand it today found its way into the *Concise Oxford Dictionary* only about 1950.[4] Organization theorists often admit that it is odd so little is known about why the object of their study exists, and sometimes they worry about how the deficiency of knowledge will hamper the field's progress.[5] Even more anxiously, others fear that because organizations have few critics, they are silently becoming the central source of power and inequality in society.[6] The lack of research and theory about the rise of organizations may stem in part from their great legitimacy: these structures are so prevalent that they hardly seem in need of explanation. But it is because of the dramatic growth and widespread acceptance of organizations that we need to direct attention to understanding why these entities exist and what is now meant by their label. Motivated by the field's lack of clarity about its main subject of investigation, in this book we focus on several core questions: Why do organizations exist? What explains their global expansion in so many sectors in recent decades? What expands the extensions of their rationalized structures into so many arenas of activity (e.g., management)? What are the essential features that distinguish them from other forms of social structure?

This book addresses these questions in two main parts. In Part 1 we illustrate the scope and scale of the contemporary organizational revolution, then discuss its emergence from cultural shifts, especially in the past half century. We also discuss main pathways through which these cultural underpinnings transform local settings. In Part 2 we turn to a more conceptual endeavor; spelling out what organization comes to mean, as people adopt it around the world. We argue that "organization" is a dominant cultural model, with clear cultural origins. This view helps us understand many features of the contemporary organizational revolution, and helps explain why the organizational idea extends to so many unlikely places in the world, institutional sectors from religion to states to businesses, and activities far removed from ordinary work. "Organization" is a dominant theme in the contemporary world;

a model as much or more than a practical reality, extending far beyond a specific set of practices.

To begin, we suggest some features that seem to be central to contemporary conceptions of organization. The analyses in subsequent chapters lead to a more complete depiction of this cultural model, presented in Part 2. One defining feature is rationalization (and consequent rationalized differentiation).[7] Organizations formally articulate means–ends relationships on more dimensions than other structures do, through everything from planning to differentiated work technologies, to inventory management. A second defining feature is that they are attributed with actorhood. We develop the concept of organizational actorhood later in the book, but as a starting point it highlights that organizations have sovereign accountability in legal and moral terms, and they are expected to define their own boundaries, purposes, and responsibilities.[8] Further, they create formal control systems linking people and activities to central decisions.

We see organizational expansion and the core features of these entities as arising more from problems of cultural integration in an expanding and globalizing social world than from alternative sources such as the pressures of practical life in polity and economy. In a chaotic and now globalized world, the expansion of scientific and quasi-scientific thought and action as a fundamental cultural principle helps bring rational order to areas of uncertainty and supports much formal organization.[9] Further, the expanded authority and capacity attributed to the individual human person creates entitled people who can, far across national boundaries, build and participate in organizations.[10] The contemporary worldwide educational revolution locates and merges these elements in the social structure, creating massive numbers of people with relatively common schooling in a rationalized culture.[11] Waves of legalization and professionalization press organization building in more local settings, and the contemporary expansion of a range of principles of accounting and financialization creates an available shared language of rationality. Given all these pressures and resources, organizing and organizations expand and become more complex. As a result, organizations, putatively dedicated to clear purposes, build a surprising degree of internal inconsistency and incoherence into their structures. In contemporary organizations there are often loose connections between formal structures, daily practices, and intended outputs. The links between all the various organizational components and activities are similarly weak.[12] These problems make up grist for business schools and furnish much of the rationale for modern managerialism, which can be seen to specialize in the integration of formerly incompatible elements, activities, and obligations.

A cultural explanation accounts more fully for the diffuse character of the contemporary organizing wave than two common alternative views. One view supposes that organization exists because it is the optimal way to achieve (often economic) goals that require collective action, and the other supposes that it expands to serve the interests of powerful elites in social control.[13] Forces of local power and interest clearly do operate to construct formal organizations, but so do many other forces, including those that resist dominant powers and interests: every institution in contemporary society becomes more organized. While organizational expansions reflect pressures for efficient coordination and control, they also often reflect efforts to resist efficiency (in the name, for instance, of environmental protection or human rights), so organizing structures may do little to improve performance related to core goals. Neither of the alternative approaches explains why the rise of organization occurs in a wave that is concentrated in a narrow post-war time period and spreads across countries and social sectors. Further, neither can readily explain the expansion of modern organization into areas (e.g., human resource management) difficult to see as reflecting obvious functional requirements or producing clear functional consequences.

In each social sector—charities, businesses, government agencies, religious denominations, hospitals, schools, and so on—we can find immediate and local theories. These have a functional cast—they depict pressures that make organization "make sense," often as a strategy of elite political control over large-scale social activity or for effectiveness in competitive markets. But it is difficult to make this case about the worldwide expansions in so many countries and social sectors. The web of organization reaches across sectors in any national society, and extends from international professions and organizations down into the local structures of any given country like Lesotho.[14]

Both the academic literature and common culture recognize the phenomenon of organizational expansion. In both arenas, it is treated as an inevitable feature of the world—like death and taxes, in a darkened view, or like progress in a rosier one: in this book, we analyze the sources of the changes rather than emphasizing normative assessments.

Sometimes new dimensions of organization are a conscious source of complaint. People commonly confront conflicting activities and policies; fill out reports and mountains of paperwork for unknown or futile purposes; and struggle to stay on top of expanding and rapidly changing policies at organizational, professional, industrial, and governmental levels. Often, the contradictions and intricacies of organizational life are so embedded in social expectations of what a proper organization should do that they are little questioned. Few would doubt, for instance, that an organization should plan, monitor, assess risk, evaluate performance, track resources, conduct audits, and the like; although in reality the ability to do such things coherently is often far weaker than in theory.[15] Faced with any problematic situation, the modern impulse is to create more organizational structures, such as task forces, reporting mechanisms, or performance monitoring.

Figure 1.1. Dilbert Cartoon

Critical reflection in ordinary social life—perhaps after working hours, or informally behind closed doors—reveals common doubts about whether routinized tasks make clear contributions to any bottom line. Cynicism about the positive value of organizational elaboration may indeed be a necessary feature of contemporary life, even as people participate in the process or accept its inevitability. Many workplace commentaries found in popular culture are rooted in these observations: television shows like *The Office* or *Parks and Recreation*, or the comic strip *Dilbert* (see Figure 1.1). The common acceptance of organizational expansion is often balanced by an awareness of the inconsistencies between formal rule and practice, and between different legitimated goals and responsibilities.

Further critical reflection on the expansion of the organizational world calls attention to the social costs involved, such as violations of human rights and the destruction of the environment. There is a common sense that organization may mean a kind of corruption—a violation of transparency and openness, at least, but perhaps also the concentration of illicit power. Coleman (1982) and others describe an "asymmetric society" where great inequalities arise from the vast power of government agencies, trade unions, professional associations, and especially business corporations (as these clearly reflect private interests) relative to individuals and society. Speaking about organizations, the sociologist Charles Perrow comments:

Their size and power is troubling. Our economic organizations—business and industry—concentrate wealth and power; socialize employees and customers alike to meet their needs; and pass off to the rest of society the cost of their pollution, crowding, accidents, and encouragement of destructive life styles.... Big noneconomic organizations also trouble me. Big churches and school systems and local, state, and federal governments also centralize power, socialize employees to bureaucratic values, "de-skill" them unnecessarily.[16]

The bleak characterization is often incomplete. For instance, it becomes increasingly appropriate to assert that organizations should minimize the harm they do to the natural world and respect human rights—the modern organizational expansion in fact partly reflects such pressures. It is increasingly enshrined in law and public opinion that firms should engage in corporate philanthropy and corporate social responsibility (CSR), becoming broadly responsible citizens.[17] In parallel, "non-economic organizations" like charities are increasingly justified by their contribution to the public good rather than by how they fulfill private concerns or goals. For example, volunteering and charitable giving are now envisioned as paths for improving society rather than demonstrations of Christian mercy and means to salvation.[18] Similarly, educational systems worldwide are increasingly expected to empower individuals and teach critical thinking skills, rather than to socialize subservient citizens and workers.[19] Overall, instances of both progress and abuse abound, as every component of society from the most virtuous to the most defective now comes to be organized.

Most important for our purposes, critical reflection about what contemporary organizations ought to do generates still more organization as a control. New organizations arise to police existing ones, and new internal structures are created to increase responsibility for the goals and obligations that arise. A major theme of this book, developed in Part 2, is that an essential feature of the present-day organization is its incorporation of multiple and contradictory elements. There are inconsistencies between what organizations ought to do and are doing, and between the multiple goals they are tasked with. These complexities, we argue, are inherent characteristics of the organization as a legitimate modern actor, rather than a pathology or dysfunction to be corrected. Organizations embody much internal conflict and have dramatically non-rational qualities, not *despite* their rationalistic goal orientations but *because of* them. They are constructed as rationalized social actors expected to attend to many responsibilities, rather than rational actors built solely to achieve core goals most efficiently or effectively.

Arguments

In Part 1 of the book we outline our view of the expansion of rationalized organization as a cultural model or template as rooted in an expanding global culture. A dramatic growth of systematic, scientific thinking turns a world of vague threats and uncertainties into defined sets of risks calling for rational collective action. Further, the rights and capacities of the individual human being, now seen as an empowered (and rational) actor on a global scale, have exploded. These changes come together in an additional worldwide change: the expansion of education, and of models of education celebrating both rationalistic analyses of society and nature and the ability of individuals to manage them. Just as economic theories assume that free market capitalism is built on the existence of *homo economicus*, we assert that the organizational society arises from the creation of *homo organizationus*—individuals socialized, often through high levels of education, to embrace scientific thinking and human empowerment: core features of contemporary modernization, now diffused worldwide.

We see the overall cultural model as having direct effects on local settings. The global construction of rationalized formal organization as a preferred model for structuring social life has direct impacts on any local setting—the model serves as an available template in the widest range of locales. But the broad cultural shifts are also transmitted indirectly. Rationalization of the immediate social environment, in the form of expanding forms of hard and soft law, elaborate ways of counting and accounting for activities and goals, and the creation of many types of professionals, often force more and expanding organization into local sites. We review processes that transmit the overall rationalized culture into local social organization in Chapter 4.

Local settings vary in how deeply they are reconstituted by the diffusion of cultural principles that drive organizing. Consequently, there are differences in organizational expansion across contexts. In a few countries with longstanding liberal traditions, organizations have been a dominant feature of society since long before World War II. This trend appears most radically in the United States (US), but also in the United Kingdom (UK) and, to a lesser extent, in parts of continental Europe influenced by social liberalism. For example, formal legal incorporation, one indicator of expansion, has ancient roots in Rome and more modern precursors in Britain, but proliferated in the US in the nineteenth century, where it was applied to businesses as well as towns, churches, schools, universities, fraternal organizations, and other charitable groups.[20] Today it exists worldwide.

The cultural origins of organization generate a model of the "organized actor," which we spell out in Part 2 of the book. They produce several undertheorized dialectical processes which we assess. The scientized rationalization of nature and social life exposes every domain to the possibility of organization. Further, empowered humans, now seen as central and rational actors, have the ability and responsibility to recognize problems and act collectively and rationally in response. This helps create defining properties of the modern "organization": it is a collective actor, with an identity and purposes of its own rather than derived from individual participants or sovereign superiors.[21] It is also a rationalized actor, using scientific and quasi-scientific means to achieve its goals. Becoming a collective and rational actor in society means having the right to pursue goals, but this autonomy carries responsibility, parallel to the national (or global) citizenship of individual human actors. Thus an organization's legitimation as a proper collective actor involves obligations as a member of society in general: becoming a legitimate organization means taking on many responsibilities that may be inconsistent with the pursuit of primary goals.

Understanding that organization is essentially cultural in character—a normative and cognitive model, more than reality, of integrated collective rational action—helps us understand two most central observations about organizations in the real world.[22] First, they claim integration, but tend to be astonishingly decoupled, policy from practice, structural element from structural element. Second, organizations, despite being modeled as unitary actors, have the widest variety of goals or foci, and commonly embody great internal inconsistencies and conflicts. The modern organization parallels Tocqueville's picture of the American individual—an empowered but deeply embedded conformist—formed as a socially controlled actor.[23]

Our arguments are rooted in a neo-institutional organization theory that emphasizes how external cultural characteristics constitute organizations and generate organizational change.[24] Most directly, we build on work by Gili Drori, John Meyer, Hokyu Hwang, and collaborators, especially as spelled out in *Globalization and Organization: World Society and Organizational Change*.[25] Our causal explanation of scientization and human empowerment as providing a basis for organizational expansion stems from this work. But we develop new arguments spelling out how cultural rationalization generates growing complexity of the institutional environment and creates unresolved inconsistencies in organizational identity and activities.

To illuminate why older social structures, like hierarchical bureaucracies, traditional firms, or informal associations, are becoming organizations, and how this process unfolds, we first provide background on three issues: (1) our approach to distinguishing between contemporary organizations and the modern social structures that are their precursors; (2) a brief description of the expansion of organization; and (3) a primer outlining where existing organizational theories provide insight into this organizational expansion and where they are limited.

Precursors to contemporary organization

Organization is a relatively new form of social structure, taking on current understandings of the word mainly in the 1950s. Figure 1.2 shows that the term entered common English usage somewhat earlier—in the period following World War I. Earlier, the term simply suggested a pattern. One might have discussed "the organization of pre-modern human societies," but this did not refer to a bounded entity, as in "the United Nations (UN) is an organization." To appreciate what is meant by contemporary uses of the word organization, we need to distinguish it from earlier modern precursors, such as states, churches, firms, charities, hospitals, universities, and armies. These older entities still exist, of course, but they are increasingly reshaped as

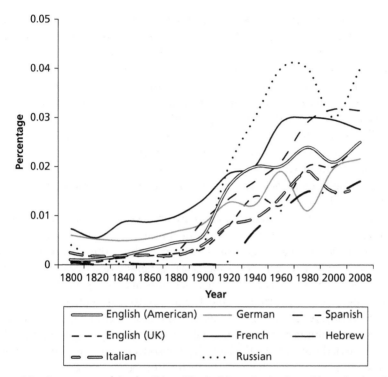

Figure 1.2. Percentage of Books Using Words "Organization" or "Organizations" (or Translation) in Google Ngram Corpus, 1800–2008

Notes: Specific search terms were: for American English (case insensitive—organization, organizations); English (UK) (case insensitive—organization, organisation, organizations, organisations; German (Organisation, Organisationen); French (case insensitive—organisation, organisations); Spanish (case insensitive—organización, organizaciones); Hebrew (case insensitive—ארגונים, ארגון); Russian (case insensitive—организации, организация)

instances of the broader category of organization. A traditional bureaucracy is not what is now meant by the term organization, nor is a firm or a charity. These earlier structures become organizations to varying degrees when they take on a set of characteristics that we spell out in this book. The transformation to organization is sometimes captured using phrases like "post-modern,"[26] "post-industrial,"[27] or "post-bureaucratic."[28] They especially capture the rapid changes since the 1970s, but reflect changes in the whole post-War period. The terms indicate a transition from modern societies dominated by structures like states, family firms, trading empires, and traditional professions to late-modern society in which organizations are fundamental units of order: an "organizational society."[29]

In keeping with everyday language, we use the word "organization" to describe both a process or set of practices and a bounded entity. Organization is often partial and can refer to certain activities or ways of thinking in structures that are not themselves complete, formally incorporated entities.[30] Phrases like "organizing" and "getting organized" are routinely applied to settings that are not officially incorporated, but still refer to the practices associated with formal organizations. For example, social movement groups and community associations can have relevant features: they are professionalized, or formalized; they evaluate outcomes, have routinized channels for governance, monitor their public perception, and perhaps employ full-time staff.[31] On the other end of the moral spectrum, it is now widely known that terrorist groups also use formal accounting practices and other organizational structures.[32] Even as modern individuals, we come to be more organized, hiring consultants or getting training to help us organize our personal and professional lives.[33]

Contemporary organizations had many predecessors, most directly in earlier Western history. Modern social forms in the background have substantial histories covering many centuries—entities such as the university, church, army, or firm.[34] The term "bureaucracies" generally describes many of these structures.[35] They were conceived of as servants of a sovereign: they lacked the autonomy of the organization, and the ability to legitimately generate their own decisions. A second central modern ancestor of contemporary organization is the voluntary association. Like contemporary organizations, these groups carried (and carry) the capacity for collective purpose, but they were weakly rationalized. To illustrate the distinction between these modern forms of social order and contemporary organizations, we discuss these precursors, bureaucracies and associations, in more detail. What is called organization, now, represents their combination.

BUREAUCRACY

Bureaucracy was (and is) conceived as a specialized instrument intended to transmit the will of a sovereign (perhaps including "the people" as a collective) down into society. As a particular bureaucracy was the tool of a sovereign, its nature and legitimacy depended on in which institutional sector it took form; such as a national or religious one. But the term also describes large firms operating under the sovereignty of an individual or familial owner. In partial measure, it also applies to the structures that arise under the authority of the old corporate occupational groups with special certified religious standing: the university and its professors, the hospital and its doctors, or the monastery and its monks.

Weber famously described a bureaucracy as having six qualities:[36] (1) Official jurisdictional areas are fixed in rules, laws, or administrative regulations that encompass the regular activities required for the structure. (2) In a hierarchical structure, subordinates are supervised by superiors; appeals of lower-level decisions can be made to higher-ups. (3) Bureaucratic structures are separated from private spheres in terms of resources, assets, hiring, decision-making, and documentation; written documents preserve the rules and decisions. (4) Placement in a bureaucratic role presupposes specialized expert training. (5) Conducting the affairs of the bureaucracy is a full-time career: official business is the primary focus rather than a secondary activity. (6) The structure is governed by abstract rules that are stable and are learned as a form of special technical knowledge. These characteristics help delineate bureaucracy from other structures that operate on alternative principles. We would add subordination to an external sovereign, with roots in authority and power, as a central defining element.

The expanding sovereign authority of kings, legislatures, and courts provided cognitive grounding and normative legitimacy for bureaucratic expansion.[37] Taxation, military control, religious standardization, and, later, welfare arrangements and family relations came under its scrutiny and direction. Even children eventually came to be governed by the authority of the school and the truant officer.[38]

Bureaucracies never worked according to the theory. The chain of command was broken at some point, as bureaucrats pursued interests of their own (now often called corruption) or reinterpreted rules in inventive ways.[39] Or rules made no sense in particular local settings and were ignored or followed only in ritual, with officials and priests repeating incantations in languages none of the locals knew.[40] Despite many deviations from practice, the ideology of bureaucratic control, carrying out the will of a sovereign certified by religious, racial, historical, or dynastic authority, has been central to modern societies, permitting social control, often successful, on vast scales.

Today, the term bureaucracy has taken a negative turn. And the term organization, with clearly altered meanings, comes into common (and academic) use, as designating proper rationalized social structure. Relative to bureaucracies, organizations are thought to be more responsive, flexible, efficient, autonomous, and accountable. Organizations retain the rationalistic orientation of bureaucracies in using formal structures to achieve goals efficiently, but substitute more associational structures for strict hierarchy and centralized authority and control. Instead of simple subordination to a single sovereign, organizations are accountable to multiple stakeholders. Instead of exercising Weber's "imperative authority," they operate through "management."

The transformation of bureaucracies is widely recognized. The absolute authority of military (or religious, or educational, or medical) leaders is undercut by calls for participation, choice, accountability, and transparency. In all social arenas, misconduct is less likely to be justified by the fact that it was carried out "under orders." Even the Catholic Church shifts from a ceremonial bureaucracy structured around charismatic authority toward a model where religious orders become non-profit organizations and the laity come to be more central.[41] In government, many changes occur, typically subsumed under New Public Management or Reinventing Government reforms.[42] Government bureaucracies have become "hybrid" organizations promoting decentralization and broadened ideas of accountability.[43] This often occurs via a process of "agencification," disaggregating public sector entities into smaller units.[44] In discussing government agencies, one scholar reflects the changing culture or ideology: "Post-bureaucratic organizations are those that have dispensed with the techniques, mind-sets, and values of bureaucracy. However, post-bureaucratic organizations need not be unsystematic or disorganized. Instead, within such organizations systems serve people, rather than people serving systems."[45]

In parallel, the prototypical corporate Bureaucracies, large firms, exhibit similar changes. There are many demands that the modern business organization should display corporate responsibility (CR), regardless of any owner's preference. Describing trends in businesses, one discussion captures the now-familiar ways in which these transformations are described:

> ... including, among others "Post-Fordist" organization (Gee et al. 1996), the "new work order" (Heckscher & Donnellon 1994; Grey & Garsten 2001), and "post-bureaucratic organization" (Heckscher & Donnellon 1994; Grey & Garsten 2001). The analyses and terminologies offered by these commentators point to a related set of ways in which they see organization as undergoing change. "...the reduction of formal levels of hierarchy, an emphasis on flexibility rather than rule-following and the creation of a more permeable boundary... as denoted by the increased use of subcontracting, temporary workers and consultants rather than permanent and/or in-house expertise" (Grey & Garsten 2001: 230). Heckscher and Donnellon expand on this list, offering nine features: worker participation through self-managing work teams; cross-functional task forces; multi-level consensus; information technology; decision-making capacity building; partnerships across boundaries; horizontal and vertical information sharing; negotiated solutions, and new managerial roles: leader, change agent, coordinator, broker, boundary-crosser.... Post-bureaucratic organization is not necessarily contingent upon [the nature of] work and environment [organizational context], but potentially exceeds traditional bureaucratic organization by being able to handle "a wider range of conditions" (Heckscher 1994: 16).[46]

Bureaucracies of all types arise under cultural frames that emphasize rational-legal forms of authority while elevating relatively few to the privileged position of sovereign.[47] Two important differences distinguish them from, as rationalized social structure, what are now called organizations. First is the locus of legitimated decision-making and agency. In a bureaucracy, that capacity inheres in the external sovereign state, owner, or corporate professional body. But in contemporary organizations the structure itself becomes a legitimated social actor: this actorhood inheres in the many managers that set plans, set goals, strategize, make decisions, and so on, on behalf of the organizational entity. Second, and related, is the status of individuals and interests beyond the sovereign. In a bureaucracy, the system is structured around the will and goals of people in power at or above the top of the hierarchy; others are expected to obey formal rules. In contrast, an organization has many functions and responsibilities, working through participation; people in differentiated, subordinate, and external positions have rights and powers that must be respected.

ASSOCIATION

Voluntary associations arose alongside bureaucracies and, in some cases, in opposition to them. Whereas bureaucracies are built around the obedience of bureaucrats and the governed masses to a sovereign power, associations arise under cultural assumptions of diffuse, and sometimes individual, authority. The common man (and, increasingly, women and minorities) could be, and was, empowered to participate in public life.[48] Therefore associational life and the principle of individual empowerment that underpins it were (and sometimes are) treated with suspicion by forms of sovereign authority such as state, firm, church, and army.[49] But with the Reformation and the Enlightenment, the idea and legitimacy of civil society became firmly established and associational life exploded.[50] Today, expanded voluntary sectors are widely taken for granted in many countries, and they are seen as forwarding many economic, political, and social benefits.[51] Globally, efforts to limit freedom of association are now decried as violations of human rights under Article 20 of the Universal Declaration of Human Rights.

A main distinguishing feature of associations is their ability to pursue a collective goal or interest on behalf of participants, which may be individuals or groups (or even national states). Unlike a bureaucracy, which derives legitimacy, goals, and interests from its sovereign, associations derive their legitimacy from integrating the interests and actions of participating members around a common aim. Many associations were built around religious goals, but civic aims were also important, as well as educational purposes and many issues of the public good (e.g., infrastructure, hunger, homelessness, fine arts). Another distinguishing feature, one that separates associations from collectivities such as families or tribes, is that participation is voluntary. This ability to exit reifies the role of participating individuals or groups in choice and decision. Initially, voluntary associations are especially characteristic of individualist contexts in Western history, most strikingly in Tocqueville's America, although over time worldwide more and more structures have taken the associational form.[52] Consistent with this discussion, the scholar Peter Frumkin defines the voluntary sector as composed of entities with three main characteristics: (1) they do not coerce participation; (2) they operate without distributing profits to stakeholders; and (3) they exist without simple and clear lines of ownership and accountability.[53]

Rationalization as well as vertical and horizontal role differentiation tended to be more limited in early associational life (outside government and religious structures that took the bureaucratic form). Whereas bureaucracies were built to serve one master, voluntary associations were created to serve many individual masters joined by a collective goal. Installing hierarchical bureaucratic controls has legitimation problems in the associational context; strict centralized authority runs against the founding principle of associations, which tends to assume that participants are constitutionally more equal rather than stratified and differentiated. Unlike bureaucracies, in voluntary associations the lines of ownership and accountability were (and are) unclear, especially across the roles played by different parties, such as members, donors, volunteers, full-time staff, clients, and board trustees.[54]

Importantly, a number of commonly recognized changes have occurred in the voluntary sector. Starting in the nineteenth century, the emergence of contemporary incorporation marked an important shift in the structure of associational life, with legally incorporated non-profit entities becoming central components of economies (e.g., professional associations), society and culture (e.g., public good groups), and political systems (e.g., towns and political parties).[55] Early in the twentieth century charitable work developed into a reasonable full-time career option, and the goals of many associations shifted away from notions of Christian duty, charity, and salvation and toward human rights and scientific approaches to curing social ills.[56] Over time, early informal associations became increasingly subject to formalization, adopting some bureaucratic features (e.g., written policies, full-time career positions), although they were not, by virtue of their collective nature, true bureaucratic hierarchies. More recently, observers have emphasized the commercial transformation of the charitable sector and reported on phenomena such as the creation of "hybrid" organizations, social enterprises, and social entrepreneurs.[57] Often these changing structures are depicted as becoming more like government bureaucracies (as they increasingly subcontract and take on formal structures), or more like businesses (as they take on practices designed to improve efficiency and effectiveness). Instead, as we discuss later, voluntary associations (and firms and government agencies) are reshaped by the emergence of a new model—what is now called organization. That is, many kinds of formerly distinctive social structures—firms, charities, and public bureaucracies—come under a common more general model.

We have emphasized bureaucracies and associations as illustrations of older structures in transition; analyses and descriptions of strikingly similar changes cut across many unique sectors of social life. The contemporary Catholic Church, for example, becomes pressed to deal with sexual abuse the way any organization would, through lawsuits, fines, and prison terms, and can no longer handle such matters privately as in past centuries. An elaborate litera-ture describes the reconstruction of medicine and hospitals.[58] Despite hetero-geneous health care systems, many countries experience similar shifts, with autonomous organizational expansion mediating between state and market: there is decentralization to lower levels of the public sector or to the private sector, and the rise of patients' rights.[59] Others analyze the rise of the univer-sity as an "organizational actor."[60] Scholars describe a shift from traditional entities with quasi-religious status to ones that are more socially embedded, applied, and consumer oriented.[61] Yet another rich body of work discusses the transformation of the professions; the classic professions (priests, professors, lawyers, and doctors) are changing to suit life in the new organizations, and new kinds of experts, such as university-trained managers, emerge.[62]

Our overarching observation is that parallel changes are occurring in once distinct social structures, turning them into instances of what is now routinely called organization. This combines the rationalization of bureaucracies (e.g., efforts to clarify lines of accountability and establish links between means and ends through activities like planning and evaluation) with the collective sovereignty of associations (e.g., the entity itself integrates the purposes of sovereign individuals and thus has its own legitimate goals, interests, and the authority to pursue them). On this latter point, James Coleman similarly notes as a distinguishing feature of organizations: that the entities themselves pos-sess a measure of sovereignty (although we would not limit this quality to legally incorporated entities):

the conception of the corporation as a legal person distinct from natural persons, able to act and be acted upon, and the reorganization of society around corporate bodies made possible a radically different kind of social structure than before....It [the corporation] could act in a unitary way, it could own resources, it could have rights and responsibilities, it could occupy the fixed functional position or estate which had been imposed on natural persons.[63]

Conceptions of organized entities like corporations as analogous to indi-vidual persons (fictive individuals in some phrasings) have long standing in a variety of legal systems.[64] The rise of the template of the contemporary organization greatly intensifies this tendency, illustrated by the recent US Supreme Court decision that private organizations have the right to freedom of speech closely parallel to the basic right of individual persons.

Organizational expansion

Alongside the transformation of older social forms, the number of organiza-tions has expanded in recent decades in what has been described as a

"Cambrian Explosion."[65] No single source collects data on the existence or growth in organizations around the world, and numerous challenges are associated with gathering such information. Indeed, there is no standard definition of the term, though an elaborate cultural conception develops in our current period. Our cultural arguments suggest that World War II and the current neoliberal era are important junctures in the globalization of organization, so it is only recently that it makes sense to begin counting and tracking organizations in much of the world. Over longer periods, counts of businesses or non-profit organizations across many countries are unavailable, untrustworthy, or incommensurable. Nonetheless, prevailing data from multiple sources suggest that a major social change has gone on in all sectors and around the world. In Chapter 2 we discuss in more detail data illustrating the international and national growth of organizations in numbers and internal complexity, in business, government, and civil society. Here, as an introduction, we show estimates of the expansion of international organizations, including multinational corporations (MNCs), inter-governmental organizations (IGOs), and international non-governmental organizations (INGOs).

International trading has existed for millennia. But the "markets" involved were organized under the aegis of national states and empires or supranational religious, ethnic, and familial structures, not formal organizations. Multinational corporate organizations, like the East India Company, were very rare until recent decades. Now there are tens of thousands of them, regardless of how one counts.[66] Their growth radically exceeds the much slower increases in international trade. By one estimate, illustrated in Figure 1.3, there were roughly 3,000 multinationals in 1900, and by the early 2000s the number grew to more than 63,000, with 821,000 subsidiaries spread all over the world.[67]

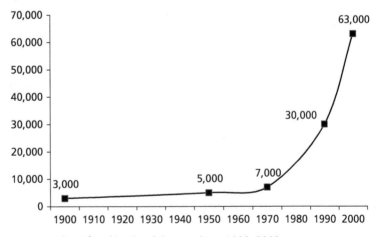

Figure 1.3. Number of Multinational Corporations, 1900–2000
Source: Adapted from Gabel & Bruner 2003: 3.

Generally, the data indicate that the number of MNCs grew slowly until recent decades, with exponential growth emerging only after the 1970s.

Similarly, IGOs and INGOs grow in numbers at remarkable rates. The Union of International Associations is the most comprehensive source for data on international organizations. It has been collecting data on the creation of these entities since the early twentieth century and publishes information about these international organizations annually. Until recently, persons and states had limited capacity for organizing on a supra-national scale, but they now do so with astonishing facility. INGO activities cover a wide range of domains, including education, science and technology, recreation, politics, and religion.[68] A comparable pattern describes the international organizations of the formal political system. IGOs have expanded in the post-World War II era: nation-states have acquired the ability to readily form political organizations of their own, although this growth is less dramatic than the exponential rise of multinationals and INGOs. Figure 1.4 shows estimates of the expansion of these organizations. The numbers include both the creation of entirely new organizations and the transformation of earlier structures into organizations. Catholic orders, for example, start to be listed as "international organizations" in these data in the 1950s, as they come to take on the proper template. Earlier it simply did not make sense to think of the church, and its internal bodies, as organizations.

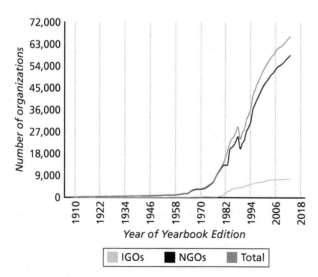

Figure 1.4. Number of Organizations in the Yearbook of International Organizations, by Year, 1909–2011

Source: Union of International Associations website 2013.

Overall, available data indicate an expansion of organized government, business, and associational life around the world. Furthermore, traditional bureaucracies and associations are transforming into more similar entities—organizations. Common explanations of function or power do not explain why such expansion would occur worldwide, in different types of social sectors, and beyond the demands of economic growth or particular political and economic configurations.

Existing theories

A well-established literature discusses the economic and political imperatives thought to produce the emergence of the corporate form.[69] Such theories make a good deal of sense: they work well in some settings, and indeed many kinds of interests and pressures in contemporary society lead to the formation of organizations. However, we focus on two overlooked points: (1) To a surprising extent, organization expands beyond what can be explained by these views. (2) The economic and political theories tend to suppose that organizations are functional for important interests because they work well. This ignores the massive disjunctions characteristic of contemporary organizations. We briefly review existing theories of function and power and their relation to our own neo-institutional approach.[70]

A first explanation, largely emphasized by economists, contends that organization is the most efficient form for achieving goals that require coordinated action. A classic account of this view is in business historian Alfred Chandler's *The Visible Hand*.[71] Focusing on the US, the text shows that before the Civil War very few entities looked like what we would now recognize as a typical business organization. Most firms were small, operated in a constrained geographic area, focused on one or two economic activities, and were run by individual or family owners. In this account, these early businesses were plagued by inefficiencies and uncertainties that hindered economic growth. Chandler argued that contemporary firms emerged because the "visible hand" of management outperformed the market's invisible hand, replacing a lesser form with a superior alternative. Specifically, managerial intervention and the move toward larger entities that incorporated some activities within firm boundaries reduced transaction costs and increased productivity.

Along the same lines, Ronald Coase and, later, Oliver Williamson argued that firms arise because of the relative inefficiency of performing some kinds of transactions in a market.[72] A contemporary application of this approach explains, "Organizational economics can help explain why the highly imperfect office of today may nonetheless represent the least dysfunctional of all possible worlds."[73] This view assumes that organizations and their highly complex structures exist because they perform more efficiently than other forms. It tends also to assume that they perform as designed. The transaction cost view has, however, been widely criticized in sociological literature for neglecting the social processes involved in organizational design.[74]

In itself, the observation that organizations sometimes facilitate efficient collective action is unproblematic. But organizations exist in greater numbers for broader purposes, in more contexts, and with more complicated structures than can be explained by functionality alone. The expansion in formal social entities called "organizations" is worldwide. Absolute numbers of organizations are higher in developed countries, but less developed ones are experiencing some of the most rapid growth. This growth is greater in scope than can be explained by increases in general socio-economic development or population, as we show in Chapter 2.

In addition, much of the expansion is in social sectors like welfare, education, and religion, where core technical requirements are relatively limited. In contrast to global shipping, for instance, schooling can take place with little coordination, fundamentally requiring little more than a teacher and some students. Structurally complex school districts and the testing, ranking, and evaluation regimes that now extend globally are new inventions. Education went on for centuries without these accessories, and given the difficulty in measuring short- and long-term effects of education for individuals and societies, it is uncertain whether such additions are indeed functional. Even in firms, arguments that structures reflect function seem limited. Certainly competitive pressures lead to particular organizational structures, but so do other circumstances such as peer influences, mimicry of high-status entities, social movement pressures, professional norms, or interpretations of legal compliance.[75] And, at times, there is little evidence that new structures or practices either achieve their goals or contribute to productivity.[76]

A second story line moves beyond assumptions of economic efficiency, instead emphasizing power and political processes. Charles Perrow spells out these dynamics in *Organizing America: Wealth, Power, and the Origins of Corporate Capitalism*, which traces the political activities of textile industrialists in New England during the nineteenth century.[77] He outlines how these powerful men shaped property and trading law in ways that enabled them to build giant companies that were the vehicles for accumulating wealth and power. Generally, he argues that the broad social changes of modern development, such as urbanization and industrialization, create possibilities (or even necessities, from some elite points of view) for large-scale social control—essentially domination. Organizational expansion arises from the interests of power-holders, who exploit the new possibilities. Earlier, James Coleman, reflecting on the same general process of organizational expansion, presented a similar view.[78] He saw the outcome of organizational expansion as an imbalance between atomized and powerless individuals and well-organized and powerful collectives.

This line of thought resonates with daily observations and experiences in many ways. Under modern cultural conditions, a variety of social interests—including concentrated and powerful elites—produce formal organizations on an enormous scale and in huge numbers, some of which generate inequalities.

The problem is not in the argument, which is reasonable. The difficulties come in the generalization of the argument to all organizations, and in emphasizing inequality as the only noteworthy consequence. The impulse to organize seems to impact most or all societies and sectors in the modern world, from the most powerful to the least. The powerful organize, but so do local religious congregations, medical service organizations, government service agencies, sports leagues, weight-reduction programs, choral groups, and family service societies. Social movement groups organize and can sometimes shape far more powerful groups.[79] Organization may be a cause of inequality, but today it is also the main proposed solution. For instance, "community organizing" is touted as a tool for empowering the poorest and most marginalized.[80] Proper governance structures, emphasizing transparency and accountability, are intended to curb the excesses of greed and corruption in both political and economic domains. Beyond the fact that the interests of power-holders lead to organization, many kinds of collective goals now come to be organized. So we must generalize arguments beyond a narrow focus on power concentration in the modern system.

A related argument is found in discussions that depict firms as contractual networks.[81] A network view of the firm asserts "that most organizations are simply legal fictions which serve as a nexus for a set of contracting relationships among individuals."[82] A vision of the firm as a network of contracts is in opposition to the transaction-cost view described above, where the essential theory of the firm is that some economic activities take place in a market and are governed by contract, whereas others take place within firm boundaries and are governed by authority. Such work often causally attributes the creation of firms that look like networks as rooted in macro-economic shifts toward financialization and a profit model focused on shareholder value.[83] The idea is that older firms, with owners that supported and employed local communities, have been replaced by transient networks of contracts aimed at increasing shareholder value, which serve mainly to concentrate wealth and power among elites. In *Managed by the Markets: How Finance Reshaped America*, Gerald Davis advances a comprehensive development of this view. Discussing the transformation of large US firms over the twentieth century and especially since the 1970s, he comments:

The corporation was no longer portrayed as a tangible institution with an inside and an outside, as in the industrial-managerialist days. Rather, it was a network, a "nexus of contracts", organized in such a way as to promote the creation of shareholder value. It had no moral commitments to various stakeholders. Its commitments were those explicitly stated in written contracts with buyers, suppliers, and customers, or implicit in its status as a for-profit enterprise.[84]

In some ways the point that the older model of a firm breaks down and is replaced by something that looks like a network is aligned with our arguments. Both network views and our approach to organization note that old-style firms, structured more like bureaucracies, are transformed into less hierarchical and less integrated structures. But we emphasize two important features of contemporary organizations that network ideas overlook. First, although network imagery and the "legal fiction" concept may be more or less descriptively correct, they downplay the fact that, as a socially constructed form, organizations are everywhere envisioned and chartered (often legally) as holistic, bounded entities. A great deal of boundary- and identity-defining work goes on in contemporary organizations and organization theory, as participants imagine their structures as unified: a whole world of managers and management is built on this view. Studies of both the causes and consequences of organizational identity, culture, and values are a burgeoning area of research.[85] Outside academia, huge amounts of legal and accounting effort go into establishing what counts as the proper boundaries of the organization.

These efforts to establish a clear identity and boundaries may become even more important and complex precisely because organizations, descriptively, look more like networks than their predecessors. Boundaries are often unclear in practice and cultural definitions (including law and accounting) are required to maintain them. But at the same time the managers, lawyers, researchers, consumers, clients, and many other stakeholders who socially construct organizations envision them as bounded entities. Thus a network view downplays the paradox that firms are also "social facts, given deference in the law and in social practice.... Corporations may not have a soul, but their participants—and sometimes the law—expect them to act as if they do."[86] In our approach, this dialectic is central.

Further, the contractual network approach was developed to apply to firms with shares, but a step back reveals that the description of network-like relationships goes beyond the ties that might maximize shareholder value. Organizations across the board have a growing range of responsibilities stemming from legal requirements and perceived social expectations. Of course many firms are responsible to shareholders, but they also have expanding obligations in arenas such as governance, CR, human resources, and accommodating the personal tastes and expectations of employees (who are encouraged in contemporary culture to have highly developed senses of their own worth). Obligations beyond production or profit make firms look more like networks because they weaken hierarchy and centralized authority. But such patterns occur in many types of businesses (not just those with public shares) and in other sectors (government agencies and non-profits are also increasingly more network-like and have accountabilities beyond their mission).[87]

Institutional theory

Our arguments are taken from a closely related group of theories that go by the label "sociological institutionalism" or "organizational institutionalism." These approaches have developed into one of the most dominant perspectives in organizational analysis.[88] A central theme is an emphasis on the cultural sources of social structures.[89] In narrow lines of this argument, the causal linkages mainly reflect the power and authority of external bodies over local situations. That is, institutions constrain and enable lower-level units; individuals and organizations must navigate the demands of their external environment. Some of what we argue can be fitted into this form. For instance, if the government requires that local structures write environmental impact statements, at least some of them are likely to actually do so. But we go further, pursuing more phenomenological lines of reasoning.[90] Here, as before, local units are constrained and enabled by their institutional environment, but in our view they are also constructed by it. Institutions create not only required action but the required actor too.[91] Thus the putative boundaries between organizations and their institutional environment are constructed, not real. This line of thought brings to the fore, and helps explain, two core features of contemporary organization that are peripheral in previously discussed theories that emphasize function or power.

(1) Decoupling. A difficulty of functional arguments—whether power-centered or efficiency-oriented—is that they presume the organizations of modern society work as intended. Structures exist because they are efficient or help elites maintain power. But a recurrent theme throughout modern research on formal organizations is that they are multi dimensionally decoupled.[92] Organizational structures are often poorly linked to their practices and to each other.[93] This raises the question: if organization arises around pressures for efficient production, but does not really control production well, why is it there? If organization arises out of the exploitive demands of the powerful to control activity, but can be altered by pressures directly against powerful interests, why is it there? Institutional theories provide a clear answer: formal organization, and the organizational identities involved, directly reflect environmental, cultural, and structural requirements rather than simply providing solutions to local exigencies.

It makes sense to see modern organization as both reflecting institution-alized cultural models and partly mediated by direct environmental pressures. As recent economic sociology has documented, even the causal chain leading to profits is constructed.[94] Certainly rhetorics of power and efficiency are involved—these are standard parts of ideologies of modernization, and are used to ground many kinds of structure and provide rationales for all sorts of activities. But they are institutionalized patterns located far beyond any particular local setting. In short, organizations are built to conform to, and enact, these ideologies, as much as to accomplish ends: we develop an account emphasizing this view in Part 1 of this book.

(2) Internal inconsistency and non-rationality: the goals or ends of organizations are also creatures of the environment, and they contain multiple and inconsistent requirements. Organizations, to be legitimate collective actors, must conform or appear to conform to a wide range of potentially conflicting obligations—to their own goals, but also to their human participants and stakeholders, to the environment, and to a variety of norms of organizational transparency and propriety. Much internal structured inconsistency—sometimes involving conflict, sometimes simple decoupling and hypocrisy—is intrinsic to contemporary organization. We develop an analysis of such intrinsic properties of "organizational actorhood" in Part 2 of this book.

Overview of the book

Part 1 of the book, consisting of Chapters 2 through 4, discusses organizational expansion, starting with indicators of this growth, then moving to its cultural roots and pathways through which these cultural ideologies shape local realities.

In Chapter 2 we outline indicators of organizational expansion. We present depictions of the expansion of international and domestic organizations, businesses, non-profits, and government agencies. We discuss the tendency of any given organization to become more formalized in the current period.

In Chapter 3 we discuss the cultural rationalization supporting the rise of organization in the post-World War II period. Scientific growth, enlarged conceptions of human powers, and educational expansion made organization seem plausible and necessary.

In Chapter 4 we show how, against this cultural backdrop, hard and soft law, rationalized counting and accounting systems, and education-fueled professionalism facilitate and require organization.

Part 2 of the book, consisting of Chapters 5 and 6, is a more theoretical effort. We seek to define the term organization more completely and consider how the cultural foundations of organization shape its features.

In Chapter 5 we come to an understanding of the contemporary meaning of "organization." We define the essential characteristics of the model or template involved. Our core point is that organizations are conceived as social actors rather than passive entities.

Chapter 6 discusses the non-rationalities of actorhood. Cultural changes, and more immediately rationalized environments, create pressures and opportunities for organizational expansion. Dialectic processes emerge, and in coming to terms with more and more rationalized environments, modern organizations acquire internal inconsistencies, conflicts, and uncertainties.

We conclude, in Chapter 7, with a discussion of the implications of this transition for society and a discussion of the potential future evolution of the "organizational society".

▨ NOTES

1. A few examples illustrate the rise of various organizational trappings: benchmarking (Davis 1998), balanced scorecard (Chan 2004), performance measurement (van Dooren 2005), planning (Berry 1994; Bryson 2011), vision, ethics, and core value statements (Kernaghan 2003), risk management (Power 2004), and sustainability reporting (Farneti & Guthrie 2009).
2. Aldrich 1999.
3. The population ecology tradition counts the existence of various types of organizations over time (Hannan & Freeman 1977, 1993), but this does not address the existence of organization in the first place.
4. Drucker 1992.
5. For example, King, Felin, & Whetten (2010: 291) observe: "The ontological status of the organization as a distinct kind of social entity is not well theorized given the present focus on social phenomena above or below the organization-level." See also Hirsch & Lounsbury 1997a, b; Gavetti et al. 2007; Heath & Sitkin 2001; Whetten 2006; Kraatz & Block 2008. In a more recent example, a post on orgtheory.net, a popular blog, bemoans the fact that "Org theory's main research programs—institutional theory, networks, field theory, population ecology— aren't about 'organizations' anymore." Accessed 6/4/2014 at <http://orgtheory. wordpress.com/page/3/>.
6. Coleman 1982; Perrow 1999.
7. Rationalization refers to structuring of social life around clear means–ends relationships. These may define instrumental accomplishment, such as an economically efficient division of labor, or the implementation of social controls over activity. Rationalization implies the specification of both means–ends relationships and the entities that enter into these relationships, such as individual roles.
8. Following Coleman, we use the term "sovereignty" to indicate a socially authorized locus for action, a "right to act" (1982: 44). This use of the term is distinct from meanings of sovereignty linked to autonomy of (especially legal) authority, as in

"the sovereign state." Later in our arguments, we diverge from Coleman in that we emphasize cultural sources of organizational expansion rather than attributing it to the "differentiation of activities" in society (Coleman 1982: 14).

9. The expansion of scientific and quasi-scientific thought and action (including social scientific domains) as a cultural principle as much as a factual knowledge base is often referred to as scientization (Drori et al 2003; Drori, Meyer & Hwang 2006).

10. In *Constructing World Culture: International Nongovernmental Organizations Since 1875* sociologists John Boli and George Thomas describe world culture as constituting the "locally situated individual as someone who can, may and should act globally" (1999: 34). Similarly, drawing on Durkheim's imagery of "the cult of the individual," Michael Elliott describes how "the increasing concern for, and elaboration of, human rights points to a world-cultural environment where the individual is increasingly regarded as sacred and inviolable" (2007: 1).

11. On the expansion of education see Boli, Ramirez, & Meyer 1985; Benavot & Riddle 1988; Meyer, Ramirez, & Soysal 1992; Schofer & Meyer 2005.

12. These weak linkages are often described using the term "decoupling" or "loose coupling." For classic accounts see Weick (1976) and Meyer & Rowan (1977). For reviews and recent discussions see Orton & Weick (1990), Boxenbaum & Jonsson (2008), or Bromley & Powell (2012).

13. Coleman 1982; Perrow 2002.

14. Ferguson 1990.

15. Power (1997), for instance, provides an insightful analysis of the inability of audits to prevent fraud.

16. Perrow 2002: 1–2.

17. Jamali & Mirshak 2007; Matten & Moon 2008; Preuss, Haunschild, & Matten 2009.

18. Sealander 2003.

19. Shor 1992; Tabulawa 2003; Bromley, Meyer, & Ramirez 2011.

20. Kaufman 2008.

21. Brunsson & Sahlin-Andersson 2000; Whetten & Mackey 2002; Drori, Meyer, & Hwang 2006; Krücken & Meier 2006; King, Felin, & Whetten 2010; Meyer 2010; Hwang & Colyvas 2011; Krücken, Blümel, & Kloke 2013; Westphal & Zajac 2013.

22. We refer here to the cultural framing of contemporary society, not to the specialized notions in the field of organizational studies that organizations may have their own distinctive internal cultures.

23. Tocqueville [1890]1972; McClay 1994.

24. Meyer & Rowan 1977; DiMaggio & Powell 1983; Greenwood et al. 2008; Scott 2013.

25. Drori, Meyer, & Hwang 2006, 2009.

26. Parker 1992; Caporaso 1996; Hirschhorn 1997; Kumar 2009.

27. Touraine 1971; Bell 1976; Masuda 1980; Huber 1984.

28. Heckscher & Donnellon 1994; Grey & Garsten 2001; Iedema 2003; Salaman 2005; Josserand, Teo, & Clegg 2006; McSweeney 2006.

29. Presthus 1962; Coleman 1982; Zald & McCarthy 1987; Cheney 1991; Perrow 1991; Drucker 1992.

30. Ahrne & Brunsson 2008, 2009, 2011 distinguish meta-organizations (organizations of organizations) and partial organizations (with incomplete control or rationalization). These ideas are most useful. But we see all organizations, in the contemporary world, as tending toward partial or meta-status. All depend on rationalized external control structures, and all are filled with incipient internal organizations of their own.

31. McCarthy & Zald 1973; Minkoff 1993; Skocpol 2013.

32. In one report Shapiro (2013) says: "Members of the Red Brigades, an Italian terrorist group active in the 1970s and early 1980s, report having spent more time accounting for their activities than actually training or preparing attacks. From 2005 through at least 2010, senior leaders of al Qaeda in Iraq kept spreadsheets detailing salary payments to hundreds of fighters, among many other forms of written records. And when the former military al Qaeda military commander Mohammed Atef had a dispute with Midhat Mursi al-Sayid Umar, an explosives expert for the Egyptian Islamic Jihad, in the 1990s, one of his complaints was that Umar failed to turn in his receipts for a trip he took with his family."

33. See, for example, the website of a Certified Professional Organizer for tips on Green Organizing, Home Organizing, Office Organizing, and Life Organizing. Accessed on 2/4/2014 at <http://www.worklifecoach.com>.

34. Naturally, there are even clearer differences between contemporary organizations and pre-modern structures, such as family, tribe, empire, or monarchy. We focus on the distinction between organization and the main structures of modernity, as it is in this shift from modern to late-modern that the conceptual lines are most likely to be blurred.

35. Brunsson & Sahlin-Andersson 2000; Whetten & Mackey 2002; Drori, Meyer, & Hwang 2006; Krücken & Meier 2006; Meyer 2010.

36. Weber 1921/1968: 956–8.

37. Cameron 1978; Skowronek 1982.

38. Boli-Bennett & Meyer 1978; Boli, Ramirez, & Meyer 1985.

39. Dwivedi 1967; Gould & Amaro-Reyes 1983; Mbaku 1996; Lipsky 2010.

40. Weber 1976.

41. Osborne 1993; Hood 1995; Putnam & Campbell 2012; Parigi 2012.

42. Osborne & Gaebler 1992; Boston, Martin, Pallot, & Walsh 1996.

43. Billis 2010. See Ebrahim (2003a) for a detailed discussion of the concept of accountability in northern and southern non-profits.

44. Christensen & Laegreid 2006; Verhoest, van Thiel, Bouckaert, & Laegreid 2012.

45. Fairtlough 2008.

46. Iedema 2003: 2.

47. Satow (1975: 1–2) elaborates: "Weber meant by 'rational' that the actor was aware of the goals and the means to achieve them.... Rational authority rests on a belief in the legality of rules and the right of those elevated to authority under the rules to issue commands (Weber 1964: 328). Weber calls it 'rational-legal' because it involves obedience to a legally established, impersonal order....That form of legitimacy is in turn rooted in a purposive-rational orientation to social action....It is implicit in Weber that rational-legal authority is a derivative of purposive-rational motivation."

48. Seligman 1992.
49. For general overviews of conflict and cooperation in non-profit-government relationships see Boris & Steuerle (2006), and for NGOs–corporation relationships see Yaziji & Doh (2009). In a more specific case, Berman (1997) describes how civil society contributed to the collapse of the Weimar Republic. For a discussion of fluctuations in tolerance of voluntary association in autocratic Russia see Lindenmeyr (1990a, b). In the US context Madison (1787) is often cited as warning against the threat of "factions" in Federalist #10. (This interpretation is sometimes contested, as Madison was concerned only with groups that abused the rights of other citizens or were otherwise detrimental to society.)
50. Seligman (1992); for a detailed history of voluntary associations in the US from 1600 to 2000 see Hall (2006).
51. Classically, Tocqueville argued that democratic governance was strengthened by a flourishing civil society; neo-Tocquevillians such as Putnam, Leonardi, & Nanetti (1994) continue to argue that civil society is crucial for "making democracy work;" see also Putnam (1995, 2000). Even scholars as typically divergent as Fukuyama (1995, 2001) and Barber (2010) agree that a strong civil society brings economic, social, and political benefits.
52. In societies around the world there are long histories of sectors outside of government, business, or the family that share some characteristics with the voluntary associations we describe. The collection of chapters in Chambers & Kymlicka (2002) provides a particularly rich discussion. For our purposes these distinctions between the precursors are less salient, as we emphasize ways in which we would expect the structures of civil society, be they voluntary associations in Europe or Islamic or Confucian models of civil society, to become more "organized."
53. Frumkin 2002: 3.
54. Frumkin 2002: 5.
55. Creighton 1990; Kaufman 2008.
56. Sealander 2003.
57. Dees 1998; Weisbrod 2000; Eikenberry & Kluver 2004; Billis 2010; Pache & Santos 2010.
58. Starr 1982; Scott et al. 2000; Anderson & Funnell 2005; Woolfe et al. 2005.
59. Marrée & Groenewegen 1997; Saltman & Figueras 1997.
60. Krücken & Meier 2006 coined the term "organizational actor" to refer to the contemporary university.
61. Frank & Gabler 2006; Ramirez 2009; Krücken, Blümel, & Kloke 2013; Ramirez & Christensen 2013.
62. Wilensky 1964; Khurana 2007.
63. Coleman 1982: 14.
64. Hansmann & Kraakman 2000.
65. Aldrich 1999; Davis & Marquis 2005: 332.
66. One report indicates that in 1970 there were some 7,000 parent multinationals, and by 2000 that number had jumped to 38,000 (Greer & Singh 2000). Another report, issued by UNCTAD, estimates that at the end of the 1960s there were about 7,000 multinationals operating worldwide; by 2006 this number had ballooned to almost 80,000 (Ghemawat & Pisani 2013).

67. Gabel & Bruner 2003.

68. Boli & Thomas 1997, 1999.

69. Coase 1937; Chandler 1977; Williamson 1981; Coleman 1982; Perrow 2002.

70. For a review see the introduction of Dobbin (2004). Chapter 1 of Khurana (2007) also provides an excellent summary of the core literature.

71. Chandler 1977.

72. Williamson 1973; Coase 1984.

73. Fisman & Sullivan 2013: 4.

74. For example, through an historical analysis of General Motors (GM), Freeland (1996) outlines weaknesses of the efficiency and cost-effectiveness arguments for the growth and proliferation of the multidivisional governance form. He contends that, in practice, GM, often held up as a model, rarely met theoretical definitions of multidivisional governance. Moreover, it experienced economic decline during the times it did conform to the textbook multidivisional form. See also Granovetter 1985.

75. As examples, multiple studies have shown that firms adopted a multidivisional structure both in response to economic imperatives and because of institutional pressures—for instance, more of their peers adopted a multidivisional structure or executives had elite business degrees (Fligstein 1985; Palmer, Jennings, & Zhou 1993). Lounsbury (2001) demonstrates that social movement activism can also shape formal job descriptions and hiring at universities. And, in a series of publications, Frank Dobbin and colleagues have amply demonstrated that interpretations of the law and the rise of human resource personnel contribute to expanded organization, such as the adoption of grievance procedures, formal promotion mechanisms, and diversity programs (e.g., Dobbin, Sutton, Meyer, & Scott 1993; Sutton & Dobbin 1996; Kelly & Dobbin 1998, 1999; Kalev, Dobbin, & Kelly 2006; Dobbin & Kelly 2007; Dobbin 2009).

76. For instance, McWilliams & Siegel (2000) discuss the mixed evidence for a link between corporate social responsibility practices and firm financial performance, outlining several measurement challenges involved. Kalev, Dobbin, & Kelly (2006) indicate that diversity programs might be better characterized as "best guesses" than "best practices," as some common practices fail to achieve their goals. Bloom, Kretschmer, & Van Reenen (2010) find no association between a firm's family-friendly work practices and productivity, net of relevant controls.

77. Perrow 2002.

78. Coleman 1982.

79. Lounsbury 2001.

80. Speer & Hughey 1995; Gittell & Vidal 1998.

81. Davis & Marquis 2005; Davis 2009.

82. Jensen & Meckling 1976: 310–11.

83. Davis 2009.

84. Ibid.: 21.

85. As examples see Albert & Whetten 1985; Gioia, Schultz, & Corley 2000; Sørensen 2002. Many studies provide evidence that organizational identity is consequential. It can be a core source of conflict (Glynn 2000), shape strategy and decision-making (Dutton & Dukerich 1991; Elsbach and Kramer 1996), and influence

outcomes like knowledge transfer (Child & Rodrigues 1996), change (Chreim 2005; Hannan, Baron, Hsu, & Koçak 2006), and stakeholder relations (Brickson 2005). A somewhat more limited body of work considers identity formation (Czarniawska and Wolff 1998; Clegg, Rhodes, & Kornberger 2007; Rodrigues & Child 2008; Gioia et al 2010), and issues of identity emergence, persistence, and selection are emerging as a core agenda in population ecology (Hsu & Hannan 2005).

86. Davis 2009: 60.
87. Rhodes 1997, 2007; Goldsmith & Eggers 2004.
88. Lounsbury 2008; Powell & Bromley, forthcoming.
89. For an overview of organizational institutionalism see Greenwood, Oliver, Suddaby, & Sahlin-Andersson 2008.
90. Meyer 2010; Meyer & Bromley 2013.
91. Westphal & Zajac (2013) insightfully note a distinction between socially situated agency and socially constituted agency.
92. For reviews of decoupling see Orton & Weick 1990 and Bromley & Powell 2012.
93. Weick 1976; Meyer & Rowan 1977.
94. For example, Zuckerman 1999 shows that stocks are discounted if they are not covered by securities analysts. See also Fourcade 2011.

Part 1

Organization: Worldwide Expansion and Cultural Roots

2 Worldwide expansion

The previous chapter reviewed the general expansion of organizations and common explanatory ideas about it. We also emphasized the international proliferation of organizations, including multinationals, INGOs, and IGOs. In this chapter we consider more general evidence of expansion, with a fuller discussion of empirical data and their interpretations.

Our central observation is that organization expands on multiple fronts. It expands on all levels, from local to national to global, in frequency and internal complexity. Organizations grow in many domains, from competitive profit-making to public administration to the ambiguous work of saving souls. Further, they expand in elements brought under managerial control, with the hyper-organization of formerly opaque matters distant from clear core functions, such as the more exotic forms of human resource management, CSR, or planning and strategy. Hyper-organization involves the extensive elaboration and structuration of social life into organizational arrangements beyond the clearly functional and demonstrably rational.

Our discussion in this chapter illustrates expansion at three levels—international, national, and intra-organizational—and draws on examples from business, the non-profit sector, and government. Recognizing the breadth and depth of this growth is essential to our arguments; first, that global cultural forces produce organizational expansion, and second, that increasing complexity and density in the external and internal organizational landscapes tend to feed hyper-organization.

Organizational expansion is not simply our conception, but a central observation and focus in the world of practice, and in the minds of researchers and the expanding data sets that they use. It is a thriving, prestigious, and rewarded feature of the articulate and self-conscious contemporary world. People build organizations and claim that their constructions are (or are becoming) real organizations: a favorite modern task is to "get organized." Intertwined with the legitimate status of being "an organization," unrealistic descriptions are put forward about the character of these entities: few such entities are as well structured as they claim to be. Formal organizations can be ephemeral, existing more in the imagination of a founder and in a few legal documents than in any concrete assembly of people, funds, and relationships. For instance, organizational scholars Göran Ahrne and Nils Brunsson depict many entities as only meta-organizations or partial organizations, incomplete on many dimensions.[1] So lists of putative organizations are likely to include many that exist only marginally if at all. Indeed, from some points of view, an organization is simply a nexus of contracts or a collection of network relationships; consequently, counts based on legal incorporation have little meaning. Certainly, in many instances, formally incorporated entities in fact have little substance, perhaps existing solely to support another organization. In one sense, it can be accurate to observe that:

With corporations, there is no there there—they are simply legal devices with useful properties for raising finance. While counting new incorporations may give the impression that we are living in a Cambrian Explosion of organizations (Aldrich 1999), counting may not be that informative. It is trivially easy to incorporate in the United States, with or without a recognizable organization. Enron had upwards of 3,500 subsidiaries and affiliates, often organized as corporations or limited liability companies—entities that were often both legal and accounting fictions.[2]

But in another sense, the claim that "there is no there there" is mis-stated. As a *model* of bounded and agentic social structure, organization is thriving. Shared cultural understandings of what "an organization" (rather than a network or contract) can and should be and do are at the heart of much collective social action and substantial managerial effort. The concept is continually reinforced through such activities as business school teaching, legal codification, and all kinds of professionalism and activism intended to expand the boundaries of organizational accountability and responsibility. In most of the world, corporate entities have legal standing. In considerable research, in popular thought, and in law, each one has a unique identity: a culture, values, and special responsibilities. For example, management enthusiasts can study corporate culture at Hewlett-Packard: the "HP Way" is built around flexible management strategies, responsiveness to employee input, and sensitivity to the needs of its customers.[3] Similarly, in recent years, there has been great interest in Facebook's "internal innovation culture."[4] Sometimes, a firm's culture can in fact shape its performance,[5] though such claims are likely to reflect the exaggerated self-images of the successful. Thus the constructed category of "organization" as a form of social structure, and as an increasingly institutionalized model, exists at the macro-cultural level: in practice, actual local entities exist on continua of how completely they fit into this claimed category.

Looking ahead, in subsequent chapters we offer a general explanation of why the cultural model called "organization" emerges and transforms local settings to great but varying degrees. We consider some specific channels through which this general and abstract model is transmitted into concrete realities. Here we emphasize that legal incorporation, and entry onto various official and unofficial lists, matter as manifestations or indicators of the social construction of the category. It is true that "the apparent growth in numbers of organizations may really reflect a change in legal procedures for registering entities that previously existed in a more informal state."[6] But, as we emphasize below, those changes in legal procedures (which are widespread) indicate the ways in which organization becomes a preferred model for social life, and they help predict the enormous expansion we find.

In fact, the growing complexity of regulations that govern core organizational functions, such as taxation or personnel management, often requires the creation and elaboration of organizations. In the Sarbanes-Oxley Act of 2002, for instance, the US implemented sweeping new laws that required publicly listed firms to enhance internal controls over financial reporting, evaluate the effectiveness of these internal controls, and increase financial disclosures.[7] Similar corporate governance reform laws have been enacted in a wide range of other countries, including, according to one study, Argentina, Australia, Austria, Canada, China, Finland, France, Germany, India, Malaysia, Mexico, Norway, Poland, South Korea, Spain, Sweden, and the UK.[8] Legal changes that alter how organizations are counted, incentivize entities to take an organizational form, or require elaborated internal structure are an integral part of modern social construction.

As we turn to indicators of organizational expansion, three points are important to bear in mind: first, organization is an abstract and global cultural model supported by, but not limited to, legal definitions. Second, there is variation in how, and how much, this model is enacted in different historical, substantive, and geographic settings. Third, the global preference for organization as a model is likely to lead to a good deal of local change, as well as the overstatement of change reflecting the awareness of preferred macro-cultural models.

International expansion

In the previous chapter we showed indicators of the exponential growth of MNCs, which increase in number much more rapidly than economic development or population growth would predict. A traditional view was that multinationals are not truly global, because their headquarters are concentrated in just a few powerful countries such as the US. Early on, characterizing the multinational phenomenon as American was largely accurate. The majority of these companies were based in the US. This is no longer the case. A report compiled at Tufts University using sources from the UN and *Fortune* magazine says:[9]

According to the United Nations Conference on Trade and Development (UNCTAD), there were about 75,000 MNCs operating worldwide in 2005. These firms are classified according to the location of the parent company, although this location is not

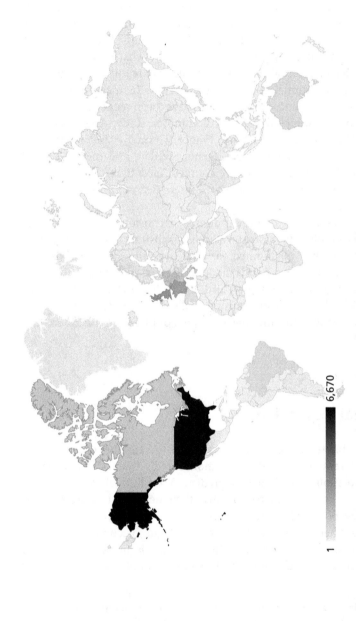

Figure 2.1. Countries in which International Organization Headquarters are Located in 2013

Source: Union of International Associations website 2015.

necessarily where most of its business is conducted. About 73% of MNCs are head-quartered in developed industrial economies.... Overall, their number has increased considerably in recent years, more than doubling since 1990, when there were about 35,000 MNCs. This growth has been especially dramatic in developing nations. While the number of MNCs in developed countries increased by 66% between 1990 and 2005, the number in developing countries increased by a factor of more than seven during the same period.

When we consider the geographic distribution of only the very largest MNCs, a greater share are concentrated in the US and Japan, although this has also been changing in recent decades. About 64% of the largest 250 industrial companies, ranked by revenues, were headquartered in the US in 1960. Except for a handful in Japan, all the rest were located in Europe. By 2006 we find only 34% of the world's 500 largest firms headquartered in the US. Japan was second with 14%, and then about 7% each in France, Germany, and Britain. About 8% of the largest MNCs are now located in developing countries, including China, Brazil, India, Malaysia and Mexico.

Aside from hegemonic concentration, transnational corporations are also known to flock to tax havens, producing, for example, an oddly high number of shipping companies in Liberia.[10] On the other hand, neither the existence of tax havens nor the power of dominant economies satisfactorily explains the full extent of growth and distribution of transnational corporations around the world.

Parallel to our discussion of businesses, in the previous chapter we also showed the global expansion of IGOs and INGOs. As with the concentration of MNCs, many international organizations are found in wealthy countries.[11] But, again like multinationals, these structures have a presence in nation-states all over the world: democracies and dictatorships, rich and poor, large and small. Figure 2.1 illustrates the worldwide distribution of international organization headquarters by country in 2013.

National growth

Beneath the global level, organizational growth is dramatic in almost all national societies. The earliest widespread use of the modern corporate form occurred in the US.[12] By the turn of the twentieth century a fairly standardized legal form of incorporation had emerged in advanced jurisdictions around the world.[13] Figure 2.2 shows the increasing number of incorporations in 13 US states between 1790 and 1810. Initially, the legal distinctions between different kinds of charters were minimal, making it difficult to clearly separate the business and charitable sectors.[14] One analysis of Massachusetts between 1781 and 1790, illustrated in Figure 2.3, suggests that at first most charters were granted to townships and polities, though religious and educational

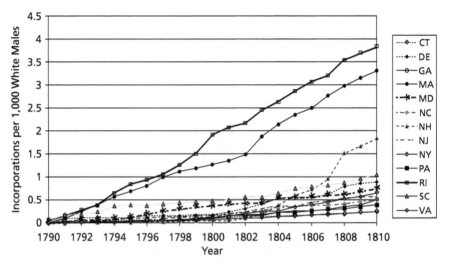

Figure 2.2. Number of Incorporations in 13 US States, 1790–1810
Source: Kaufman 2008: 414.

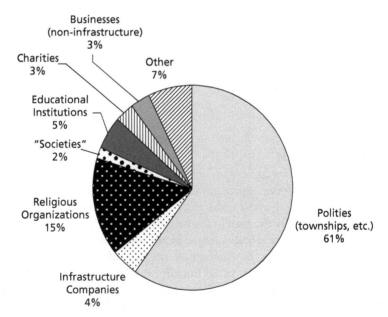

Figure 2.3. Type of Charter, Massachusetts (1781–90)
Source: Kaufman 2008: 415.

groups also received a substantial proportion. In sharp contradiction to lines of thought that see organizational expansion as a special creature of the private economy, at the time businesses were a minority of incorporations in the US. Only later was the situation sharply reversed: in 2011 there were 7.34 million businesses[15] and 1.46 million non-profits registered with the US Internal Revenue Service.[16]

Recent data suggest that the number of businesses continues to grow in many countries around the world. It is difficult to know the extent to which these structures take the form we now call "organization", but it is obvious, given all the material and non-material incentives, that increasing proportions do. In 2004 the World Bank began tracking the number of new businesses registered each year. Even over the short period since 2004 there has been a worldwide increase in the density of new businesses registered, from 2.7 to 3.4 per 1,000 people aged 15–64.[17] Globally, this means that there were an estimated 17.2 million new businesses registered in 2004, growing to 23.5 million new registrants in 2011. The data (not presented here) show that economic constraints matter, as is evidenced by the worldwide drop in 2008 and 2009 following the global financial crisis, but that growth occurs in every region of the world except the Middle East and North Africa. In absolute terms, developed economies tend to have higher numbers of new businesses registered (e.g., compare the European Union to the developing economies of Central Asia). Figure 2.4 shows an estimate of the density of new registered businesses by country in 2012, which ranges from a maximum of 45.27 new registrations per 1,000 people aged 15–64 on the Isle of Man to a minimum of 0.02 in the Democratic Republic of Congo. However, economic context does not explain all the variation we observe, and it seems less important for rates of growth, which are relatively consistent around the world (with the partial exception of the Middle East and North Africa).[18]

To further emphasize the trend of worldwide organizational expansion, we consider data from another source. The International Finance Corporation (IFC) has collected data from 132 economies on the number of formally registered micro, small, and medium enterprises (MSMEs), a category that includes businesses with fewer than 250 employees.[19] Many of these entities obviously fall short of expectations about what constitutes a true organization, despite their formally registered status. At the same time, many undoubtedly take on fashionable characteristics of the organizational form, a point we consider further below in discussing intra-organizational expansion. As a simple count, worldwide, the number of MSMEs per 1,000 people grew by 6 percent per year from 2000 to 2009, with growth of up to 15 percent per year in Europe and Central Asia, as shown in Figure 2.5.[20] Now, the growth in MSMEs is a truly global phenomenon. A recent report indicates that there are 125 million of them, of which 89 million operate in emerging markets.[21] On average, countries with higher incomes per capita report more

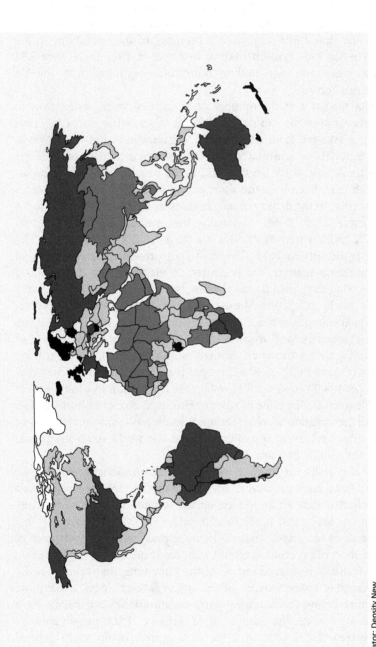

Indicator: Density New
Year: 2012
☐ No Data ☐ 0.00–2.00 ☐ 2.00–4.00 ■ 4.00–6.00 ■ 6.00–4.39K

Figure 2.4. New Business Density (New Registrations per 1,000 People Aged 15–64), 2012

Source: World Bank Entrepreneurship Database Online. Accessed 3/19/2014 at <http://www.doingbusiness.org/data/exploretopics/entrepreneurship/time%20series>.
Notes: Darker shades indicate higher density. New business entry density is defined as the number of newly registered corporations per 1,000 working-age people (those

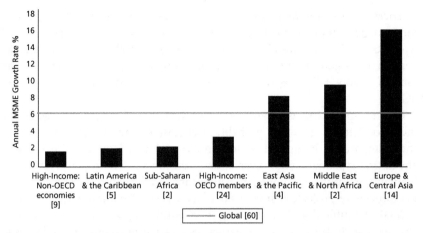

Figure 2.5. Growth of Micro, Small, and Medium Enterprises by Region, 2000–9

Source: Kushnir et al. 2010: 4.

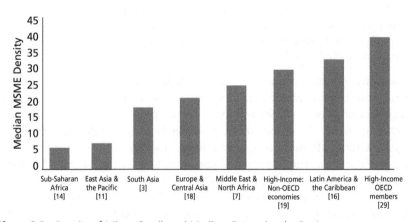

Figure 2.6. Density of Micro, Small, and Medium Enterprises by Region

Source: Kushnir et al. 2010: 3.

Note: Name of the region [#] signifies the number of economies from the region included in the analysis. The figure uses the most recent data available from 117 economies after the year 2000.

MSMEs, but the five countries with the highest density are an eclectic assortment that includes Brunei Darussalam, Indonesia, Paraguay, the Czech Republic, and Ecuador. Figure 2.6 illustrates the per capita density of MSMEs worldwide.

Recalling our theoretical discussion, one view of organizations suggested that they exist because they are a vehicle for elites to amass wealth and power. In contrast, the empirical data indicate that much expansion occurs in tiny, small, and medium-sized enterprises, which undoubtedly offer less potential for social domination and exploitation than large firms. Certainly, organization can be a tool of inequality, but the diffuse nature of organizational expansion calls into question whether a main causal process behind the creation of organizations is the consolidation of wealth and power. The point is doubly salient as we now turn to look at trends in non-profit and NGOs.

The non-profit or associational sector within each country is generally understood to be growing, probably even faster than the business sector. The Comparative Nonprofit Sector Project at Johns Hopkins University is "the largest systematic effort ever undertaken to analyze the scope, structure, financing, and impact of nonprofit activity around the world."[22] The leaders of this impressive project, Helmut Anheier and Lester Salamon, have discussed in detail the difficulties in classifying these entities across countries and over time, but conclude that the evidence suggests a widespread growth of domestic non-profit sectors.[23] Based on data collected in the 1990s, they report:

Reliable time-series data on the more tangible dimensions of the nonprofit sector have been lacking for all but a handful of countries.... Even without these more comprehensive data, however, initial investigation through the Johns Hopkins Comparative Nonprofit Sector Project documented a striking increase in the scale of the nonprofit sector in the early 1990s.[24]

Drawing on seven countries (Hungary, Japan, Sweden, Germany, the UK, France, the US) for which data could be compiled on a consistent range of organizations between 1990 and 1995, the Hopkins researchers found substantial increases in employment, volunteering, and individual memberships.[25] Calling attention to these findings, Anheier and Salamon note that non-profit sectors around the world appear to be growing "despite the attention generated by political scientist Robert Putnam's assertion that Americans and others are increasingly 'bowling alone'."[26] Their point is directly related to our own overarching theme: organization, as opposed to other formal and informal structures, has become a central mode of structuring social life in the contemporary rationalized society. Cross-sectionally, the research shows that civil society organizations have come to employ a substantial portion of the workforce in many countries (Figure 2.7). The contemporary non-profit sector, organized and formally funded, is now far removed from Adam Smith's characterization of charitable work as "unproductive labor."

Details about workforce participation and individual membership or volunteering rates are not, of course, direct measures of the scope and scale of organizational structures, although they are certainly correlated with them. Noting the complementary, but distinct, nature of the different types of data available, sociologists Evan Schofer and Wesley Longhofer compiled a large cross-national data set on non-profits, using information from the *Encyclopedia of Associations: International Organizations*.[27] The *Encyclopedia* is a directory

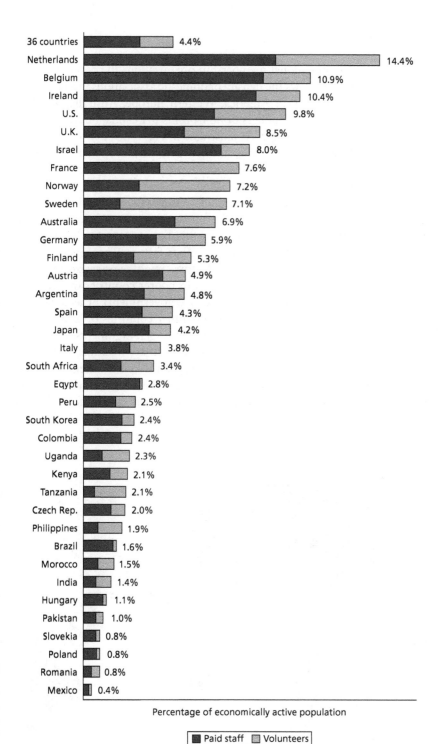

Percentage of economically active population

■ Paid staff ☐ Volunteers

Figure 2.7. Civil Society Organization Workforce as Share of the Economically Active Population in 36 Countries, 1995–2000

Source: Salamon et al. 2004. Retrieved 1/31/2015 at <http://ccss.jhu.edu/wp-content/uploads/down loads/2013/02/Comparative-data-Tables_2004_FORMATTED_2.2013.pdf>.

of national and multinational membership organizations in countries around the world. Figure 2.8 shows the density of domestic associations in a country in 2006. Unsurprisingly, North America, Western Europe, Australia, and New Zealand have the greatest numbers of non-profits per capita, but this figure is growing most rapidly elsewhere. As illustrated in Figure 2.9, between 1991 and 2006 parts of Eastern Europe, Asia, and Africa experienced increases of 200 percent or more in the number of associations per capita—growth far higher than any estimates of growth in businesses.

Using a statistical analysis, Schofer and Longhofer found that links to world culture and educational levels (i.e., the universalistic, rationalizing cultural shifts that are the focus of Chapter 3 of this book) increase the predicted numbers of domestic associations, net of other factors. Theoretically realist accounts, more dismissive of cultural factors, might emphasize that such associations arise out of need (i.e., perhaps in poorer countries or less stable ones or countries where there is less effective government) or as a result of purely technical factors (i.e., perhaps in wealthier countries or as a result of population growth or political structures). Some such arguments have some, though uncertain, empirical support. Countries that are wealthier, have larger populations, are more democratic, and have expanded governments also have larger non-profit sectors. Notably, the size and significance of the effects of a number of these predictors shrink after the researchers control for linkage to world society, suggesting the degree to which overall expansion is linked to global culture more than to immediate, local, and instrumental factors.

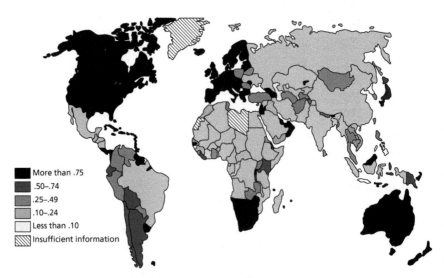

Figure 2.8. Association Density per 100,000 People, 2006
Source: Schofer & Longhofer 2011: 563.

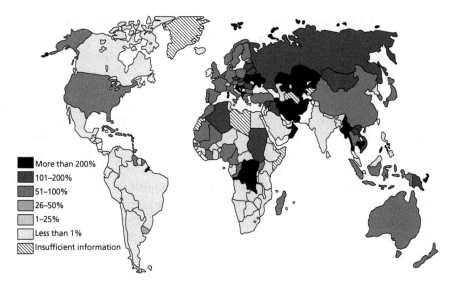

More than 200%
101–200%
51–100%
26–50%
1–25%
Less than 1%
Insufficient information

Figure 2.9. Percentage Change in Associations per Capita, 1991–2006
Source: Schofer & Longhofer 2011: 564.

The rapid expansion of non-profits calls further into question whether organizations should be understood mainly as tools for the powerful to perpetuate inequality. It is a stretch to think of the founders or leaders of most voluntary associations now turning into formal organizations (e.g., churches, schools, hospitals, and civic clubs) as driven to exploit the weak for personal gain. Some instances of personal benefit occur, but it seems unlikely that the overall trend is driven by the aggregation of self-interested rational people pursuing wealth and power via non-profit organizations. A power-based explanation of organization works best when we consider the creation of some large firms, though even in this context questions can easily be raised. (For instance, it doesn't make intuitive sense for greedy leaders to offer expensive same-sex benefits or pursue other CR initiatives purely of their own volition.[28]) We are hard-pressed to use sub optimizing power and self-interest as a general account for organizational expansion.

A more common explanation, often put in economic terms, is that non-profits exist as a response to the failures of government and the market to meet social needs.[29] Such theories may explain why some of these organizations are created, perhaps especially service providers, but they do not capture the full range of associations, including myriad hobbyist and expressive groups. They certainly fail to account for the general trend of parallel expansions in the non-profit, business, and government sectors.[30] Early theories posited that government expansion would "crowd out" civil society, but more recent research, including the analyses of domestic associations described above, documents that governmental expansion in fact supports the growth of the voluntary sector.[31]

On the one hand, mere counts of organizations are not the whole story, though they are a useful indicator of the dramatic changes we have emphasized. As others have noted, "The number of organizations is a notoriously imperfect variable through which to gauge the growth of this [non-profit] sector, however, since organizations vary so fundamentally in size and complexity."[32] On the other hand, even very imperfect numerical accounts—probably reflecting hopes as well as realities—demonstrate the extraordinary prestige and legitimacy associated with the organizational form. Moreover, organizational expansion occurs not only in numbers but also in the elaboration of these entities. We turn now to discuss the internal expansion of contemporary organizations.

Intra-organizational elaboration

When we reach down to survey the terrain inside organizations, data become even scarcer. Tracking activities like internal management practices within organizations over time and around the world is rare. Most studies are limited to case studies of particular firms or practices, often within a single country.[33] One exceptional multi-year project has documented changes in US firms over the twentieth century on multiple dimensions. Sociologist Frank Dobbin and colleagues have compiled comprehensive data on many facets of firm structure in the US. Some of the results are catalogued in the book *Inventing Equal Opportunity*.[34] Dobbin brings together data from multiple surveys to outline the huge changes involved, showing sharp increases in recent decades (as indicated below) in the percentages of employers with the following formal structures:[35]

- Antidiscrimination policies for women (1960–1980)
- Antidiscrimination policies for minorities (1960–1980)
- Seniority Policies (1939 and 1946)
- Training Programs for Supervisors (1929–1946)
- Management Training Programs (1971–1985)
- Affirmative Action Officers (1970–1986)
- An Equal Opportunity Office (1970–1986)
- A Personnel Office (1956–1986)
- Diversity Performance Evaluations for Managers (1971–2002)
- Non-union Grievance Procedures (1956–1986)

- Disciplinary Hearings (1956–1986)
- Formal Job Descriptions (1956–1986)
- Required Job Postings (1971–2002)
- Salary Classifications (1956–1986)
- Performance Evaluations (1956–1986)
- Discharge, Hiring, and Promotion Guidelines (1971–2002)
- Diversity and Equal Opportunity Policies (1971–2002)
- Diversity Training (1965–1997)
- A Diversity Task Force (1971–2002)
- Attitude Surveys (1956–1986)
- Culture Audits (1971–2002)
- Networking or Mentoring Programs for Women and Minorities (1974–2002)
- Maternity Leave, Paternity Leave, Medical Leave, Leave for Ill Family Members (1965–1997)
- Policies for Flextime, Compressed Work Weeks, Job Sharing, Work-at-Home, Part-time/Full-time Transition (1971–2002)
- Dependent Care Expense Account, On-site Child Care, Child Care Vouchers, Dependent Care Referral Services (1971–2002)
- General Harassment Grievance Procedures, Sexual Harassment Grievance Procedures, Sexual Harassment Training (1977–1990)

Worldwide, two recently developed cross-sectional surveys are notable exceptions to the general dearth of international information on internal firm structures. Unfortunately, both sources lack sufficient numbers of temporally repeated observations within individual countries for longitudinal analyses at the country level (in the future such data are likely to be available). The studies can, however, show general global trends. Between 2002 and 2014 the Enterprise Analysis Unit of the World Bank surveyed more than 70,000 firms from 120 countries.[36] Data on some indicators are available for a handful of West European countries for comparison purposes, but the project focuses on emerging economies. The researchers note that constructing panel data to observe changes within firms over time is a current priority, but at present most countries are sampled only once. Therefore we pool the observations over time to look at regional patterns. As Table 2.1 shows, the vast majority (more than 80 percent) of sample firms are formally registered when they start operations, and those that are not registered remain in an informal state for 1.1 years or less. Outside the Middle East and North Africa, firms in emerging economies use internationally recognized quality certifications and license technologies from foreign firms at roughly the same rate as the developed economy comparison cases. Worldwide, it is a prevalent practice to hire external auditors to approve annual financial statements, and (again with the exception of the Middle East and North Africa) firms in developing

Table 2.1 Survey of Firm Practices

	Firms formally registered when they started operations (%)	Number of years firm operated without formal registration	Firms with an internationally recognized quality certification (%)	Firms using tech. licensed from foreign companies (%)	Firms with an annual financial statement reviewed by external auditors (%)	Number of visits or required meetings with tax officials	Firms offering formal training (%)
East Asia & Pacific	86.4	1.0	17.8	18.4	49.7	1.4	45.2
Eastern Europe & Central Asia	97.0	0.3	20.8	19.3	37.1	1.5	39.1
Latin America & Caribbean	86.8	1.1	16.7	12.8	60.2	1.6	43.7
Middle East & North Africa	75.0	0.9	5.5	3.7	35.3	3.2	15.4
South Asia	89.3	0.8	11.6	8.1	46.6	1.5	26.0
Sub-Saharan Africa	81.4	0.7	16.1	16.5	47.9	2.9	31.7
Germany	.	.	.	.	54.1	1.3	35.4
Ireland	.	.	17.2	.	94.6	1.3	73.2
Portugal	.	.	12.7	.	80.0	1.6	31.9
Spain	.	.	21.3	.	58.3	1.5	51.3

Source: World Bank Enterprise Surveys Unit. <http://www.enterprisesurveys.org/methodology>.

economies offer formal training for staff at about the same rates as those in West European comparison countries.

Even in emerging economies, firms are quite formal and complex. Much daily work is entailed in maintaining quality certifications, participating in external audits, providing formal training opportunities for employees, licensing foreign technology, and so on. To carry out such practices, there must be people inside a firm (perhaps consulting on a temporary basis) playing roles like surveying resources, gathering and disseminating information, applying knowledge of specific laws or guidelines, and generating written reports. Overall, internal firm structures are highly elaborate on many dimensions. We interpret this trend in more depth in Chapters 5 and 6 of Part 2, where we argue that organizational expansion begets the rise of more non-rational or hyper-organizational qualities in existing organizations. Increasing organizational density as a feature of society generates organizational expansion beyond effective capacities for functional coordination and control—and thus beyond the reach of conventional theories of organizational expansion.

A second impressive large-scale data collection effort, led by economists Nick Bloom and John Van Reenen, examines management practices in more than 10,000 organizations in 20 countries and four industries (manufacturing, retail, health care, and education). These scholars go to considerable lengths to produce survey data of high quality, and have made available detailed discussions of their sampling and survey methods.[37] In Table 2.2 we present data from manufacturing firms on the prevalence of six management practices that indicate formalized internal complexity and elaboration—the presence of metrics, measures, targets, performance reviews, planning, and documented

Table 2.2 Cross-National Prevalence of Formal Management Practices in Manufacturing, 2002–10

	Tracking (1–5)	Reviews (1–5)	Measure Clarity (1–5)	Targets (1–5)	Planning (1–5)	Rewards (1–5)	Average (1–5)
Japan	3.4	3.7	3.2	3.8	3.6	3.3	3.5
United States	3.6	3.6	3.0	3.2	3.3	3.1	3.3
Germany	3.6	3.6	2.7	3.3	3.5	2.7	3.2
Sweden	3.8	3.9	2.3	3.4	3.6	2.3	3.2
Canada	4.0	4.0	2.0	4.0	3.0	2.0	3.2
Chile	3.5	3.5	2.5	3.0	4.0	2.5	3.2
France	3.8	3.6	2.6	3.2	3.2	2.6	3.2
Argentina	3.5	3.0	2.0	3.0	3.5	3.5	3.1
Great Britain	3.6	3.4	2.7	3.0	3.1	2.4	3.0
Italy	3.4	3.3	2.7	3.1	3.1	2.5	3.0
Poland	3.1	3.3	2.7	3.1	3.0	2.7	3.0
Republic of Ireland	3.1	3.3	2.5	2.9	3.0	2.5	2.9
China	3.1	3.2	2.9	2.4	2.6	2.9	2.9
Australia	3.0	3.4	2.6	2.5	3.0	2.5	2.8
Northern Ireland	3.1	3.1	2.5	2.7	2.9	2.6	2.8
Portugal	3.4	3.3	2.2	3.0	2.7	2.2	2.8
Greece	3.1	3.1	2.4	2.9	2.7	2.3	2.8
Brazil	3.5	2.5	2.5	2.5	2.0	3.0	2.7

Source: Data from World Management Survey. Accessed 3/17/2014 at <http://worldmanagementsurvey.org/?page_id=183>.

Notes: Tracking tests whether performance is tracked with meaningful metrics and with appropriate regularity. *Reviews* tests whether performance is reviewed with appropriate frequency and communicated to staff. *Measure Clarity* tests how easily understandable performance measures are and whether performance is openly communicated to staff. *Targets* tests whether targets cover a sufficiently broad set of metrics and whether financial and non-financial targets are balanced. *Planning* tests whether organization has a "3 horizons" approach to planning and targets. *Rewards* tests whether there is a systematic approach to identifying good and bad performers and rewarding them proportionately.

communication. Each item is scored on a one through five scale, with five indicating a higher score in organizational elaboration. Countries are ordered by their average score across the six items. Japan, the US, and Germany top the list in using many highly formal practices in manufacturing, and Portugal, Greece, and Brazil score the lowest overall. The rank order corresponds in some measure to economic development, but a more remarkable point is that the cross-national variation is limited. On average, countries score within a point of each other in the prevalence of formal management practices; data not shown here indicate far more variation within countries than between them.

For a more limited sample of countries, the authors also report management scores in different sectors, covering manufacturing firms, retail firms, hospitals, and schools.[38] A striking feature of this research is that it assumes the existence of a standard set of "good" and "bad" managerial practices that apply to all entities called "organizations," a term that can include firms and schools and hospitals. The organizations can be owned by the government or private citizens, and they can reside in any country in the world. These assumptions would have seemed unreasonable at the turn of the twentieth century because of the diversity of countries and social arenas involved. Now they reflect (and in a small way contribute to) the global social construction of organization as an overarching phenomenon.

In addition, these assumptions suggest that modern management practices requiring professionalized managers are core features of contemporary organizations, in contrast with other types of social structures, a point we emphasize in Chapter 4. Governments have bureaucrats or officials, schools have teachers and principals, hospitals have doctors and administrators, firms have owners and employees—but they are all organizations now, and, as organizations, are very likely to have managers.

Looking across sectors, Bloom, Van Reenen, and colleagues find that government-owned entities score somewhat lower than private businesses on management practices. Figure 2.10 illustrates the management score for schools and hospitals by ownership type, available for Canada, Germany, Sweden, and the UK. The researchers also find that family-owned firms (family Chief Executive Officers (CEOs)) and founder-owned firms (where the founder is the CEO) score even lower than government agencies. It seems that structures that are linked to alternative sources of authority and legitimacy (e.g., the traditions observed by government or family firms, or personal charisma) are slower to adopt all the trappings of formal organizations. We discuss the matter in subsequent chapters. Variation exists, but the use of modern management practices is widespread, across sectors and around the world. Even governmental agencies are becoming managed organizations, albeit more slowly than firms.

In addition to firms and government agencies, civil society associations around the world are becoming more elaborately structured. For example, in the US non-profit sector, studies have documented the rise of strategic plans,

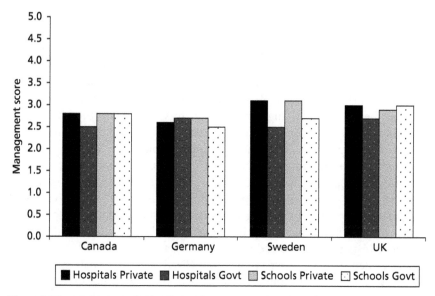

Figure 2.10. School and Hospital Management Practices by Government/Private Ownership

Source: Data from World Management Survey. Accessed 3/17/2014 at <http://worldmanagementsurvey. org/?page_id=183>.

independent financial audits, quantitative program evaluations, codes of conduct, outcomes measurement, and performance measurements.[39] A rare large-scale study outside the US shows that in a nationally representative sample of Cambodian NGOs, including a wide range of organizations, 60 percent conduct external audits, 91 percent prepare annual budgets (budgets are on average updated quarterly), 76 percent collect data, 52 percent use interviews or questionnaires to conduct needs assessments, and 13 percent use quantitative evaluation methods.[40] Similarly, a large random survey of Ugandan NGOs found that 90 percent had boards of trustees or directors (with an average of seven trustees or directors), 88 percent prepare annual reports, and 80 percent prepare yearly balance sheets and income statements. Two-thirds claim that their statements are reviewed by external auditors.[41] Other studies show that formal structures linked to accountability and self-regulation, such as voluntary standards or codes of conduct, are on the rise among civil society organizations worldwide.[42]

It would be easy to assume that organizations adopt formal managerial practices because they improve productivity or performance. Some case studies and experiments suggest that certain managerial practices do increase performance.[43] But in fact there is little systematic knowledge about the effects of most formal structures. One challenge is that it is difficult to pinpoint the effects of any specific organizational element, as groups of practices often appear together and exist in many inter-related combinations.[44] In non-profits, a particular challenge is finding appropriate indicators of performance. True outcome measures of social missions (e.g., student learning) are far more difficult to quantify than such alternatives as organizational survival, input resources (e.g., revenues), or outputs (e.g., clients served per dollar).[45]

Even in firms, the issue of measurement is a thorny one.[46] Moreover, existing theories and findings are contradictory, leading to the observation that many "researchers remain skeptical about the importance of management practices for explaining variations in firm performance."[47] Some of the most rigorous longitudinal research shows no relationship between practices and performance, especially when we look over an extended period of time and hold firm-level characteristics constant.[48] Regardless of the effectiveness of any particular practice in helping a firm or non-profit optimize performance, numerous internal elaborations are related to obligations that conflict with efficiency (e.g., compliance and regulatory structures).

The evidence of weak effects of rationalized organizational policies and practices—and, more strikingly, the absence of much evidence on the issue—calls sharply into question the common economic and political theories of why organizational expansion is endemic in the contemporary world. The putatively powerful political elites, and interested economic ones, cannot know that all this organization and hyper-organization is effective. And when researchers study the question, they get the most modest results. The implication, and the core of our arguments, is that expanding organization is a culturally driven process as much or more than an economic or political one.

The special case of public and state organizations

Our focus has been on non-profits and businesses, but these do not cover the whole domain. A distinctive set of issues arises in discussing the long-term worldwide expansion of formalized public and state structures.[49] The expansion has a long history, and it was greatly intensified in the late nineteenth and twentieth centuries.[50] After World War II, there was a period of growth in governments in the developed countries of the world, as well as an explosion in the peripheries with decolonization and subsequent state-building. Trends in numbers of employees and fiscal size in the period since World War II are shown in Figures 2.11 and 2.12. The dramatic expansion is even more apparent when viewed through a longer historical lens, as shown in trends in the fiscal size of government in the UK, US, and Australia in Figure 2.13.

Recent discussions of the retreat of the state obscure the much more pervasive and longer term trends in the other direction, both in the size of government and the extent of its responsibilities. As an indicator of these

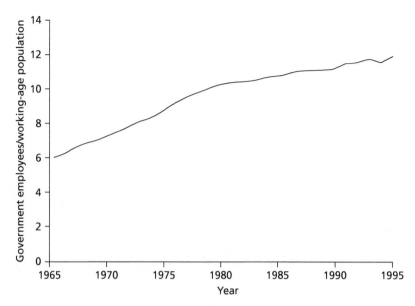

Figure 2.11. Public Sector Employment in OECD Member Nations, 1964–94
Source: Lee & Strang 2006: 885.

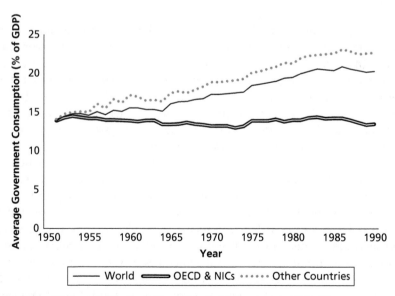

Figure 2.12. Changes in the Fiscal Size of Central Government, 1950–90
Source: Kim, Jang, & Hwang 2002.

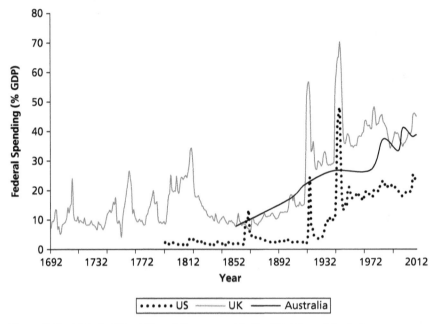

Figure 2.13. Historical Fiscal Size of Government in the UK, US, and Australia

Sources: Australia: <http://ipa.org.au/library/publication/1367829888_document_paper_-_australias_big_government_-_may_2013.pdf>. UK:<http://www.ukpublicspending.co.uk/spending_chart_1692_2013UKp_13c1li011tcn_F0t#copypaste>. US: <http://www.usgovernmentspending.com/spending_chart_1792_2>.

expanding responsibilities, Figure 2.14 shows the increase in national ministries representing various substantive areas in countries around the world, and Figure 2.15 shows the specific increase in the proportion of countries with ministries of human rights, environment, science, and education. Much of this historic expansion lies in the background of our study. It consisted of the enormous growth of bureaucracies, not autonomous organizational actors, and enhanced the authority of external state sovereigns, not organizational decision-making, accountability, and responsibility.[51]

A historical view illustrates that in some ways the calls for deregulation and privatization that emerged (especially in the 1990s) under labels like the Washington consensus, neoliberalism, or New Public Management barely dented the overarching trend of state expansion. But in other ways these pressures have contributed to a dramatic shift. The traditional civil service bureaucracies in much of the world have tangibly shifted toward becoming more like non-profit structures, and sometimes private organizations, albeit with much variation between countries.[52] One collection of studies, for example, documents changes toward accountability and technical rationality in financial management systems in Australia, France, Germany, Japan, New

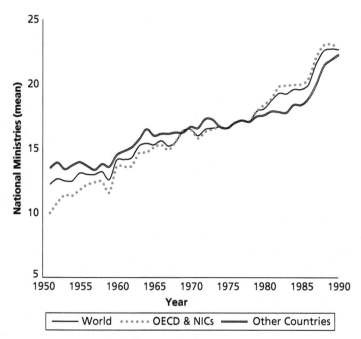

Figure 2.14. Mean Number of National Ministries

Source: Adapted from Kim, Jang, & Hwang 2002.

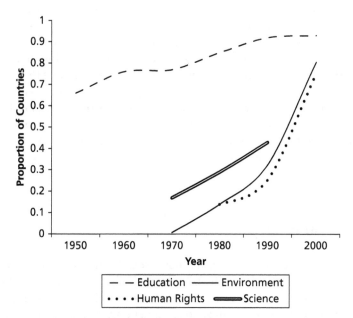

Figure 2.15. Increase of National Education, Environment, Human Rights, and Science Ministries or Institutions

Sources: Environment: Frank, Hironaka, & Schofer 2000. Human Rights: Koo & Ramirez 2009. Science: Jang 2000.

Zealand, Norway, Spain, Sweden, Switzerland, the UK, and the US.[53] Another considers New Public Management reforms in Europe, North America, Africa, and East Asia.[54] The declining prestige of bureaucracy as a form of social structure laid the foundation for reassembling states as sets of accountable, autonomous organizations.

Neoliberal and New Public Management rhetorics overlook crucial dimensions of rapidly shifting state–society relations. Many changes involve a new approach to governance rather than the abandonment of government activities. Large bureaucratic structures are reorganized as more specialized and autonomous agencies,[55] often involving the expanded participation of new stakeholders. Neoliberal rhetoric also masks the fact that deregulation and privatization often involve the elaboration of internal managerial and administrative controls, such as increased reporting, monitoring, and evaluation requirements. In line with these observations, public administration scholars increasingly discuss a New Public Governance that involves "self-organizing inter-organizational networks as distinct from the bureaucratic hierarchies of classic public administration and the contractual relationships of New Public Management."[56] This view emphasizes the partnerships between government and non-governmental providers in delivering public services, and implies a pluralist state and participatory decision-making. There is an emphasis on accountability,[57] but this is broadly defined and includes a range of stakeholders rather than a narrow focus on efficiency concerns.[58] Case studies have shown changes toward greater participation by diverse stakeholders in housing subsidy programs in South Africa,[59] in Brazilian municipalities[60] and health care,[61] and participatory governance in Asia.[62] In the developed world such changes are widely apparent, most strongly in the discourse on "governance without government" in Europe, but also spreading to the US and elsewhere.[63] Clearly, state agencies have changed less than most business firms (family firms aside) and have evolved less than non-profit organizations, as shown by the research by Bloom, Van Reenen, and colleagues discussed above. Assessments of the success of all these changes vary. But there is widespread agreement that dramatic change has occurred.

Chapter summary

Much evidence suggests that organization expands and elaborates at multiple levels around the world—internationally, domestically, and intra-organizationally. This occurs in multiple sectors—business, government, and non-profit. It covers more and more organizational functions: bureaucracies turn into organizations, and organizations become elaborated hyper-organizations covering a wide range of activities and responding to an expanded range of stakeholders. We use such statistics as are available. But an equally important task is to consider the social meaning that underpins the existence of these expanding data sets. The figures, and the heroic efforts researchers make to collect them, are manifestations of the growing cultural construction of organization. Legal and scientific activities that generate the data represent efforts to define organization as a category, a process that is ongoing and the subject of much discourse. The trends are overwhelmingly in the direction of expansion. But the evidence should be understood as illustrative of broad patterns and reflective of the emergence of a category called "organization" rather than a mirror of on-the-ground realities. Getting more and better organized is a modern virtue for firms, state agencies, churches, schools, hospitals, and indeed contemporary individual persons.

Any particular data set has a great deal of error, and of course the prestige-laden quality of being an organization leads to hyperbole. It seems wise to be skeptical about whether there were, for example, exactly 2,998,449 MSMEs in Mexico in 2003. It is also sensible to observe many actual and reported differences throughout the world. At the same time, the striking consistency and magnitude of the trends suggest that it would be rash to deny a general pattern of cross-national organizational expansion, both in cultural-cognitive efforts to define these structures and in their actual existence.

NOTES

1. Ahrne & Brunsson (2009: 6) highlight that many kinds of organization occur outside the boundaries of a formal entity and are thus incomplete, but still a form of organization. They define organization as: "active, decided upon attempts to achieve special orders that differ from already existing ones, for example those that are culturally determined. Such a definition eliminates the distinction between organisation and environment. It entails, in this respect, a broader definition than the traditional one. We can find organisation not only within but also outside and between formal organisations. There can be elements of organisation within markets, networks and institutions." See also Ahrne & Brunsson 2008, 2011.
2. Davis & Marquis 2005: 332.
3. Packard 1995.
4. Jana 2013.
5. Sørensen 2002.
6. Anheier & Salamon 2006: 100.
7. A recent survey estimates that compliance with a central section of Sarbanes-Oxley cost, on average, 1.2 million dollars in 2007–2008 (Alexander et al. 2013).
8. For a detailed analysis of corporate governance reforms in 26 economies see Kim & Lu 2013.
9. Roach 2007: 3.
10. See, for instance, reports by the Organization for Economic Cooperation and Development (OECD 2014). A recent comprehensive study of effective tax

rates based on an analysis of financial statements finds that Japanese-based multinationals pay the most; and France and Germany have slightly higher rates than the US (Markle & Shackelford 2013).

11. Beckfield 2010.
12. Creighton 1990; Kaufman 2008.
13. Hansmann & Kraakman 2000.
14. Creighton 1990; Kaufman 2008.
15. US Census Bureau 2011.
16. National Center for Charitable Statistics 2011.
17. World Development Indicators Online. Accessed 3/19/2014 at <data.worldbank. org/indicator/IC.BUX.NDNX.ZS/countries/1W-ZJ-EU-7E-Z4-ZQ? display=graph>.
18. The recent Arab Spring uprisings are in part a testament to the globalized and culturally contested nature of organizational expansion. Activists were calling largely for more participatory governance and equitable justice systems aligned with global cultural definitions of how contemporary state agencies should operate. Further, they drew on assistance from INGOs to advance their cause. An article in the *New York Times* reports (Nixon 2011: 14, A1): "A number of the groups and individuals directly involved in the revolts and reforms sweeping the region, including the April 6 Youth Movement in Egypt, the Bahrain Center for Human Rights and grass-roots activists like Entsar Qadhi, a youth leader in Yemen, received training and financing from groups like the International Republican Institute, the National Democratic Institute, and Freedom House, a non-profit human rights organization based in Washington, according to interviews in recent weeks and American diplomatic cables obtained by WikiLeaks.... 'We learned how to organize and build coalitions', said Bashem Fathy, a founder of the youth movement that ultimately drove the Egyptian uprisings."
19. IFC website 2014. The site contains a detailed discussion of the data collection methodology.
20. Kushnir, Mirmulstein, & Ramalho 2010.
21. Ibid.
22. Comparative Nonprofit Sector Project website 2014.
23. Salamon & Anheier 1992a, b; Salamon & Anheier 1997; Anheier & Salamon 2006.
24. Anheier & Salamon 2006: 100.
25. Ibid.
26. Ibid.
27. See Schofer & Longhofer (2011). For example, the authors note that the *Encyclopedia* is a directory compiled by personnel in countries around the world and does not represent a complete census of associations. They check the reliability of the *Encyclopedia*'s counts by comparing estimates with three other sources of data (finding a 0.72 correlation between different data sources). They also describe reconstructing longitudinal details by using the founding date of associations in the 2010 directory to estimate prior years. A comparison of their retrospective count with figures in a prior volume yielded a 0.8 correlation.
28. Briscoe & Safford 2008.

29. Hansmann 1987. For an overview of "failure theories" see Steinberg 2006.
30. For a more detailed critique of these failure theories see Salamon 1987 and DiMaggio & Anheier 1990.
31. Salamon 1981, 1987; Schofer & Longhofer 2011.
32. Anheier & Salamon 2006: 100.
33. Another study in the US surveyed about 3,000 organizations on employee recruitment, work organization, meetings, and modern production practices (Black & Lynch 2001).
34. Dobbin 2009.
35. Ibid. Source data come from Dobbin et al. 1993; Sutton et al. 1994; Kalev, Dobbin, & Kelly 2006; and Dobbin & Kelly 2007.
36. A detailed overview of the methodology is available online at <http://www.enter prisesurveys.org/methodology>.
37. See especially Bloom & Van Reenen 2007.
38. See Bloom et al. 2012 for a detailed discussion of the management practices index.
39. Hwang & Powell 2009; Alexander, Brudney, & Yang 2010; Barman & MacIndoe 2012; Bromley, Hwang, & Powell 2012; MacIndoe & Barman 2012; Bromley & Orchard, forthcoming; Hwang & Bromley, forthcoming.
40. Marshall & Suárez 2014.
41. Barr, Fafchamps, & Owens 2005.
42. Gugerty & Prakash 2010; Prakash & Gugerty 2010a. For a study of Africa see Gugerty 2010; for Europe see Bies 2010. Ebrahim 2003b discusses global trends.
43. For example, Ichniowski, Shaw, & Prennushi (1997) collected detailed monthly performance and management data on 36 steel lines owned by 17 firms. Other examples include Huselid 1995; Bandiera, Barankay, & Rasul 2005, 2010; and Bartel, Ichniowski, & Shaw 2007.
44. Bloom et al. 2012.
45. Lynch-Cerullo & Cooney 2011.
46. Becker & Huselid 1998.
47. Bloom et al. 2012: 22. These scholars elaborate on the skeptical view of links between managerial practices and productivity: "The argument against the importance of management is that profit maximization will lead firms to reduce costs. As a result, any residual variations in management practices will reflect firms' optimal responses to differing market conditions. Hence, different management practices are not 'good' or 'bad', but the optimal response to different market circumstances. This view also underlies the contingency theory of Woodward (1958)."
48. In a study using a nationally representative sample of 3,000 US firms, Black & Lynch (2001) find it is not whether particular management practices are adopted that matters for productivity, but rather how they are implemented. Neumark & Cappelli (1999) similarly note a "weak" statistical case for linking high-performance human resource practices to productivity. A longitudinal study of seven practices in 308 firms over 22 years found that no operational practices (e.g., total quality management, supply chain partnering, or just-in-time production) were linked to increased productivity; empowerment and training improved performance (Birdi et al. 2008). In New Zealand, Guthrie (2001) found that the use of high-involvement work practices reduced employee productivity.

49. Bendix 1964; Tilly 1975; Thomas & Meyer 1984; Iversen & Cusack 2000.
50. Tilly 1975, 1993.
51. Meyer et al. 1997.
52. For example, Hood (1995) discusses variations of the New Public Management doctrine in OECD countries; Aucoin & Peter (1995) compare Canada, the UK, Australia, and New Zealand; and Barzelay (2001) discusses the value of comparative New Public Management research.
53. Olson, Guthrie, & Humphrey 1998.
54. McLaughlin, Osborne, & Ferlie 2002.
55. Verhoest, van Theil, Bouckaert, & Laegreid 2012.
56. Osborne 2006; McCourt 2008: 472.
57. For example, Bovens 2007, 2010.
58. See Osborne 2006, 2010 for a more detailed discussion of the contrasts between bureaucracy, New Public Management, and New Public Governance.
59. Mitlin 2007.
60. Wampler 2010.
61. Shankland & Cornwall 2007.
62. Sneddon & Fox 2007.
63. Rhodes 1997, 2007; Peters & Pierre 1998.

3 Cultural foundations: science, empowerment, education

Organizational expansion transcends anything that could have been produced solely by forces of power or interest particular to specific social sectors or national locations. Large-scale cultural change, extending worldwide and across all domains of social life, created the context for the global expansion of organization—and hyper-organizational expansion into arenas difficult to account for in functional terms.

We focus here on three dramatic trends of the post-war period that promoted the proliferation of organization in a growing array of national settings and social domains:

(1) *The re-envisioning of nature and of social life as subject to scientific (including social scientific) analysis.* The worldwide expansion of science provided a basis for thinking of most natural and social realms as subject to human understanding and potential human control—as though nature and society follow standardized, integrated, and lawful rules. The expansion of science thus supports the rise and spread of rationalized formal organization.

(2) *The reconceptualization of individuals as having expanded and standardized capabilities and responsibilities.* The expanded and rationalized actorhood attributed to individual humans facilitates their assembly into rationalized and purposive formal organizations.

(3) *The intersection of science and human rights in the explosive worldwide growth of education.* The rise of schooling—especially expanded higher education throughout the post-war period—produced a population for which rationalized organization is a possible, and indeed natural, form of social relations.

We turn now to a more systematic treatment of these cultural shifts. We start by reviewing why the period since World War II was a particularly important historical moment for rationalized cultural globalization. Next we discuss the three core changes—expansions in science, individual empowerment, and education—and how they support the rise of organization. We conclude with an illustration of the process through which cultural trends generate organization.

Cultural globalization following World War II

Contemporary organizations existed long before World War II, of course. In some societies, like the US, the transformation of modern social structures, such as firms and charitable groups, was well under way by the early twentieth century.[1] But World War II is a turning point for the globalization of the model of an organizational society. Several causal factors are involved:[2]

Global interdependence, actual and perceived: politically, World War II was fought on a supra-national scale, over ideologies that transcended narrower nationalisms. It led directly to a Cold War conflict of a similar sort, organized around issues and coalitions far beyond the interests of specific national states. Technologically, a nuclear age carrying prospects for global destruction rendered traditional national military and political strategies obsolete. The war also followed closely on a collapse of the world economy, whose disasters were understood to reflect the failures of economic nationalism. All this made it obvious that in Europe and the world, economic as well as political coordination was essential—ideologies celebrated an open world economy rather than closed national ones.[3] Communism provided one vision of this sort, and in reaction a global liberalism intensified, ultimately turning into a set of more extreme neoliberal doctrines.

Stigmatization of the past: under different conditions, one could have imagined a post-war world involving resurgent nationalist claims of the sort that had marked the world in the aftermath of World War I. But World War II had evolved into a fight against authoritarian statism and corporatism. As it wore on, even the leaders of imperialist Britain and the racist US could promulgate an Atlantic Charter spelling out an extended version of human equality and freedom and organized supra-national cooperation. After the war, the United Nations Charter, along with its Declaration of Human Rights, asserted these doctrines as global truths (against some American and British resistance). The discovery of the extent of the Holocaust further undercut overtly racist ideologies. The awareness of the consequences of uncontrolled nationalist and corporatist statism was overwhelming: the Holocaust remains a dominant worldwide iconic symbol of the evils involved.[4] The search for supra-national civility became central.

Breakup of empires: World War II weakened or destroyed many existing governance structures, especially the administrative and bureaucratic capacities of the great world empires.[5] Further, the discursive evolution of the war into a conflict of freedom against corporatist statism greatly weakened the legitimacy of empire. Both organizationally and culturally, explicit colonialism suffered a mortal blow, and the contemporary world filled with national states rather than other forms.

In the face of fears of extreme disorder and Communist expansion, the question of social order in a world with all the new national states became central. In line with liberal ideologies, notions of the equality and commonality of both individuals and nations, and reciprocal responsibilities among them, were natural principles on which to base a post-war world order. These principles were built into the theories and structures of the global social architecture, including a whole array of world organizations.

American, and liberal, dominance: the war left the US in a hegemonic position, controlling more than 40 percent of the gross world product. As a victor, the country was held up as an exemplar of liberal virtues dramatized in the ideological conflict between democracy/capitalism and communism. Alternatives were greatly weakened in power and legitimacy (the European core) or stigmatized (the Soviet Union). Thus liberal ideologies and institutions flourished at the global level, and a dominant culture reflecting Anglo-American cultural forms has been central in the world through the whole post-war period. Tocqueville's order in a nineteenth-century America[6] with a very weak state became a global cosmology.[7]

Global statelessness: the cultural authority of liberal ideologies and institutions was greatly reinforced by the absence of anything like a supra-national government.[8] The UN and its agencies never played a state-like role. Even the European Union was a very limited and problematic structure. Fantasies, hopes, and policies lay in other directions such as soft law and decentralization and deregulation.[9]

Taken together, these consequences of the war drastically weakened the charisma of national states (although it increased their number) and strengthened the sanctity of individuals on a global scale. Changes in the foundations of social authority and legitimacy, from states to individuals and from national to global levels, provided the basis for a new vision of social order. The Cold War and rise of neoliberalism intensified these pressures. These historical junctures globalized three main cultural trends that were prominent in liberal ideologies, providing the foundation for the construction of organizational societies worldwide: (1) the scientific reconstruction of natural and social worlds, (2) individual empowerment, and (3) the transmission of these values through educational expansion. The globalization of these three cultural principles provided a basic mythology or cosmology from which a new world order emerged, favoring organization over other forms of social structure (such as bureaucracy or association). These trends are, of course, reversible. Conflicting trends, such as resurging nationalism in Europe or increasing religious fundamentalism (rooted in Christianity in the US, or in Islam in the Middle East), undercut both globalization and the cultural foundations of organization. We return to this point in the conclusion of this book.

Expansion of science

Scientific expansion has an extensive history. As a cultural matter, faith in a lawful and orderly nature is rooted in the evolution of Christianity, especially Protestantism;[10] in the Enlightenment; and very much in American history. Properly endowed humans could comprehend nature and could use their understanding of its laws to manage the natural world and society. Such notions were particularly strong in nineteenth-century America.[11] A faith in science combined with more directly religious commitments supported social control through associational life in a relatively stateless society. Scientific ideas and ideologies expanded rapidly.[12] They covered domains far beyond those involved in directly instrumental purposes: science (including all sorts of pseudo-sciences and quackeries) functioned as a quasi-religious cosmology. Following World War II, for many of the same reasons, the continuous process of scientific expansion became far more global,[13] with social scientific expansion especially prominent.[14]

The universalization of nature and social life through the expansion of science creates domains that are suitable for, and that often require, rational formal organizations.[15] Diverse domains are treated as subject to the same scientific laws (e.g., the effects of pollution or, more controversially, economic theories of development), and thus potential foci of standardized and rationalized structures of adaptation and management.

Over time, scientific ideologies and activities expanded across every social domain, stemming from evolving cultural foundations that assume both the systematic nature of the world and the human ability to understand. With rapidly increasing globalization in the post-World War II era, scientific authority emerged in a wide array of countries.[16] The expansion of science generates organization in two ways simultaneously. First, the development of new scientific theories expands the arenas of nature and life that can be understood and potentially managed by humans. Second, it provides a framework for the proper methods of organization itself—the way action in these arenas should be structured.

Indicators of scientific expansion: the global explosion of science is widely recognized: it has famously been said that 90 percent of all the professional scientists who have ever lived are alive at the time of writing.[17] One scientist noted that this statement has been true at any given moment for nearly 300 years, an observation based on the exponential growth of scientific journals.[18] Similarly, according to one statistic, more "data" were amassed in 2002 than in all prior human history.[19] An overall pattern of expansion remains throughout the period. For instance, in the 1970s the rate of doctorates awarded per year in the US decelerated but then continued its increase in the 1990s, as shown in Figure 3.1. Overall, the number of PhDs increases by about 5 percent per year, according to a recent report released by the National Research Council

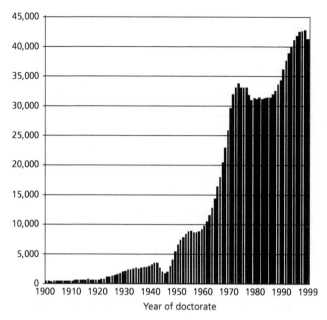

Figure 3.1. US Doctorates Awarded, 1900–99
Source: Thurgood et al. 2006: 7.

entitled *Trends in the Early Careers of Life Scientists.*[20] The rising number of natural and social scientists is particularly striking, as shown in the field of doctoral degrees awarded, in Figure 3.2. This increase in doctoral degrees is worldwide. Although the US has historically awarded the majority of doctorates, a substantial proportion of these have always been to non-US citizens. In the 1960s, for instance, roughly 13 percent of doctorates from US institutions went to non-citizens, and in the 1990s this proportion rose to more than 30 percent.[21] The number of degrees granted in other countries is also increasing. Figure 3.3 shows an increase in doctorates awarded between 1998 and 2006 in some countries for which data are available. Numbers of doctorates and scientists are, of course, simply indicators—the central point is that the creation of trained scientific professionals is an indicator of the expansion of scientific authority, influence, and activity.

Another rough indicator of scientific expansion is the number of members of scientific professional associations. The Federation of American Societies for Experimental Biology (FASEB) issues an annual directory of fourteen US societies, ranging from anatomy to biophysics. Membership has increased at a rate of just over 6 percent per year, from 469 members in 1920 to 56,469 members in 1997–98.[22] For trends outside the US, Perutz reports:

European trends are harder to measure, because there are no organizations comparable to FASEB. From 1920 to 1970, the British Biochemical Society grew at an average

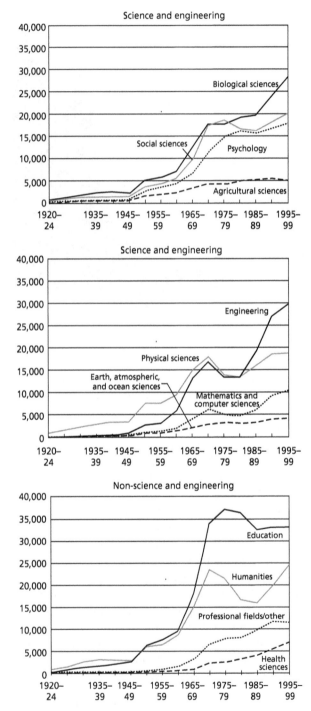

Figure 3.2. US Doctorates Awarded by Major Field, 1920–99
Source: Thurgood et al. 2006: 14.

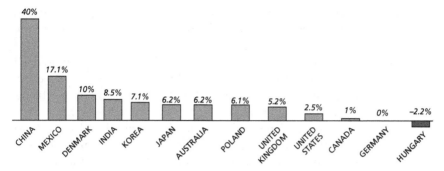

Figure 3.3. Average Annual Growth in Doctoral Degrees Awarded in all Disciplines across 13 Countries, 1998–2006
Source: Cyranoski et al. 2011: 277.

annual rate of 5.8%; from 1950 to 1970 the [German] Gesellschaft für Biochemie und Molekularbiologie grew at an annual rate of 16%. After 1970, their rates of growth slowed to 2.4% and 10%, respectively; the societies now have memberships of around 10,000 and 5,000, respectively. The growth rate of the German society outstrips that of FASEB, probably because it started later.[23]

Generally, existing data suggest that the increase of scientific activities is widespread. For instance, government expenditures on medical sciences in the US, UK, and Germany have expanded, particularly in the decades immediately following World War II.[24]

Many of the examples above are drawn from the natural and medical sciences, but in the twentieth century the social sciences expanded even more substantially. The social sciences—essentially absent in the nineteenth-century university—grew exponentially in the post-war period.[25] For example, what we now think of as sociology, a standard discipline with multiple subfields in undergraduate and graduate programs, barely existed in 1900. A few universities offered courses on moral philosophy that covered ethical debates on the nature of a perfect society, but stand-alone courses—and particularly those with an applied focus on understanding society in order to improve it—were virtually non-existent.[26] In universities, social science disciplines such as political science, sociology, and anthropology grew rapidly, and newer ones, such as organizational theory, finance, public administration, psychology, and education, also expanded and became established fields of academic study. Data collected by the United Nations Educational, Scientific, and Cultural Organization (UNESCO), for instance, show that enrollments in social sciences, business, and law account for much of the worldwide growth of tertiary expansion since 1999.[27]

Science and organization: beyond instrumental benefits, science functions as a universalizing and rationalizing cosmology in the post-war era. It is celebrated as a unifying collective world good in global structures—most strikingly in the form of UNESCO, which acquired its "S" in the process.[28] It is seen as an essential instrument in the efforts of national states and societies to progress. Scientific thinking provides a rationalized order which applies everywhere, and in which all can in theory participate.

Knowledge expansion is widely seen as a worthy human goal unto itself, not simply useful in an instrumental sense. Much legitimate scientific effort, past and present, has little immediate utility. Who needs to know whether there is ice on a moon of Jupiter? Or whether human language has a single point of origin? Biological research can develop medical and agricultural uses, but it also tracks the pre-history of extinct species. Anthropological research might usefully trace genetic migration patterns, but it also attends to the distant pre-histories of humanoid behaviors. Thus science expands with military and economic uses, but so does our knowledge of the moons of Jupiter and pre-modern history. Science provided a universalistic set of principles and a way of thinking that facilitates global cultural expansion and integration.

Since World War II, arena after arena of social life has been brought under scientific scrutiny. In each case, the application of scientific principles creates elements of organization—and hyper-organizational extensions. New organizations emerge, and existing organizations come under pressure to manage issues distantly related to their original purposes—finance, human resources, air or water pollution, the safety of workers and customers, the protection of the environment, or the proper management of transportation. Whole departments arise, as contemporary organizations create programs for personnel management covering matters formerly little scientized or organized (e.g., the protection of rights related to gender, race, or ethnicity).

Scientific findings and theories sometimes have direct and instrumental consequences. For example, when problems were discovered with the atmosphere's ozone layer, with clearly defined links to skin cancer, worldwide rules to reduce ozone depletion developed rapidly, impacting all sorts of organizations. Many effects, however, are more diffuse, less direct, and less immediately instrumental. For instance, the long-term development of the field of psychology has had clear effects on the rise of human resources programs and policies. But for decades there was no direct link. In the American case, national organization around the war effort sped up the process. The rise of political issues around affirmative action and inter-group equality gave further impetus to the expansion of rationalized organizational structures around personnel issues. As the field expanded and became institutionalized, secondary effects occurred, so that human resources programs in organizations broadened their jurisdictions far beyond the original agendas.[29]

Two examples help illustrate how the scientization of any context supports expanded organization.

Example 1. The invention of scientific management: the development of scientific principles for managerial activities underpins a great deal of what we now call organization. This trend took real form in the early twentieth century. The link to a systematic, scientific, evidence-based approach was explicit, whereas by now it has become taken for granted and rests more implicitly in the background. In 1911, Frederick Winslow Taylor published *The Principles of Scientific Management*, which described how the application of the scientific method to management could improve productivity.[30] In his words, the goal of the text was:

> *First.* To point out, through a series of simple illustrations, the great loss which the whole country is suffering through inefficiency in almost all of our daily acts.
>
> *Second.* To try to convince the reader that the remedy for this inefficiency lies in systematic management, rather than in searching for some unusual or extraordinary man.
>
> *Third.* To prove that the best management is a true science, resting upon clearly defined laws, rules, and principles, as a foundation. And further to show that the fundamental principles of scientific management are applicable to all kinds of human activities, from our simplest individual acts to the work of our great corporations, which call for the most elaborate cooperation. And, briefly, through a series of illustrations, to convince the reader that whenever these principles are correctly applied, results must follow which are truly astounding.[31]

Taylorism, as it is sometimes called, spelled out an early scientific approach to management. Taylor's philosophy recommends that managers be held responsible for planning work using scientific principles. This includes developing work methods based on the scientific study of tasks, monitoring workers to ensure that the proper methods are being used, and purposefully and actively selecting and training each worker for a specific task. Thinking of this kind is at the core of modern management. The general idea that outcomes should be achieved using evidence-based methodologies (in rhetoric if not in reality) is now applied not only to managing production, as Taylor intended, but also to the many other issues organizations must now attend to (e.g., performance assessments and incentivizing employees, labor and environmental protection, public relations, marketing, information management).

Although Taylor's *Principles of Scientific Management* may be the best known initial application of scientific management, he was not alone. Others, such as Henri Fayol and Henry Ford, were developing similar ideas at about the same time.[32] Still others were taking the idea that science could solve social problems and applying it to the charitable world.[33] Andrew Carnegie was among the first to create a professional foundation aimed at giving away money in a systematic way.[34] Some of his largest philanthropic projects were explicitly founded to develop scientific knowledge that could uncover the root cause of social problems. For instance, within a decade of its 1910 creation the

Carnegie Endowment for International Peace had produced 240 monographs analyzing the origins and outcomes of World War I. As one historian of philanthropy says, "They [the monographs] were a weighty testament—even as memories of the conflict remained vivid—to scientific philanthropy's belief that if only enough facts were unearthed, if only root causes were explored, a solution to warfare could be found."[35] The expansion of scientific thinking generated a belief in a human ability to prevent war and provided the means to putatively solve this problem—leading to the creation of a structure with a peculiarly (for the time) social scientific character.

Example 2. The construction of finance: the evolution of financial theory illustrates how the expansion of science also provides a foundation for organizing and organization by expanding human knowledge.[36] Sociologist Donald Mackenzie traced the development of financial theory in *An Engine, Not a Camera: How Financial Models Shape Markets.*[37] He provides a richly detailed evolutionary tale of the options pricing theories that started in academia in the 1950s and 1960s and become well established in the real (or surreal) world of finance in the 1970s.[38]

Options pricing models of the 1970s relied on unrealistic assumptions, such as the absence of transaction costs and the possibility of unlimited short selling, but nonetheless enabled an options market to grow. Although options trading had existed in various forms for centuries, it was considered highly speculative and generally unethical, more like gambling than investing. Academic models brought legitimacy to the practice, leading to the creation of the first options exchange in Chicago.[39] Initially, these academic models generated controversy, and practitioners resisted them on grounds of the questionable empirical validity of the theories and the unrealistic assumptions required. But faculty at the University of Chicago worked with investors and regulators to get their models onto trading floors, and eventually formal scientific models of financial valuation caught on. These models offered two benefits to practitioners. First, scientizing obscure financial transactions helped to legitimate and standardize the practice of options trading. Options could be listed on a reputable stock exchange and derivatives investing moved from the realm of immoral (and sometimes illegal) gaming into respectability. Second, the theories facilitated voluminous transactions (especially when later combined with automated trading technologies) and offered much profit potential.[40]

The scientized basis of financial theory (rather than its accuracy) brought great cultural legitimacy, contributing to a moral and legal foundation for the subsequent establishment of much finance-related organization. As Mackenzie describes, in 1970 there was almost no trading in financial derivatives, but by 2004 $273 trillion in derivatives contracts existed worldwide. As the models created new markets, they generated corresponding differentiation in the available jobs (e.g., a derivatives analyst), developed new types of firms (e.g., many hedge funds), required new forms of regulation and risk management (e.g., parts of the Dodd-Frank Act), and stimulated other organizational supports (e.g., classes offered in Master of Business Administration (MBA) programs and in-house in firms, or new certification systems).

Further, the generation of financial theory produced a phenomenon described in the literature as financialization.[41] As financial models evolved, managing share price (or maximizing shareholder value) became a central goal unto itself, rather than a natural outcome of producing some good or service. In early theories, share price was based on the fundamental underlying value of the firm. But it is now widely understood that both random fluctuations and socially constructed elements can also shape share prices. A recent study shows, for instance, that firms in lower status industries (e.g., waste management) face a higher share price penalty after an earnings restatement than firms in higher status industries (e.g., luxury consumer goods).[42] Other work shows that analysts' ability to easily categorize a firm's activities also shapes price.[43] Financialization involves the reorienting of firm activity away from its actual production operations and toward the management of share prices. To take on this additional obligation, the organizational and professional apparatuses of financial management expand. Figure 3.4, for example, shows the increasing prevalence of Chief Financial Officer (CFO) positions in US firms between 1963 and 2000. The expansion of finance as a legitimate enterprise rooted in scientific principles, as both an investment tool and a firm strategy for increasing profits, generates formal internal complexity as corporations create new roles and rules to manage these interests.

Behind any modern organization, or any component of a modern organization, lies a substantial history of scientific development. However, science

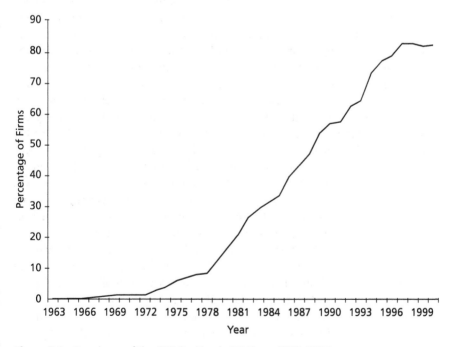

Figure 3.4. Prevalence of the CFO Position in US Firms, 1963–2000
Source: Zorn 2004: 351.

alone can produce bureaucracies, built on top-down authority, rather than contemporary organizations. What makes organization distinct is that it simultaneously integrates related, and equally powerful, assumptions about individual rights, capacities, and responsibilities that produce and legitimate organized actors and action in properly rationalized domains.

Expansion of individual capacities, rights and responsibilities

The global expansion of institutions celebrating individual rights and capacities is extraordinary.[44] Just as with the expansion of science, much of the source can be tied to the long-term erosion of traditional forms of authority and the rise of models of supra-national society and order. The nation-state arose with a long history of religious sanctification, which provided legitimation for its sovereignty and capacity for collective action. Over time, with secularization, sovereignty shifted from kings to peoples.[45] Formal bureaucracies developed under the sovereignty of the state, in part replacing earlier bureaucracies of the Church. In later developments, private structures could— with state certification—take the form of corporations under the sovereignty of state-licensed owners. And traditional professions, operating as guilds with religious sanction, gradually came under state licensing provisions too, thus generating entities for education, charity, medical care, and legal professions. Over their long history, all these sorts of structures became regulated by the state. These early forms, less independent actors and more servants of state and church-defined public needs, are precursors to the contemporary organization.

In early modern Western and later world history, a parallel source of sovereignty became built into the religious and social system: the individual person, and the associations entered into by such persons. Individuals directly were the locus of salvation and were thus sacralized. All the expanding organizing systems included components validating the individual. Indeed, the tension between the political or religious collective and the status of the individual person was historically central to the expansive Western organizational dynamic. The state evolved into the nation-state, with members seen as individuals and ultimately as citizens.[46] The property rights of the owners of the firm had natural law justifications, then state-certified ones, but they also (especially after the Reformation) had an individualistic religious character. Similarly, the organizational forms of religious, educational, and charitable life were in part associational, resting on the special religiously located status of the professionals involved.

The events of the first half of the twentieth century dramatically changed the balance of legitimacies. In the first part of the century, the state and competitions among states were seen as driving forces in human progress. But the pointlessness of World War I, the disastrous failures of the subsequent nationalist peace, the rise of fascism and communism, the Depression (seen as resulting from autarkic nationalism), the Holocaust, and the utterly destructive second war made it obvious that the state was as much a problem as a solution in a globalizing world.

The main alternative ontological base for a universalistic and global order was the individual person. In the contemporary period, the status of the individual has continually expanded and pressed against every alternative structure, including the state. The ultimate sovereignty of the state itself is weakened vis-à-vis the rights of the individual. The traditional professions and their authority structures are weakened too—priests, professors, lawyers, and doctors all came to be subjected to regulation. And all came to be organized in the modern order. Similarly, in the sphere of private property, the authority of the owner was sharply constrained.[47]

The legitimacy and authority of the individual also increases relative to familial and community structures. Structures around the world—and sometimes directly global ones—regulate matters such as abortion, sexual identities, and behaviors;[48] protect children as individuals from their parents; protect wives from spousal abuse; and protect the individual's right to choice in marriage.[49] In freeing the individual from family and community (and state), rights to individual choice in language, religion, self-expression, and free association are now celebrated on a global scale.

Indicators of the expansion of human rights and capacities: the striking expansion in global assertions of human rights is documented in Figure 3.5, taken from the research of Michael Elliott.[50] The figure shows the rising number of international human rights legal instruments over time. It can be paralleled by research on rights as asserted at national levels around the world. Figure 3.6 shows the rising percentage of countries with one or both of two types of national human rights institutions—a conservative count of such structures, because it excludes sub national bodies and those that do related work using a different name (e.g., under the auspices of issues related to women or children).[51] The values espoused by these global and national structures are reflected in public opinion surveys as well. A poll conducted in 2008 in 25 countries found that majorities in all countries surveyed, including authoritarian ones, supported the following principles:

- people should be free to express their opinions, including criticism of the government;
- people should have the right to demonstrate peacefully;
- the media should be free of government control;
- people should be treated equally irrespective of religion, gender, race, or ethnicity;

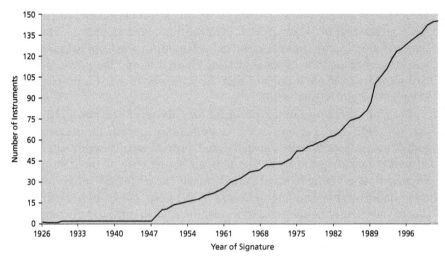

Figure 3.5. Number of International Human Rights Instruments (n=145)
Source: Elliott 2007: 354.

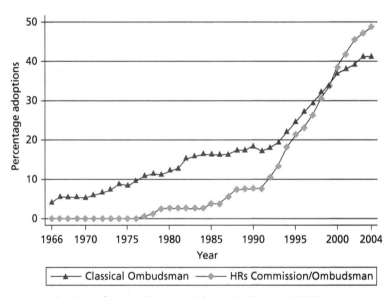

Figure 3.6. Adoptions of National Human Rights Institutions, 1966–2004
Source: Koo and Ramirez 2009: 1327.

- governments should be responsible for ensuring that their citizens can meet their basic needs for food, health care, and education (this includes large majorities of Americans);
- the will of the people should be the basis for the authority of government, and government leaders should be selected through free elections with universal suffrage.[52]

One focus of the rights discourse expanding in the post-war period remains on the classic entitlements and protections—expanding from civil protections to political rights to socio-economic welfare rights,[53] and now to psychological and cultural rights (e.g., to receive health care coverage for mental illnesses or mood disorders, or protections for special languages or religious customs). Figures 3.7 and 3.8 illustrate the rise of individual rights.[54] They depict, respectively, the range and prevalence of social participants entitled (and sometimes obligated) to support various rights of themselves and others in 145 contemporary human rights instruments (e.g., the Universal Declaration of Human Rights), as well as the types of violations listed. The traditional notions of rights as norms to be protected by states are transcended by modern assertions of rights as everybody's business. The implication is that all, or almost all, individuals have the ability (and, by implication, responsibility) to take action. Increasingly, the rights of the individual are not only protections and entitlements, but also political, economic, and cultural choices. The modern individual is seen as an empowered actor, capable of making legitimated choices in a wide range of social, cultural, economic, and political arenas.[55]

Individualism, science, and organization: the empowerment of the modern individual is expressed in the expansion of associational structures, such as self-help groups, community associations, and other voluntary groups. These, as discussed above, carry the legitimated capacity (and sometimes real capacity) for choice and action. However, the expansion of rights and individualism in the post-war era goes beyond the capacity for associational participation. Individual

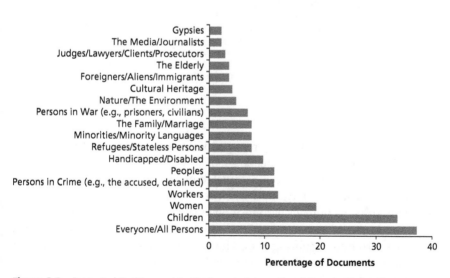

Figure 3.7. Protected Entities and Institutions in International Human Rights Documents (n=145)

Source: Adapted from Elliott 2007: 355.

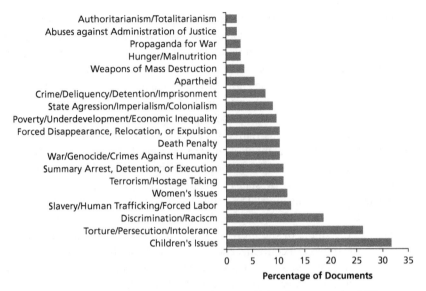

Figure 3.8. Rights Violations in International Human Rights Documents (n=145)

Source: Adapted from Elliott 2007: 356.

Notes: (1) Children's Issues include Child Abduction, Child Begging, Harmful Child Labor, Child Marriages, Child/Infant/Maternal Mortality, Child Pornography, Child Prostitution or Sexual Slavery, Child Sex Tourism, Forced Religious Conversion of Children, Children and Domestic Violence or Abuse, Sale or Trafficking of Children and Organs, Use/Procuring/Offering of Children for the Production and Trafficking of Drugs, Forced/Compulsory Use of/Displacement of Children in Armed Conflict, and Discrimination against Children with HIV/AIDS. (2) Women's Issues include: Female Infanticide, Gender Inequality, Sexual Harassment, Dangerous/Unhealthy/Arduous Work regarding pregnant or nursing women, Violations of the human rights of women in situations of armed conflict [incl. murder, systematic rape, sexual slavery/enforced prostitution, forced pregnancy, any form of indecent assault], Physical/Sexual/Psychological violence against women occurring in the family [incl. battering, sexual abuse of female children, dowry-related violence, marital rape, female genital mutilation, non-spousal violence, violence related to exploitation], Physical/Sexual/Psychological violence against women occurring within the general community [incl. rape/sexual abuse/sexual harassment/kidnapping/intimidation at work/educational institutions/and elsewhere, torture, trafficking in women, forced prostitution], Physical/Sexual/Psychological violence perpetrated or condoned by the State.

decisions—covering everything from political to economic to cultural choice—are legitimated as part of the public good.

The modern human is seen as capable of legitimate strategic choice and action, a capacity facilitated by a scientized environment imagined as subject to lawful rules. As humans become individual rational actors drawing on their scientized environments to make decisions, bureaucratic or associational societies turn into organizing ones. This overall picture is of a cultural system built around a universalistic cosmology in which collective action is feasible without state coercion, and filled with individual persons capable of acting within this cosmology. Formal organization is a consequence.

The discussion in the literature reflects Bell's "cultural contradictions of capitalism."[56] That is, the system contains the seeds of its own destruction, following Schumpeter.[57] Bell observed that individuals in capitalist systems developed a need for (and right to) personal gratification, a need that eroded the disciplined work ethic that created their initial success. One can stress either side of this issue—seeing scientization as creating a leviathan of social control, or seeing individualism as run rampant outside of social control and generating anomie.[58] We do not take either view here: expanded scientization and expanding individualism go together. Both science and individualism are closely related features of contemporary culture, and both are central in the construction of an organizing society. Expanded scientization without individualism supports bureaucracy. Expanded individualism without scientization supports a world of association. Expanded scientization and individualism together create the world of formal organization.

Education as obligation and global right

The expansion of science and individualism underpins much of the worldwide explosion of education. Education links the empowerment of people with command over the rationalized knowledge system. The enormous educational systems of the world, strangely combining compulsory and entitlement provisions, are principal mechanisms through which people everywhere are understood to acquire scientific thinking and their capacities and rights. To an astonishing degree, in recent decades, the ideal of universal mass schooling has been put into practice—and higher education has expanded rapidly.

Educational expansion is foreshadowed in the rise of modern national states and societies. It is especially early and prominent in liberal societies (e.g., the US). The assumptions of a liberal order are heavily dependent on the political, economic, and social choices of presumably responsible and rational individual persons. The answers to various social problems—for example, failures of democracy or the economy, or modern health issues like obesity and diabetes—ultimately tend to include the core institution of education. Education is the solution for enlightening people so they may solve social problems. As these individualist liberal cultural assumptions were globalized, particularly after World War II, compulsory education and higher education expanded everywhere.[59]

The forces supporting educational expansion were worldwide. That is, it was clearly and increasingly the responsibility of people in all countries to support education in all countries. This obligation is institutionalized in the contemporary global Education for All movement[60] and related declarations of human rights. It is supported by the major world organizations, such as the World Bank, UNESCO, and the international aid programs of the leading countries.

Mass education expanded dramatically in all parts of the world. By now elementary education is practically universal—and failures are now seen as urgently requiring repair. In most countries, legal rules make it compulsory. Secondary education has also expanded rapidly. Universal enrollment in at least some secondary education is in the offing, and there are movements to make it a global rule (e.g., the Project on Universal Basic and Secondary Education (UBASE)). Pre-primary education also trends upward. Figure 3.9 shows gross enrollments at all levels worldwide since 1970.

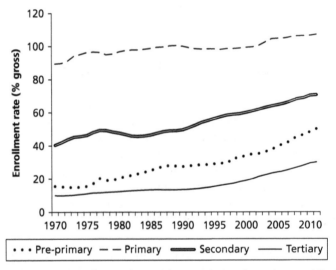

Figure 3.9. Worldwide Enrollments in Pre-primary, Primary, Secondary, and Tertiary Education, 1970–2011

Source: World Development Indicators Online (2013).

Notes: Tertiary, % gross: total enrollment in tertiary education expressed as a percentage of the total population of the 5 year age group following on from secondary school leaving (accessed 12/3/2013 at <http://data.worldbank.org/indicator/SE.TER.ENRR>). Secondary, % gross: total enrollment in secondary education, regardless of age, expressed as a percentage of the population of official secondary education age. Gross enrollment rate can exceed 100% due to the inclusion of over-aged and under-aged students because of early or late school entrance and grade repetition (accessed 12/3/2013 at <http://data.worldbank.org/indicator/SE.SEC.ENRR>). Primary, % gross: total enrollment in primary education, regardless of age, expressed as a percentage of the population of official primary education age. Gross enrollment rate can exceed 100% due to the inclusion of over-aged and under-aged students because of early or late school entrance and grade repetition (accessed 12/3/2013 at <http://data.worldbank.org/indicator/SE.PRM.ENRR>). Preprimary, % gross: total enrollment in pre-primary education, regardless of age, expressed as a percentage of the total population of official pre-primary education age. Gross enrollment rate can exceed 100% due to the inclusion of over-aged and under-aged students because of early or late school entrance and grade repetition (accessed 12/3/2013 at <http://data.worldbank.org/indicator/SE.PRE.ENRR>).

The significance of expanded mass education for the nature of social organization has long been recognized.[61] Education brings people into more universalized roles and facilitates their organization in associations. But it also makes them fit subjects for life in organized structures—indeed, the basic early modern theory of organizations presupposed a population of schooled people, as Stinchcombe emphasized.[62]

The most dramatic expansion is in higher education.[63] Universities have exploded in number and size, and the world population is schooled in them to an extent that would have seemed astonishing (and threatening) 50 or 60 years ago. Figure 3.10 shows enrollment rates in higher education since 1970—for the world as a whole, and also for main regional groupings.

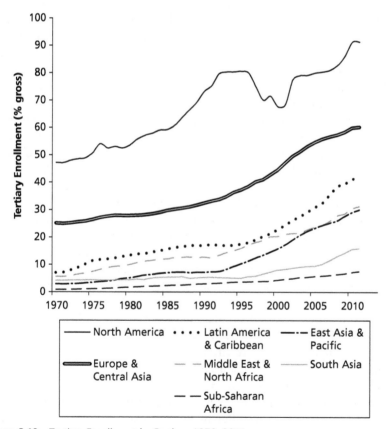

Figure 3.10.   Tertiary Enrollment by Region, 1970–2011

Source: World Development Indicators Online (2013).

Note: Gross enrollment rate (%) is total enrollment in tertiary education expressed as a percentage of the total population of the 5 year age group following on from secondary school leaving (accessed 12/3/2013 at: <http://data.worldbank.org/indicator/SE.TER.ENRR>).

To put the expansion in context, over 20 percent of the relevant age cohort is now enrolled in academic higher education. Roughly a quarter of the world's young people get some post-secondary education, often in gigantic universities. For instance, the University of Phoenix is widely recognized to be the largest private provider of higher education in the US. In 2000 its enrollment surpassed 100,000 students, and in 2010 enrollment peaked at 600,000 students. More than 25,000 faculty members teach in 20 different degree programs.[64] Many large universities elsewhere in the world are even bigger than this. For example, the Indira Gandhi National Open University in India had more than 3 million enrolled students in 2014.[65] More recently, massive open online courses (MOOCs) have attracted a wave of attention and millions of students. Coursera, one of the most successful examples, has paired with elite universities to offer free online classes, and more than 11 million students had enrolled by the start of 2015.[66]

The education involved, both mass and elite, goes on in institutions that have remarkable commonalities around the world, despite enormous national differences in culture and resources.[67] Curricular topics and degree programs, though varying widely in quality, are nevertheless translatable essentially everywhere. A basic university degree in any subject is intended to be meaningful globally—in the basic and applied sciences, in the basic and applied social sciences, and even in the declining humanities. The aspirations are celebrated in the global evaluation systems, which see universities as having so much in common that they can be ranked across countries on main single dimensions (as with the Shanghai rankings). In the same way, the quality of mass educational systems can be assessed globally (as with the International Association for the Evaluation of Educational Achievement (IEA) and Programme for International Student Assessment (PISA) tests).[68]

The person schooled with higher education is empowered with extended human rights and is culturally mapped onto a scientized world. Such people are socially fit to create and function in formal organizations. If mass education equips people to function in bureaucracies, higher education renders them suitable to be participants in the post-bureaucratic realities of the modern organization. Indeed, the theory and practice of modern organizational life is mainly about the orientations and behavior of these highly schooled participants.[69] Overall, thus, the expansion of education—particularly higher education—in any domain increases the rate at which organizations form and expand.

As people pour out of universities, worldwide, they flow into the differentiated roles of the modern organizational system. Many enter into positions for which their training has suited them—engineering students often work as engineers—and sometimes the link between training and work is legally enforced (as with medicine). But often the links are looser, and educated people can be found in roles for which their training provided no special skills. The point is that a well-schooled person is thought to be able to take rational action in a variety of highly differentiated roles. Someone with training could take on a public relations position for a dental association concerned to protect the teeth of children from the consumption of sugar. The same person, the next year, could plausibly work in marketing for a firm making candy bars.

Education has particularly direct effects on the rise of modern organization in the area of management training. The MBA degree began at Harvard University in 1908 with an incoming class of 80 students.[70] The growth of such programs has been dramatic—linked closely to the development of a quantified and scientific curriculum.[71] It is difficult to count programs exactly, but one way is through accreditation. Three of the better known accrediting agencies are the Association to Advance Collegiate Schools of Business (AACSB International), the Accreditation Council for Business Schools and Colleges (ACBSC), and the International Assembly for Collegiate Business Education (IACBE). As of 2013, the US had 1,546 programs accredited by one of these agencies. Further, of the 1,650,000 bachelor's degrees conferred in the US in 2010, the greatest numbers of degrees were conferred in business (358,000). Figure 3.11 shows the rising number of bachelor's degrees in business in the US since 1970. At the master's degree level, the greatest numbers of degrees were conferred in the fields of education (182,000) and business (178,000).[72]

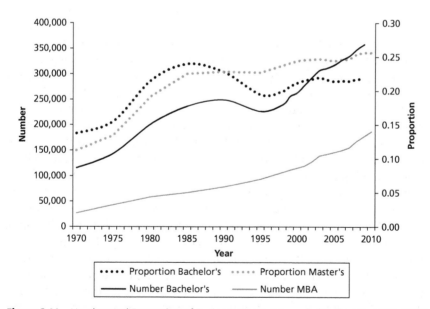

Figure 3.11. Number and Proportion of Business Degrees Awarded in the US, 1970–2010

Source: National Center for Educational Statistics website (2013a, b). Accessed 12/3/2013 at: (Bachelor's) <http://nces.ed.gov/programs/digest/d11/tables/dt11_286.asp>; (MBA) <http://nces.ed.gov/programs/digest/d12/tables/dt12_314.asp>.

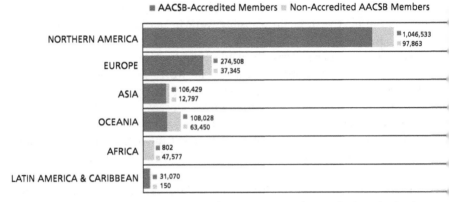

Figure 3.12. Number of Students Enrolled in AACSB Member Institutions by Region, 2012–13
Source: AACSB website 2013.

The expansion of business education is global. In 2013 outside the US there were 350 MBA program certifications (by either the AACSB, ACBSC, or IACBE) in 67 countries. A great many other programs are granted charters in alternative ways. Worldwide enrollment for AACSB-accredited programs was above 1.6 million students in 2012–13, with the majority in North America but more than half a million on other continents, as shown in Figure 3.12.

The relatively standardized and scientized (and internationally ranked) education provided in business schools produces people suited for management: they are assumed to learn generic skills like decision-making, leadership, and planning, more than specific substantive knowledge of a particular industry. Entities that have trained professional managers—MBAs, in contemporary parlance—are especially likely to have all the markers of the modern rationalized formal organization. Some studies suggest that executives with MBA degrees behave differently from those without, and in ways that predict conformity to models of "formal organization."[73] Those with business school training are more "action-oriented" and follow "textbook guidelines" more closely when making their investment decisions.[74] They are also more attuned to market trends and more prone to taking action when a shift in circumstances occurs.[75] Firms led by executives with MBAs are also more likely to respond to requests to disclose environmental performance.[76] Such trends are evident in the non-profit sector as well. Non-profits with leaders who have managerial training are more likely to adopt a range of rationalized practices, including quantitative outcomes measurement, formal audits, and the use of consultants.[77] Conceptions of management are closely and reciprocally linked to models of formal organization; the ideas involved are transmitted through contemporary education.

An illustration: organizing childhood

In this chapter we have argued that schooled rights and science work together to create hyper-organization and organizing. An example helps to illuminate how the process unfolds. The expansion of the rights of children is one of the most wide-ranging cultural shifts in the twentieth century. The rights of children are mentioned in 34 percent of human rights documents, and violations specific to children appear in 32 percent of them. A well-established body of thought notes the changing status of children in societies around the world.[78] We highlight that under contemporary cultural frames the changing status of children also leads to increased organization.

Science provided one set of grounds that legitimated the value of children and childhood. Childhood was invisible in the early twentieth-century university—almost no references to it occur in US university course catalogues. All this changed in the first half of the twentieth century, and childhood as a topic exploded in the post-war period. Children became a focus of scientific analysis in many fields—education, several areas of medicine, law, sociology, psychology, anthropology, and even literature and the arts. As part of this growth, in the 1960s a theory of human capital emerged, linking education and training to future wage productivity.[79] This theory helped initiate a newfound emphasis on education in the early years of life, on the premise that it would increase individual productivity and, by aggregation, increase the national Gross Domestic Product.

Human rights provided another equally important set of grounds for transforming children into individuals with rights. With the expansion of an international human rights regime, compulsory minimum education laws expanded worldwide, as shown in Figure 3.13. The United Nations Convention on the Rights of the Child, established in 1989 and now signed by all countries except the US and Somalia, sets out and monitors guidelines on issues such as minimum years of schooling and minimum age for employment or marriage. The methods for protecting human rights are rooted in social scientific principles, generating much organizing activity. National constitutions routinely discuss children and their rights.[80] Extensive data are collected, analyzed, and reported to monitor progress on these issues.

Nation-states and international organizations create new policies and offices related to children, but the landscape within organizations changes as well. New organized groups are created to protect youth, and others are under pressure to respond (often by developing policies to protect children and sometimes by changing their practices). For instance, NGOs such as Save the Children, the Fair Labor Association (FLA), and the Clean Clothes Campaign develop new programs to deal with the newly defined problems of child labor and labor exploitation more generally. Many of these

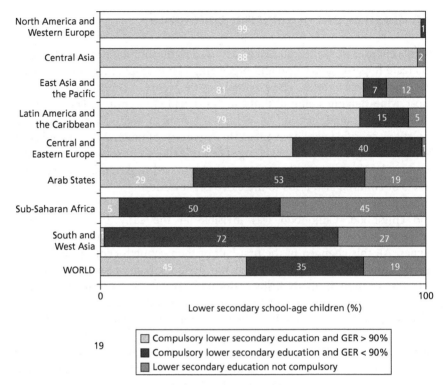

Figure 3.13. Global Prevalence of Compulsory Education Laws in 2011

Source: UNESCO Institute for Statistics 2011: 22.

Note: Gross Enrollment Rate (GER) is the ratio of the number of students who live in a country to those who qualify for the particular grade level.

programs themselves follow systematic, scientific principles to achieve their goals. For instance, the FLA generates standardized metrics of labor practices, monitors and reports on those metrics, and provides accreditation to companies found to be in compliance. All parts of a supply chain are measured against a set of benchmarks developed by the FLA based on recommendations by the International Labor Organization. These cover such matters as child labor, harassment, forced labor, non-discrimination, safety, and compensation. Emphasizing their scientific approach, these organizations liken their methods to visiting the doctor—with a check-up, diagnosis, remedy, and follow-up.

As new global principles, organizations, and programs emerge to protect children,[81] existing organizations change in parallel, in a predictably scientific fashion. When, in 1996, *Life* magazine featured a heartbreaking story about Tariq, a 12 year-old Pakistani boy who worked stitching soccer balls at a Nike subcontracting factory for the equivalent of 60 cents per day, the organizational response was rapid and extensive.[82] Following the soccer ball exposé, Nike developed additional departments and policies; hired relevant personnel; and raised the age limit for workers in its shoe factories to 18 and for other garments to 16. Nike now monitors its overseas facilities, generates regular reports (as illustrated in Figure 3.14), and invests heavily in reputation management and marketing (themselves now scientized fields),[83] including supporting and helping to found related NGOs. For Nike, this organizational elaboration occurs not only in the realm of labor, but also in regard to its impacts on energy and climate, including chemicals, water, and waste; community; and people—where it also has set policies and goals,

Beyond the breakdown of factory ratings, we also look at trends in the types and severity of violations found through our auditing processes. We made a significant shift with the incorporation of NIKE, Inc. Affiliate brands in our auditing and reporting. We moved from 68 percent non-rated factories in FY07 to 89 percent rated in FY11 (see previous table). By comparing the percentage of C (serious) and D (critical) rated incidents found during factory audits, over time we can see where changes are taking place.

TOP ISSUES OF LABOR NON-COMPLIANCE IN CONTRACT FACTORIES - NIKE, INC.

	FY07	FY10	FY11
AGE	1%	1%	1%
FREEDOM OF ASSOCIATION AND COLLECTIVE BARGAINING	0%	2%	2%
HARASSMENT	7%	4%	3%
HIRING	3%	4%	4%
HOURS	52%	38%	41%
OTHER	20%	19%	13%
WAGES	17%	32%	36%
TOTALS	100%	100%	100%

Additional information on each area is available online, including descriptions linked to our Code Leadership Standards outlining what is expected of factories in each of these areas.

Over the five years from FY07 through FY11, the most common issues were those related to hours worked and wages. In FY11, 41 percent of overall noncompliance incidents were related to hours, down from 52 percent in FY07. Hours issues entail the serious (C-rated) incidents of contract factories with workers putting in between 60 and 72 hours per week or not providing one day off in seven. Other issues in the general category of hours include critical (D-rated) issues of no verifiable timekeeping systems, exceeding daily work hour limits, working more than 72 hours per week, or not providing one day off in 14. Wages represented 17 percent of noncompliance incidents in FY07, when assessing NIKE Brand only, compared with 36 percent of incidents found in FY11 with inclusion of all brands across NIKE, Inc. Most wage-related incidents were miscalculations of wages or benefits, rather than an overall failure to pay workers the agreed wage for work performed. These kinds of incidents are systemic within factories across the industry, as understanding and correctly paying social security-type benefits can mean navigating confusing and complex laws and standards. We recognize the complexity of and interest around the broad issue of wages, and we address our efforts in this area both below and in the Manufacturing section of this report.

Other categories tracked have remained relatively steady over the five-year period and the inclusion of Affiliate brands. Age-related incidents remained steady at 1 percent. Freedom of Association remained relatively low, from 0 percent to 2 percent of incidents. Harassment decreased from 7 percent to 3 percent of noncompliance incidents, which we believe to be partly due to the HRM training.

The category of "other"—which includes issues of dishonesty, such as coaching workers to lie about conditions, denial of auditor access, falsifying statements and unwillingness to comply with standards—has decreased from 20 percent to 13 percent of incidents over five years. We believe this indicates increased transparency in the supply chain.

We have continued to analyze the root causes of noncompliance. The three main causes we saw in FY10 and FY11 are broadly consistent with previous years: lack of systems, lack of commitment and lack of knowledge.

Figure 3.14. Excerpt from Nike Annual Report on Labor Compliance
Source: Nike website 2013.

monitors and generates reports, and has created other similar organizational structures.

A case study of Nike's transformation into an organized corporate citizen based on detailed interviews describes the organizational elaboration involved:

In response to the growing criticisms, Nike created several new departments (e.g., Labor Practices (1996), Nike Environmental Action Team (NEAT) (1993)) which, by June 2000, were organized under the Corporate Responsibility and Compliance Department. Last year, in an effort to strengthen the links between production and compliance decisions, the compliance department was moved into the apparel division. Today, Nike has 85 people specifically dedicated to labor and environmental compliance, all located in countries where Nike products are manufactured. These employees visit suppliers' footwear factories on a daily basis. In apparel, given the much larger number of suppliers, Nike managers conduct on-site inspections on a weekly or monthly basis, depending upon the size of the firm. In addition to its corporate responsibility and compliance managers, Nike has about 1000 production specialists working at/with its various global suppliers. All Nike personnel responsible for either production or compliance receive training in Nike's Code of Conduct, Labor Practices, Cross Cultural Awareness, and in the company's Safety, Health, Attitudes of Management, People Investment and Environment (SHAPE) program....

For example, all potential Nike suppliers must undergo a SHAPE inspection, conducted by Nike's own production staff. The SHAPE inspection is a preliminary, pre-production inspection of factories to see if they meet Nike's standards for a clean and healthy workplace, respectful labor-management relations, fair wages and working conditions, and minimum working age. After this initial assessment, labor practices are more carefully audited by Nike's own labor specialists as well as by outside consultants like PriceWaterhouseCoopers (PWC)....In addition to developing internal expertise and capacity in the area of standards and corporate responsibility and working with its own suppliers to improve their performance in these areas, Nike has been active in founding and/or supporting an array of different international and non-profit organizations, all aimed at improving standards for workers in various developing countries.[84]

Principles of rights and science transform such problems as child labor into arenas that can be systematically understood and controlled in ways that link local settings (e.g., a soccer ball factory in Pakistan) all the way up to the centers of world society (e.g., the Convention on the Rights of the Child). Sometimes existing organizations change through direct pressure as in our Nike example (e.g., from social movements[85] or legal mandates[86]), but change may also occur as diffuse cultural responses to new expectations, mimicry, or assumptions about appropriate ways of talking and doing.[87]

As the social value of children increases, any sort of organization is likely to come under some pressure for expansion to deal with issues related to children. Child care becomes an obligation, along with special rules supporting parenthood. Child safety becomes an endemic concern, and dangerous toys and recreational equipment are inspected and regulated. Liabilities come to be an issue, and specialist legal organizations attend to them. In an ironic twist, the university, with its institutes producing scientized knowledge dedicated to the welfare of children around the world, is ultimately altered by the knowledge it created and is forced into organizational expansion along mundane dimensions. Universities may facilitate child care arrangements for students and staff and enable school children to visit. They make sure facilities are not dangerous for children; pools must be appropriately fenced and guarded; and child care centers are created and regulated. Children also are to be protected from researchers through regulations (e.g., Institutional Review Boards in the US). In partial conflict with this protection, in order to generate, test, and monitor scientific and quasi-scientific theories about childhood, it is important to gather data, record information, analyze, evaluate, and generate reports, not to mention establish planning processes to do these tasks.[88]

Chapter summary

The worldwide expansion in formal organizations in the contemporary period is rooted in dramatic changes in dominant cultural frames. The post-war world was one of expanding actual and perceived interdependence—military, political, economic, social, and cultural. But the older controls over interdependence, through nation-state powers and the expansion of the state system, were demonstrable failures. On the other hand, expansive fantasies of a global state, or even a European one, were unrealistic. A weak UN was the best that could be done.

In this vacuum—as with the relatively stateless nineteenth-century America as seen by Tocqueville[89]—authority shifted to expanding cultural controls. Science and social science provided a base on which, in the absence of positive law, orderly rule systems could be promulgated. Empowered and standardized individuals, schooled in a common global educational culture, provided an ontological base on which collective action could be grounded.

Thus the natural and social and psychological worlds were reconceived in a scientistic vein, providing grounds for common rationalized action everywhere, and for the standards regulating such action. Humans of all sorts were redefined, beyond national citizenship (and also beyond age, gender, race, and disability), as having enormous commonalities of rights and capacities, and as entitled to and capable of legitimate decisions.

Both the scientism and the empowered individualism of constructed world culture are built into many global institutions. Governmental and non-governmental organizations carry the standards of rational analysis and human rights, as do a wide variety of professional associations. But a most central institution integrating the empowered individual with a scientized environment is the university, which generates a population able to assume the professionalized roles of the modern organization, including a huge population of prospective managers.

In a world where science, rights, and education are pervasive, there are more things to formally organize around, more prescriptions about how to organize, and more people equipped to do and participate in the organizing. The organizations involved can reach into more and more aspects of human life, as these are scientifically rationalized and within the legitimate capacities of empowered humans to take responsibility for. Thus any given structure is likely to be hyper-organized beyond any locally functional or rational requirements.

In this now-global society, organizations can reach around the world, integrating formerly very disparate people in common cultural enterprises. The schooled contemporary person can organize, for instance, to protect the rights of children in countries he or she has never seen, and could not find on a map. And in response, any given organization anywhere becomes more likely to incorporate components dealing with such rights. We turn now to consider some core mechanisms by which great contemporary cultural rules are transmitted to local settings, or intensified within them.

▦ NOTES

1. See, for example, Coleman 1982; Perrow 2002; Kaufman 2008.
2. For a more detailed discussion of the historical cultural factors underpinning globalization see Drori, Meyer & Hwang 2006 and Krücken & Drori 2009.
3. Djelic & Quack 2003.
4. Bromley & Russell 2010.
5. Porter 2002.
6. Tocqueville [1890]1972.
7. See also Putnam, Leonardi, & Nanetti 1994; Putnam 2002.
8. See Weiss & Wilkinson (2014) and Finnemore (2014) for a recent discussion of the concepts of globalization and "global governance" in contrast with "government."
9. For example, Hallström 2004; Mörth 2004; Djelic & Sahlin-Andersson 2006; Higgins & Hallström 2007.
10. Weber 1958.
11. Tocqueville [1890]1972.
12. Drori et al. 2003.
13. Drori et al. 2003.
14. Drori & Moon 2006; Frank & Gabler 2006.
15. Drori, Meyer & Hwang 2006.
16. Finnemore 1993.
17. Price 1961.
18. Goodstein 1994.
19. As cited in Bail 2014.
20. National Research Council 1998.

21. National Science Foundation 2006.
22. Perutz 1999.
23. Perutz 1999.
24. Perutz 1999: 301.
25. Drori & Moon 2006; Frank & Gabler 2006.
26. Sealander 2003.
27. UNESCO Institute of Statistics 2014. See also Drori & Moon 2006; Moon & Wotipka 2006.
28. Finnemore 1993.
29. Dobbin 2009.
30. Taylor's principles were derived from a series of experiments he called time studies, in which he observed repetitive tasks to determine the most efficient way they should be done and the characteristics of the worker who could do them best. For instance, a study of shoveling productivity determined that the optimal weight for a worker to shovel without tiring was 21 pounds. By providing shovels of different sizes that corresponded to a 21-pound scoop (depending on the density of the material), employers could expect that workers could shovel three to four times more per day than if they were using a shovel that picked up a sub-optimal weight.
31. Taylor 1911.
32. Khurana 2007.
33. Friedman & McGarvie 2003; Hwang & Powell 2009.
34. Recall that organizational attention to equality is not equivalent to actual increased equality. Both Carnegie and Rockefeller were simultaneously two of the largest philan-thropists of all time and ruthless businessmen. In the words of Sealander (2003: 229): "The founders of scientific philanthropy cared deeply about democracy, but they were not democrats. They saw no reason to give their own employees a significant voice. Rockefeller, Sr. and Carnegie opposed independent unions; some of the era's bloodiest strikes occurred at companies they owned. What could only be labeled all-out class warfare occurred in the coalfields of Colorado in 1913 and 1914, when the United Mine Workers tried to organize Colorado Fuel and Iron, a Rockefeller subsidiary. Mine owners dug trenches, installed searchlights, and brought in private armies, supple-mented by the Colorado governor's compliant decision to send National Guardsmen to protect company property. Strikers, in turn, got their own guns. Disaster was inevitable when the miners' wives and children got caught in the crossfire of a firefight between strikers and guardsmen, burning to death in an underground pit in which they were hiding. The "Ludlow Massacre" became for many a searing image of injustice. There-fore, the accomplishments of scientific philanthropy must be framed in this context. They were top-down reforms, and those meant to benefit were not generally consulted."
35. Sealander 2003: 228–9.
36. A fascinating description of finance before it became scientized can be found in the cult classic *Reminiscence of a Stock Operator*. The story helps us to envision the world of finance before its contemporary hyper-organized condition. Published in 1923, author Edwin Lefèvre provides a thinly disguised biography of the stock-market speculator Jesse Liver-more (called "Lawrence Livingston" in the book), an investor renowned for making profits as the markets plummeted in 1907 and 1929 (he was worth an estimated $100 million

following the Crash of 1929). The teenaged Livermore was developing and testing theories of stock fluctuations in a rudimentary way, when stock quotes were written on chalkboards, before real-time price information was available. Livermore described his initial forays into stock market theorizing this way (pp. 1–3): "I went to work when I was just out of grammar school. I got a job as quotation-board boy in a stock-brokerage office. I was quick at figures. At school I did three years of arithmetic in one. I was particularly good at mental arithmetic. As quotation-board boy I posted the numbers on the big board in the customers' room. One of the customers usually sat by the ticker and called out the prices....I noticed that in advances as well as declines, stock prices were apt to show certain habits, so to speak. There was no end of parallel cases and these made precedents to guide me. I was only fourteen, but after I had taken hundreds of observations in my mind I found myself testing their accuracy, comparing the behaviour of stocks today with other days. It was not long before I was anticipating movements in prices. My only guide, as I say, was their past performances. I carried the 'dope sheets' in my mind. I looked for stock prices to run on form. I had 'clocked' them. You know what I mean." The violations of contemporary principles of organizing are numerous: Livermore was a teenager (probably a labor violation by current standards), there were no grand financial theories he had been trained in (he carried these in his head), a customer was involved in clocking the prices (likely some kind of Securities and Exchange Commission violation in the contemporary world), and so on.

37. Mackenzie 2006.
38. An "option" is essentially a contract to buy or sell an asset or instrument (e.g., a stock) at a given price before a given date. In order for a large market to exist, there needed to be tools for establishing the value of options. The Black–Scholes–Merton model of option pricing that evolved in the 1970s provided such a foundation.
39. Although the initial fit between the models and actual prices was poor, for a time they became more aligned. Drawing on Callon, Mackenzie calls this *performativity*: the theory of how options behaved became a self-fulfilling prophecy, with theory subsequently shaping how the market worked even if it was off-base to start.
40. A critical word here is the "potential" to make profits. Many people made money, or hoped they would, from these theories. But social scientific theories are not like the laws of physics. The world can behave in ways unpredicted by the theories, as shown by the unexpected role of derivatives in the collapse of the stock market in 1987 and the Long Term Capital Management crisis in 1998. In other words, it is not the case that the theories straightforwardly emerged as true reflections of reality and enabled great profits. They emerged as a theory of reality and generated both great gains and losses. The pursuit of social scientific knowledge can exist in tension with any practical applications.
41. Fligstein 1990; Krippner 2005; Davis 2009.
42. Sharkey 2014.
43. Zuckerman 1999.
44. Stacy 2009; Lauren 2011; Reus-Smit 2011.
45. Bendix 1980.
46. For example, see Davidson (1997) for Australia, Weber (1976) for France, or more generally Anderson (2006) for the creation of the modern nation-state populated by citizens.
47. Berle & Means 1991.
48. For example, Frank, Camp, & Boutcher 2010.

49. Arland Thornton (2013) and his colleagues have demonstrated that the norms involved are shared around the world on a very widespread basis.
50. Elliott 2007.
51. Koo & Ramirez 2009.
52. World Public Opinion 2011.
53. Marshall 1950.
54. Elliott 2007.
55. Meyer & Jepperson 2000.
56. Bell 2008.
57. Schumpeter 1942.
58. Durkheim 2012.
59. Meyer, Ramirez, & Soysal 1992; Schofer & Meyer 2005.
60. Chabbott 2003.
61. For an overview see Hannum & Buchmann 2003. For a detailed analysis see Baker 2014.
62. Stinchcombe 1965.
63. Schofer & Meyer 2005.
64. Apollo Group website 2015.
65. Indira Gandhi National Open University website 2014.
66. Coursera website 2015.
67. Meyer, Kamens, Benavot, Cha, & Wong 1992a.
68. Meyer & Benavot 2013.
69. Drori, Höllerer, & Walgenbach 2014.
70. Harvard Business School website 2015. See Anteby 2013 for a rich discussion of Harvard's MBA program.
71. Moon & Wotipka 2006.
72. National Center for Education Statistics website 2013a,b.
73. Not every dimension depends on advanced business training. Other empirical evidence finds no differences between firms that employ executives who have advanced business degrees and those that do not in levels of innovation or in research and development spending (Kimberly & Evanisko 1981; Barker & Mueller 2002).
74. Bertrand & Schoar 2003.
75. Grimm & Smith 1991; Finkelstein et al. 2009.
76. Lewis, Walls, & Dowell 2014.
77. Hwang & Powell 2009.
78. Ariès 1960; Zelizer 1981, 1985; Burman 1996.
79. See, for example, the lecture series on labor economics by Daron Acemoglu and David Autor, available online at <http://economics.mit.edu/files/4689>. They identify four main sources of human capital, three of which are related to education: (1) innate ability, (2) years of schooling, (3) school quality, and (4) training.
80. Boli-Bennett & Meyer 1978.
81. For example, Bartley & Child 2014.
82. Schanberg 1996.
83. McDonnell & King 2013.
84. Locke 2002: 16–18.
85. For example, Soule & Olzak 2004; King & Soule 2007.
86. For example, Soule & Zylan 1997.

87. For example, Sharkey & Bromley 2015.
88. The assumptions in the models of causality implied are often rather heroic (see, for example, many of the "theories of change" or "logic models" found in the philanthropic world or, more disastrously, the models a decade ago assuming that housing prices in the US could not decline). But in a science-based culture, it is seen as more reasonable to make good faith efforts at systematically controlling outcomes based on science-like assumptions than to leave things up to the gods or fates. Models of strategy take preference over models of prayer.
89. Tocqueville [1890]1972.

4 Transmitting culture: law, accounting, professionalism

A hegemonic culture of expanding science, human empowerment, and education underpins the expansion of contemporary organization. In this chapter, we consider the mechanisms through which this culture restructures older forms and builds much new organization. Sometimes there is a direct link from macro-cultural trends to expanded organization, as when local participants—now contemporary legitimated actors—directly incorporate new cultural elements (e.g., concerns about air pollution, or conceptions of legitimate sexual identities). However, the causal processes involved are in good part transmitted and reinforced by more immediate social structures.

We distinguish three main vehicles in contemporary social contexts that transmit rationalizing cultural principles through explicit and visible paths, pressing and facilitating organizational expansion:

(1) *Legal and quasi-legal rules.* These involve certificational pressures defining an entity's existence, what it can and should do, and how activity should be structured. Hard laws of nation-states expand with the rise of social rights and rationalizing science. And as nation-state charisma wanes, soft-law pressures and forms of private regulation, such as standards and accreditations, gain influence as well.[1] As hard and soft laws expand, organizations arise and become increasingly complex, to conform to expectations (for example, about "greenness," preventing discrimination, ethical business conduct, safety, accountable transparency, or core production procedures). Such pressures may be weaker in more centralized polities, but occur almost everywhere.

(2) *Counting and accounting.* If the law distinguishes acceptable and unacceptable forms, the accountants assess the value of organizations and activities. Ways of tracking past, present, and future monetary flows are central for many organizations (e.g., firms). Increasingly, other social activity is evaluated and quantified (e.g., university rankings, social return on investment measures, green certifications), and sometimes given monetary meaning.[2] As tools for counting expand to comprehend the formerly unclear, more complex organizational structures become plausible. They are often required to conform to new requirements.

(3) *Professionalism.* Macro-cultural shifts create populations of empowered, scientifically minded, highly educated people who form the basis of

modern-day professionalism as a characteristic of virtually any occupation or person. The "professionalization of everyone"[3] creates a cadre of people able and willing to cope with (and create) the legal and accounting pressures in the environment, but also to define and provide solutions for newly constructed problems not fully specifiable by legal and accounting rules.

Together, these three mechanisms—law, accounting, and professionalism—reshape the widest variety of local settings around the world by generating more organization. In Part 2 we will examine how, as these forces increase the internal complexity in existing structures, they create organizations with ambiguities, inconsistencies, and dialectic elements.

Expanding uncertainties

Expanding cultural principles of scientization, empowerment, and education directly affect local settings. They carry widely accepted knowledge and standards into a setting, thereby building organizations. For instance, as knowledge develops that air pollution harms people and the natural world, new organizations arise and old ones expand. Cultural ideologies, however, also provide assumptions and expectations about future knowledge where actual understanding is poor. For example, supermarkets can profitably sell organic and genetically pure food although the specific health advantages of many products are unknown. They can offer ethically produced fair trade and animal products, or sell goods that support local small farms, although consumers have an extremely limited ability to judge the products. Stores routinely offer such an abundance of products—in the name of expanded individual market choice—that the options far exceed human ability to calculate decisions (e.g., it is unclear whether it is better to buy "organic" instead of "grass fed" ground beef, or to purchase a wooden table from a "sustainably farmed" forest rather than one where the logging company plants 100 trees for every one cut down). In some instances cultural change provides relatively clear solutions (e.g., reducing air pollution by cutting back on coal-generated power plants or eliminating chemicals that attack the ozone layer). More often, these expansions provide grounds for competing legitimate claims, making solutions more difficult to determine (e.g., closing coal-generated power plants increases the cost of energy, placing a greater financial burden on families and creating unemployment).

In reality, the expansion of scientific development or human rights principles frequently constructs new problems. Recognized uncertainties, turned into "risks," expand in the modern order, as science and human empowerment penetrate a growing number of dimensions of social life (as in the organic food examples above, or in the increasingly analyzed family and gender relations). The idea that empowered human actors can and should do something about such uncertainties expands, as is evidenced by the burgeoning activities geared toward various types of risk management.[4]

Uncertainties are partly managed by expanded (and professionalized) legal and accounting principles. Although we are unlikely to know how much a child learns or the setting where learning is best accomplished, we can establish the child's score on a test, or define the criteria to become an accredited school.[5] There are, of course, great gaps between the uncertainties of actual teaching and learning and the certainty of a test score or accreditation requirement. There is a similar chasm between the legally determined specific number of parts per million of a chemical that a manufacturing plant can emit into the air and our understanding of the corresponding harm to humans or nature caused by that particular number of particles. We do not know the optimal level of pollution when we balance all the economic, social, and environmental interests involved, and informed opinions will vary. Nonetheless, the law and formalized counts and accounting measures convert imagined social constructions into institutionalized realities.

Common solutions to uncertainty involve the creation of professions, which have expanded enormously. These authorities translate unknowns and uncertainties into the artificial certainties (or expertise-based solutions that often remain mysterious) of the law, accounting, and a host of substantive professions. If something must be done, but exactly what should happen is unclear, it is important and often necessary to bring in a professional. At the center of the modern organizational explosion we find the rise of the modern manager as a professional, perhaps free of any specific content knowledge, but trained and empowered for the core rituals of decision-making, risk management, and planning.

Professionals, in addition to functioning as solutions, play active roles in constructing the problems they supposedly solve, and in articulating these problems in local settings.[6] The larger point is that contemporary culture reinforces both the re-imagining of uncertainties as calculated risks and the rise of professionals to manage these risks—setting them in reciprocal causal relation with each other. In practice, the transmission of wider cultural principles into local settings involves a great deal of decoupling and professional mediation, sometimes discussed as translation or editing.[7]

Rationalized rules: law and accounting

The rules that build organizations take varying forms. First, there are some rules that define a situation (e.g., what counts as a hospital or firm, and what features it should have). Here we find the power of the law, including soft-law regulation, setting standards for the conduct of a given activity. Education, for instance, is legally proper when carried out by certified teachers in an accredited school. Over and above legal requirements, soft-law pressures push for adherence to less formalized norms (perhaps schools, and firms, should not discriminate against anyone on the basis of sexual preference, even if no law prohibits discrimination). These legal and quasi-legal rules draw boundaries between conformity and deviance, acceptability and unacceptability, good and bad, real and fake.

Second, there are rules that assess variation in value from high to low, or better to worse. Some of these are formal accounting rules, defining costs and benefits, assets and liabilities, success and failure. Some kinds of accounts are less quantitative, evaluating local structures in hierarchies of prestige and status. So university departments vary on their *US News & World Report* rank, but they also vary in academic status, depending, for instance, on how many PhD programs they have. Countries are arrayed on scales such as "underdeveloped, developing, and developed."[8] These counting and accounting rules make assessments of worth, creating a common metric for external evaluation of status or rank.

Hard and soft law: nation-states have expanded greatly in number, activities, and functions since World War II, though their sovereignty is increasingly constrained by external norms.[9] All sorts of human activities and rights come under their purview, and nearly every aspect of nature and social organization has become subject to regulation. The actual capacities and normative commitments of national states and their representatives are limited, however, leading to a great deal of decoupling. It is routine for a state to completely fail to manage air pollution or the rights of prisoners, despite formal commitments.[10] But the rules are generally there, and almost all countries commit themselves in treaties and legislation to the new world of social rationalization.[11]

Relative to earlier periods, any social activity is now more likely to come under state regulation and this generates increased organization. An informal athletic club may, when properly organized, be eligible to receive public resources or use public lands. It may also be liable for participant injuries and may have difficulty finding a sporting venue if the liabilities are not properly managed. It may be subject to laws prohibiting certain types of discrimination or exclusion. It may be subject to rules protecting the environment—a rowing club disturbs the fish, a paint-gun club defaces the trees, and a football game ruins the grass in a park. Similarly, laws and policies constrain the behavior of coaches and supervisors, and the participants too may be expected to follow a code of conduct. All these types of rules increase formal organization as the governed entities strive to display compliance and convey the outside rules to internal participants.[12]

In the same way, restaurants must conform to health codes and employee regulations or risk losing their certifications, and they must contend with expert assessments of their value not only on food taste but also on décor, service, and other dimensions.[13] In education, legal requirements dictate what elements the school must have by way of space, equipment, and (professionally certified) teachers.

New legal rules are rarely justified on primordial national grounds or legitimated in racial, religious, cultural, or historical terms. Instead, new rules are rooted in contemporary scientific and human empowerment doctrines, and they are put forward with testimony from the relevant legitimate experts. Many of the rules and standards expand internationally.[14] More peripheral entities are likely to adopt the formal rules automatically, although actual conformity may be weak.[15]

The legal rules of the national state support a penumbra of associated bodies—themselves often taking the form of organizations—dedicated to the promulgation of the relevant practices. For example the "discovery" of child abuse in the post-war period, now an official business grounded in medical and psychological developments, has produced a worldwide explosion of organizations devoted to the spread of practices against the abuse and neglect of children—matters formerly left to family and community. By the end of 2014, for example, 44 countries had complete bans on any form of corporal punishment for children—naturally in school settings, but also in the home.[16] This ban is advocated most vocally by a group called the Global Initiative to End All Corporal Punishment of Children, which draws support from the UN. Using human rights language ("children hold human rights too"), the group carefully monitors national laws, assembles media accounts, and collects anecdotes, producing regular country, regional, and global assessment reports.[17]

Any given organizing situation is exposed to the influence of state law, and also to collateral bodies dedicated to enforcement. Many organizations exist, not to accomplish their own private ends, but to carry out collective rules requiring other groups to become more organized. These act as "others" to focal participants seen as responsible actors.[18] A school that permits students to be abused must organize to deal not only with agents of the state but also with mobilized parent and community groups, some of which are highly professionalized and funded at national and even supra-national levels. The informal rules of the old churches to quietly transfer abusive priests to other locations have come under sustained attack from the new antagonists of child abuse, and the churches must organize to deal with the problem. Much organizational expansion follows.

An additional cadre of "others" is available to provide solutions to new collective rules and responsibilities. In area after area of social life, consultants and consulting organizations make up powerful growth industries, drawing on

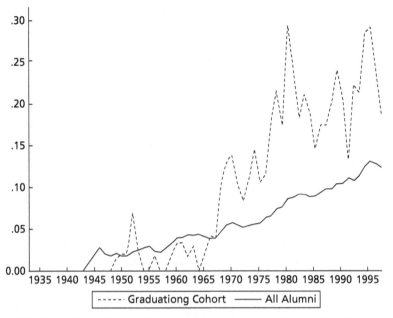

Figure 4.1. Proportion of Sampled Business School Graduates Employed as Management Consultants in the US, 1933–95
Source: Ruef 2002: 87.

external scripts to create and solve the problems of local people.[19] One survey of all alumni of a large US business school indicates that consulting has become one of the most common professions for graduates, as shown in Figure 4.1. In this sample, during the 1950s less than 2 percent of a graduating cohort became consultants, but by the 1990s this figure was slightly over 20 percent, outpacing placement in other fast-growth industries such as investment banking and management in high-tech companies.[20]

The hard law of the state as an organization increasingly generates (and may be replaced by) the softer law of collateral structures.[21] In the modern system, the nation-state has lost much of its charisma. Its ability to make and enforce law is one of the few remaining areas of its relatively unique authority. However, even in this realm, states are more subject to international pressures (and domestic structures transmitting them) than they were, as scientific and human rights doctrines now penetrate societies. Variably among national societies, some states transfer their authority to third parties and are thus even more susceptible to soft-law pressures. For instance, countries sometimes delegate legal decision-making power to the accrediting bodies that certify schools, hospitals, and businesses. Similar bodies define who is a professional (psychologist, engineer, lawyer, hairdresser, or whatever) and what the requirements are to become one.

Some associations define what a proper organization or product is on supra-national legal terms. At the extreme, supra-national certification includes requiring UN recognition to become a legitimate country, or, more routinely, involves the thousands of criteria established by the International Organization for Standardization (ISO) for cars or tourism, appliances or transportation, drinking water or financial services.[22] Figure 4.2 shows the number of ISO rules issued annually. Organizations can be certified by the ISO on an enormous array of issues, not only related to technical matters that facilitate industrial coordination (such as establishing a set volume and dimensions for freight containers to facilitate global shipping), but also now for energy management, risk management, environmental management, and information security.

Supra-national soft-law organizations are most visible in Europe, where emergent integration produces a great many organizational bodies setting standards.[23] Soft laws drift toward hard-law status as the surrounding net of social control is more and more reinforced by a variety of third parties—trading agreements, court actions, professional bodies, and so on.

Any given social setting, from family life (under expanded rules of child neglect and spousal rights) to large-scale production, is now surrounded by many structured social bodies transmitting supra-national rules (stemming from globalized cultural principles) to local settings. Legal bodies attend to the human rights of participants, many dimensions of the environment, and a variety of requirements of rational social life. Increased organization is the solution to structuring local activity in ways that meet these collective requirements.

Rationalized, globalized cultural principles can be seen as partially external to any given setting. However, this depiction is complicated by the fact that internal participants, especially when schooled and professionalized, are linked to the wider environment. So any person can, for example, press for conformity to wider rules of human rights, environmental protection, or organizational rationality. Even within family life, a spouse or child can bring to bear international human rights conventions in disputes over authority, sex, or money. Local people can themselves organize, becoming simultaneously part of the local setting and instruments of the wider environment, as we discuss in Part 2. The carriers of contemporary culture are both internal and external to modern social settings.

Overall, the rise of hard and soft law in any specific environment increases the extent of organization-forming in that environment. Continuing our illustration from the previous chapter, as childhood is rationalized, organizations arise and expand to manage its various dimensions. So it would not now be particularly surprising to learn that Google, Goldman Sachs, or General Electric provides on-site day care, offers parental leave for sick children, has rules to protect minors who might be on the premises (e.g., perhaps young people are not

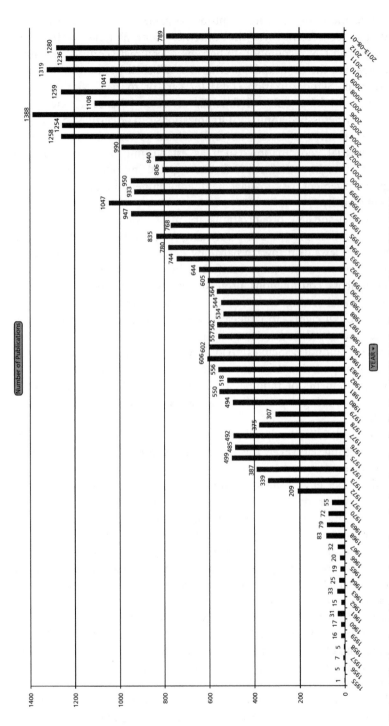

Figure 4.2. Number of International Organization for Standardization (ISO) Publications per Year, 1955–2012

Source: ISO 2013.

allowed on factory floors), has recommendations for protecting children from potential harm from any of its products (e.g., perhaps minors can't or shouldn't search the Web unaccompanied, open bank accounts, or operate blenders), has policies prohibiting child labor, or has a staff person who is knowledgeable about labor laws at national and international levels. To see these things in a firm would have seemed odd in 1950, and odder still in 1900.

Countings and accountings: hard and soft laws determine what makes an entity an organization and greatly influence its internal structure. A related system of social structures produces social control, not through ontological categorization, but through evaluation and stratification. An entity can be a better or worse school, non-profit, firm, or government agency. And if the people and setting can be defined as, say, a university, there are clear advantages to being a good one.

The most crystallized and deeply institutionalized structure for assessing value is in the monetarized accounting system. A local social entity can be defined by monetary units that are integrated into a standard, and to some extent globalized, currency. (Helpfully, the ISO can provide guidance for integrating multiple currencies with Standard 4217: 2008.) Multiple accounting criteria can be involved and there are multiple ways of assessing value. A firm might have, for instance, financial accounting statements prepared in accordance with Generally Accepted Accounting Principles for investors, creditors, and regulatory bodies. It might separately conduct forms of cost accounting or managerial accounting intended to help with internal decision-making and budgeting. Further, entities might try to conform not only to local or national standards, but to global guidelines as well.[24] In the various types and levels of accounting, it is not immediately obvious how to calculate assets and liabilities, expenses and revenues, profit and loss, and so on, especially over varying timeframes. There are no natural solutions, only constructed ones. Highly developed accounting rules provide the necessary guidance, making the uncertain real.[25]

Naturally, monetary value and profit matter more to a business than to a church or a government agency. But, increasingly, ratings and rankings on multiple dimensions are on the rise, providing grounds for evaluating many kinds of social goods.[26] Sometimes these remain in monetary terms, as in evaluating a school or hospital in terms of resources per student or patient. But other forms are non-monetary, as with test scores or patient outcome measures.[27] Thus schooling or medical systems are ranked on indicators of their prestige and general status (e.g., their possession of highly certified personnel and elaborate equipment), but also on their success in producing various outputs. Businesses are assessed on dimensions of CSR, worker safety and satisfaction, and effectiveness in producing goods and services. Governmental agencies are evaluated by surveys, or measures of output, outcomes, and impact.[28]

Monetary accounting systems have, of course, spread worldwide, but so have less monetarized ones. Whole educational systems are ranked according to test scores, and within them particular schools and schooling types are rated.[29] Universities are now rated on global scales and can aspire to become World Class Universities according to such scales.[30] Similarly, large multinational corporations are evaluated on their "greenness" and related dimensions.[31] National health care systems are scored, and within them particular hospital organizations are ranked.[32] Even cities are evaluated on formal criteria.[33]

A central feature of accounting in all its forms lies in its specification and reification of the entity being accounted. One cannot have a properly defined profit or loss without a clear delineation of the entity being accounted. The accounting involved must be assumed to be complete; we presume to know all the costs, resources, and gains. Furthermore, to construct a proper modern account, one must have a theory of the functioning of the entity involved, so one can distinguish costs, investments, benefits, and various sorts of resources. To be accounted requires organizational articulation, and the more the environment demands and produces accounting, the more local social structures become organizations with defined boundaries and explicit internal differentiation.[34]

Each new dimension of accounting requires differentiated responses in local organizational settings, and each one instructs locals in how to produce these responses. So if the legal environment requires environmental impact reports, local organizations must create structures that produce these reports. The monetary accountants then assess the costs involved as legitimate. Internal and external constituents evaluate the adequacy of the organizational response involved, perhaps with a "greenness" rating scheme. The respectable organization tries to do it all right, or appear to do so.[35] In either case, organization expands.

Counting and accounting pull articulated dimensions out of the inchoate complexity of all environments. Uncertainties become defined risks, and responsible actors must deal with them. So, as the higher educational system, globally, comes under counting and accounting scrutiny, with rankings reaching up to the world level, each entity in that system becomes more organized.[36]

Law draws the line around what counts, and accounting determines how to value it. These processes both assume and construct a world where social structures are theorized as more comparable than older cultural systems ever imagined.[37] In some fields, such as financial accounting, there are relatively standardized and widely applied methods for how to determine value. We know these processes do not actually include all costs (e.g., a firm's damage to the environment or health burdens) or potential benefits (e.g., to the self-esteem of employees with good jobs). The estimates of value are "best guesses" based on social scientized methods, and the legal lines around an organization's boundaries are socially determined rather than fully encompassing all relevant spheres of impact. The norms involved often remain in place until new knowledge (or a disaster) reveals the extent of the gap between reality and the rules (e.g., scandals at Enron and WorldCom or the 2008 subprime mortgage disaster in the US). In newer fields, such as measuring social impact, the accounting rules are less taken for granted, and the flaws seem more obvious. How many generations out should we suppose in our calculations that the effects of a public library system will be felt? Should we make assumptions just about direct benefits to library users, or also about secondary benefits to non-users in the community? Legal rules work similarly. If a student is injured during an off-site field trip, is the school or the secondary location liable? If a student has a profitable idea, is her university automatically entitled to a share of the intellectual property or only if the idea is developed on campus?[38] The boundaries are not clear in practice, but become specified by rule systems and institutionalized over time.[39]

Professionalism

We chart above the core rule systems that mediate between wider cultural principles and local realities—law-like rules defining requirements, and measures accounting their value. Often such rules can be transmitted directly into local behavior with simple enforcement mechanisms and socialization. People in most countries drive on the right and often conform to speed limits. The relevant behaviors are taught in training programs, incorporated into planning by road builders, and managed and enforced by traffic officers. A good deal of organization is involved, but much of it is straightforward, and traditionally bureaucratic.

But even in an arena like traffic control, social enactment is not simply direct and linear.[40] Too many things cannot be clearly specified, and social control works not only through the regulation of behavior but also through the construction of appropriate social identities—identities we now understand to be professional. Traffic engineers, police officers, and driving teachers are all professionalized: socialized through schooling to manage the uncertainties involved even in a straightforward arena.

Professionalism is endemic in contemporary society, and professionals of various sorts make up by far the largest category of the "labor force" (a misnomer, given the relatively few laborers involved). Figure 4.3 shows the managerial shift in the occupational distribution of American society over time. The size of the managerial class is growing in the US, both in number and as a proportion of employees in US firms.

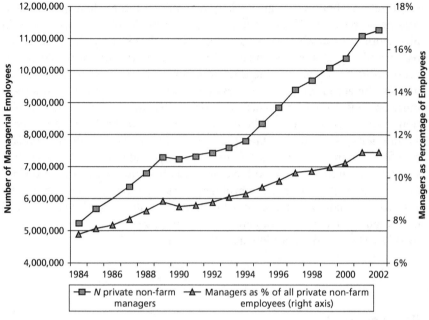

Figure 4.3. Managerial Employment Growth in the US, 1984–2003
Source: Goldstein 2012: 275.

An extensive literature defines the concept of professionalism.[41] It is well recognized that the modern professional is very different from the classic Western forms. The earlier form encompassed just a few occupations (doctors, lawyers, priests, and professors/teachers) with authority derived from universalistic knowledge, located in a corporate group with distinctive status (and its own saints). In recent centuries, and dramatically in the post-war period, the conception has changed in two ways. First, the corporate group character of the professions is greatly weakened; the professional is now seen as a disciplined individual person rather than a subordinate member of a group with corporate authority. Second, the recent expansion of knowledge seen as universalistic or scientific in character means that nearly any role can be professionalized, as in Wilensky's classic notion of "the professionalization of everyone."[42] The term is now used very broadly—anybody can be seen as "really professional." The knowledge involved still tends to be located in the university—but a dramatically expanded university.[43]

The literature on early modern organization treated the traditional professions as problematic for organizations and looked for conflict between the corporate authority of the professional group and hierarchical bureaucratic practices.[44] But the expected dramatic conflict was rarely found, in part because of the erosion of these older forms of authority (traditional professions and traditional bureaucracy). Instead, the modern professional—a skilled and committed individual person seen as able to solve problems by absorbing uncertainties in some area—is ideally suited for the expanded organization now required. For example, if we need better relations with our community, we can hire a community relations officer with appropriate training in the relevant social sciences.

An enormous range of uncertainties now comes under attempted social control. Some of it can be dealt with through expanded organizational processes controlling activity, as with making sure everyone drives on the right. But often—and increasingly with expanding cultural rationalization—it is not easy to muster effective administrative control. Under these more complex conditions, modern structures produce rules specifying required processes like professional certification rather than required output.[45]

Uncertainty and the professionals: we have discussed the ways the modern rationalized environment creates spaces of uncertainty that call for professionalism as a solution. New problems are codified, and responsibilities created with no clear specifiable solution. Here the professional, rooted in the educational system, can step in and provide an answer: organizations facing the uncertainties created by empowered personnel can hire human resources professionals. It might not actually help, but it gives all the appearances of a rational and legitimate solution to the problem.

Causality runs the other way too, and the literature often emphasizes the professions as purposive projects in the modern system.[46] That is, the professionals, typically emerging from the educational system, construct and codify the problems for which their services are required as solutions. Indeed, they might write the problems into the law and define proper costs for the accountants. This possibility is emphasized in some of the studies of the rise of modern human resources policies and practices: lawyers and personnel experts translate vague laws into programs requiring professional services by the same people.[47]

This line of argumentation often plausibly emphasizes the role of the professionals as highly self-interested actors, manipulating outcomes to their advantage. It is important, however, to also note that it is their social duty to discover uncertainties in their domains and to propose solutions to these newly defined problems. Biased or not, professional dental societies ordinarily support the fluoridation that undercuts their business. The responsibility of the professionals to actively deal with uncertainties in their domains creates a tension in organizational life that we discuss in Part 2. The professionals—mini-organizations in their own right—have a clear duty to society over and above the purposes of the organizations in which they are encased.

In the contemporary environment, many dimensions of life surrounding any organizing situation call for and come under professional controls: cultural change expands both the professions and the uncertainties they manage

and sets them in causal relation with each other. Different kinds of professionals are involved. We comment here on four types: lawyers and accountants transmitting the elemental components and requirements that constitute
organizations; substantive professionals mediating responses to specific
dimensions of the environment; substantive professionals managing uncertainties in core work processes; and professionalized managers.

Lawyers, accountants, and proto-professionals: laws and law-like rules, as
well as various forms of counting and accounting, are carried into organizations by lawyers and accountants, and by proto- or quasi-professionals of
these sorts (e.g., experts in measuring social impact). The expansion of law-
like rules, discussed above, creates uncertainties in local situations. Over time,
interpreters of these rules expand their roles, reinforced by courts and other
third-party adjudicators (e.g., evaluators in media). Grounds for protagonists,
antagonists, and mediating consultants expand greatly. Especially in open
liberal societies like the US, great arenas of uncertainty requiring much
interpretation arise; strong and centralized state bureaucracies may limit
such spaces for interpretations.[48]

Thus, just as the contemporary environment contains much law-like rule
structure, it also generates lawyers and similar professionals who press these
rules on local settings. Local activity is organized to deal with them, and
organizations expand. One response, when external requirements are clear
and workable, is simply to conform. But often the external requirements are
unclear or aspirational and cannot reasonably be met in a straightforward way.
Exactly how, for instance, is a school or factory to deal with off-site instances
of harassment among its students or workers? How is an elaborate manufacturing facility truly going to know and manage every chemical involved in
production, or a restaurant to definitively disclose all potential allergens in its
ingredients?

Under such conditions, organizations are likely to absorb external pressures
by employing lawyers and related professionals to manage the complex
relations involved. The inclination to do this has spread rapidly, and internal
legal departments try to balance actual and potential external legal demands.
Exactly the same processes work in the arena of the accountants and other
evaluators who assess the worth of local organizing settings. The external
world—tax authorities, investment advisors, unions, and community
bodies—defines what organizations can and should do. These definitions are
carried out and transmitted by a variety of accounting processes and by
expanded accountant populations. A common consequence is internal role
expansion and differentiation; in order to meet the external demands for
reporting, organizations internally incorporate the professions and rules that
parallel external ones.

Substantive professionals linked to environmental pressures: beyond legal
and accounting requirements, local settings come under external pressures in

a wide variety of substantive areas. Sometimes conformity is possible in obvious ways, but often areas of uncertainty arise. A routine solution is to delegate these uncertainties to the relevant professionals, on the often-untested assumption that their training and competence will do the job. Beyond this faith, there is the core matter of legitimacy—delegating problems to professionals often provides good defenses in legal and other fora.

For example, the expansion of human rights principles generates human resources departments, staffed by human relations and resources professionals. Similarly with expanded demands for proper relations with the natural environment (e.g., sustainability officers), with surrounding social communities and their organizations (e.g., community or public relations and marketing people), with issues of safety and matters of organizational transparency (e.g., compliance officers), the relevant professionals are incorporated. Populations of them expand, together with elaborate training programs, professional associations, and so on. It is often unclear what these people know and can do. It is precisely this lack of clarity that makes their professionalism so valuable and necessary. They are legitimated loci for absorbing uncertainties that the contemporary world has turned into risks requiring management.

Substantive professionals managing core work processes: core work processes in contemporary settings also require properly trained personnel to get technical work done. For example, classically in government agencies trained bureaucrats perform work tasks, or in mechanical or electrical projects trained engineers are needed. With contemporary expansion, external requirements and expectations expand, even over internal processes. So with the associated expansion of perceived risks comes an associated expansion of the relevant professionals, who make sure that internal work is done in ways validated by expanding external standards. More engineers are needed to manage work flow and technical processes (and may need, for example, additional training in communicating across gender and cultural lines); more professionalized supervisors manage the enforcement of rules (and so need to know what the rules are). The whole range of activities involved is likely to include much professionalism. One can now legitimately speak of a supervisor of janitors as "very professional."

Professionalized management: the most striking expansion of professionalism comes in the arena most central to the contemporary conception of organization. If the most distinctive feature of the organization, now, is its status as an integrated, purposive, and sovereign actor, displays of purpose and sovereignty become crucial. At its center, the contemporary organization has decisions: choices to be rationally made in pursuit of goals.[49] The actualities and rituals associated with such decisions are crucial: they display the externally required purposes and value that are central to the modern allocation of authority and responsibility (including liability). It is not a coincidence that organizational scholars treat decision-making as a core defining element of modern organization.[50]

How are decisions to be made and sovereignties exercised? The old ways—through ownership, the charisma of the traditional professions, or the imperative authority delegated by an external sovereign—are no longer adequate. Dealing with the scientized environment requires rational action. And dealing with populations of internal and external participants—workers, customers, suppliers, and so on—infused with expanded rights and capacities, requires action justified under norms of rationality rather than imperative authority. We thus find the rise of the professionalized manager. This role involves notions of technical competence over and above any specific organizational activity—training and skills in coordination rather than the exercise of imperative authority, and in rational decision-making rather than substantive knowledge.

Worldwide, there is an extraordinary expansion of business schools producing training in management and decision-making independent of any substantive knowledge and competence. Engineering solutions often may work at operational levels,[51] and engineering professions expand in many substantive areas. But this technical approach falls short in management, where broad organizational knowledge (i.e., the capacity to coordinate multiple internal and external stakeholders) and knowledge of constitutive rules and values (i.e., legal and accounting requirements, and quasi-law/accounting calculations such as various types of ratings and rankings) are at the core. A good manager can run a paper company without knowing what a tree is, or a hospital knowing nothing about medicine.

The myth of the manager is a dominating one, worldwide, and the programs producing managers are extreme examples of professional and educational expansion. The idea is to transform the ugly old coercive authority with the contemporary notions of rationality and competence. The managerial presence in large firms has expanded over time, even through periods of strong shareholder value rhetoric, layoffs, and cost-cutting. In lean times, managerial expertise is still considered a necessity, as reflected in both numbers and wages (Figure 4.4).

Examples of professionals: a few examples help to flesh out the differences between forms of professionalism. Table 4.1 shows a sample of executive positions in three contemporary organizations, Walmart, the Red Cross, and the US Department of Transportation, classified by our typology of professionals. Professionals of the first two types largely have an outward orientation. (1) There are professionals who can help the organization meet the criteria it needs to stay an organization, or a certain type of organization—accountants, legal counsel, and, for public companies, chief financial officers. (2) There are also professionals who are experts in something other than a core work process, such as Walmart's executives for People, Logistics, Marketing, Customers, Information, and Corporate Affairs. (3) Looking inward, some professionals, like Taylor's factory managers, are experts in improving

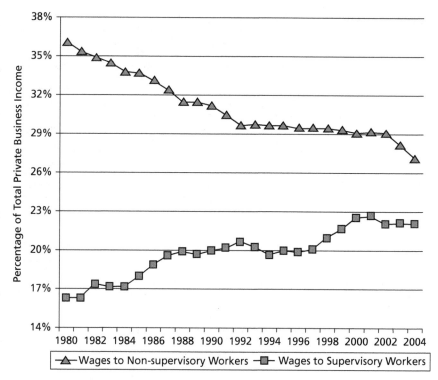

Figure 4.4. Wages Paid to Supervisory and Non-Supervisory Workers as a Proportion of Total Business Income in the US, 1980–2004

Source: Goldstein 2012: 274.

Note: Supervisors' share of total business income is calculated by subtracting total wage and salary earnings for production and non-supervisory workers from total wage and salary payments to all private non-farm workers and then dividing by total non-farm business income.

core work processes. For Walmart, they are the people who mainly oversee producing and selling things, such as the president and CEO of Walmart Latin America or the executive vice president of the Grocery Division. (4) Then there are the professionals who know about the administration of an organization itself (rather than the core task), people like an executive secretary, a chief operating officer, a chief administration officer, and experts in strategy and planning. These are, of course, conceptual categories; in empirical settings a single role could span multiple types of professionalism or the type of professionalism could vary by time and place.

Cultural changes are greatly intensified by social processes that transmit them into local settings. Legal or quasi-legal forms, standards, and counting or accounting systems also institutionalize and embody the wider cultural rules. Law specifies what a proper school or firm or product is, whereas ranking and accounting systems assess its value on various dimensions. Some aspects of

Table 4.1 Types of Professionals in Modern Organizations

	Lawyers, Accountants & Proto-Professionals	Substantive Professionals Linked to Environmental Pressures	Substantive Professionals Linked to Core Work Processes	Professionalized Managers
Walmart Executive Team 2013	• Senior Vice President (VP) and Controller • Executive VP, Treasurer • Executive VP and General Counsel • Executive VP and Chief Financial Officer	• Executive VP, Corporate Affairs • Executive VP, People Division • Executive VP, Global Customer Insights • Executive VP, Walmart US People • Executive VP, Chief Information Officer • Executive VP, Chief Marketing Officer	• • Executive VP, Merchandising • Executive VP, Grocery Division • Executive VP, Logistics	• Executive VP, Chief Administrative Officer • Executive VP, Strategy and International Development • Executive VP, Chief Operating Officer • Executive VP and Corporate Secretary
Red Cross Corporate Officers and Executive Leadership 2013	• Chief Audit Executive • General Counsel and Chief International Officer • Chief Financial Officer	• Chief Information Officer • Chief Public Affairs Officer • Chief Marketing Officer • Chief Human Resources Officer • Corporate Ombudsman • Chief Development Officer • Chief Diversity Officer	• President Humanitarian Services • President Biomedical Services • President, Preparedness and Health and Safety Services	• Corporate Secretary and Chief of Staff
US Department of Transportation Key Officials 2013	• Acting General Counsel • Acting Chief Financial Officer and Assistant Secretary for Budget and Programs • Chief Counsel	• Assistant Secretary for Governmental Affairs • Pipeline and Hazardous Materials Safety Administrator • Research and Innovative Technology Administrator • Chief Information Officer • Director, Office of Civil Rights • Director, Office of Drug and Alcohol Policy and Compliance • Director, Office of Small and Disadvantaged Business Utilization	• Secretary of Transportation • Deputy Secretary of Transportation • Under Secretary for Policy • Assistant Secretary for Aviation and International Affairs • Federal Highway Administrator • Administrator of the Federal Aviation Administration • Federal Motor Carrier Safety Administrator • Federal Railroad Administration	• Director, Executive Secretariat • Assistant Secretary for Administration

- Director, Office of
  Intelligence,
  Security, and
  Emergency
  Response
- Chief Human
  Capital Officer
- Senior
  Sustainability
  Officer

(FRA)
Administrator
- Federal Transit
  Administrator
- Acting Maritime
  Administrator
- National
  Highway Traffic
  Safety
  Administrator
- Inspector
  General for the
  US Department
  of
  Transportation

Note: These titles are illustrative rather than comprehensive.
Source: Red Cross website (2013), US Department of Transportation Website (2013), Walmart Website (2013).

Table 4.2 Examples of Law, Accounting, and Professional Influences Generating Organization

Law	Accounting	Professionals
Hard Laws	**Monetarized**	**Constitutive Lawyers/Accountants**
• Subnational and national laws of nation-states	• Return on investment	• General counsel
• International treaties and Security Council resolutions	• Cost-benefit analysis	• Accountants
	• Financial accounting statements	
	• Profit/loss statements	
Soft Laws	**Non- or Partially Monetarized**	**Substantive/External Demands**
• Certifications	• Ratings	• Human resources
• Standards	• Rankings	• Information and communications technology
• Accreditation	• Social return on investment	
• Resolutions	• Social, environmental, labor, or other related audits	• Diversity
• Declarations	• Impact assessments	• Health and safety
• Codes of conduct, ethics		**Substantive/Core Work Process**
• Action plans, stated objectives		• Physicians
• Guidelines		• Teachers, academics
• Principles		• Social workers
		• Engineers
		Organizational
		• Chief operating officers
		• Executive secretaries
		• Consultants

nature and social life cannot be easily captured in legal and accounting rules: to address the remaining uncertainties, educated professionals become central. They develop and interpret constitutive legal and accounting rules, as well as those that govern an organization's primary and secondary tasks, and the administration of the organization itself. Table 4.2 provides an overview of some of the core forms of legal, accounting, and professional pressures that generate expanded organization.

We are not alone in observing how macro-cultural changes lead to the rise of forms of counting and law-like pressures, such as certifications. As a concrete example, sociologist Tim Bartley has extensively studied the fair trade movement.[52] In a series of publications, he documents how three main trends create these certification systems: (1) the rise of multiple actors, especially states, NGOs, and social movements; (2) compromises and negotiations among these actors; and (3) neoliberal ideologies that channel solutions away from states and toward the private sector.[53] Consistent with our arguments in the preceding chapter, these three trends can be seen as rooted in the demise of traditional sources of social order and authority, and their replacement with principles of science and human rights and capacities. We turn to a more detailed depiction of this situation.

An illustration: the fair trade industry

In 1946, Edna Ruth Byler, a volunteer for the Mennonite Central Committee, left her home in central Pennsylvania to visit Puerto Rico.[54] On her trip, she saw extreme poverty and wanted to help. She was particularly moved by women who lived in desperate conditions despite working long hours creating beautiful needlepoint. Byler began carrying pieces of their handiwork back to the US to sell, and returned the proceeds back to the women. Initially operating as the Overseas Needlepoint and Craft Project, her organization eventually grew into the non-profit organization Ten Thousand Villages, one of the world's first "fair trade" organizations (and now the largest fair trade retailer in North America). Just a few years after Byler's trip to Puerto Rico, in 1949, a similar project emerged in Europe. Sales Exchange for Refugee Rehabilitation and Vocation (SERRV International) was founded to help refugees in Europe recover from World War II. Today, the organization supports artisans in more than 35 countries.

Since its emergence shortly after World War II, the fair trade industry has expanded enormously. Reliable statistics do not yet exist for the total size of this industry worldwide, but a few indicators speak to its reach. In the UK in 2011, retail sales of products certified by one organization, the Fairtrade Foundation, reached 1.32 billion pounds. This was a 12 percent increase from the previous year and included 42 percent of all retail sugar sales in the UK. Thus a consumer who eats a Dairy Milk or Kit Kat chocolate bar in the UK can take extra enjoyment from a socially conscious decision to buy fair trade chocolate. Another estimate from 2011 puts retail sales in the UK at more than 3 billion US dollars, and the US market at 1.4 billion.[55] A third group, Fairtrade International, estimates that in 2010 shoppers around the world spent 4.36 billion euros on products with its logo.[56] Fair trade certifications cover a wide range of goods, including coffee, tea, cocoa, sugar, spices, honey, some produce (especially bananas), grains and beans, wine and spirits, flowers, apparel and linens, body care products, and sports balls. In addition to thousands of smaller groups, major retailers, such as Starbucks, Costco, Marks & Spencer, Tesco, Safeway, Nestlé, and Cadbury, are involved in importing fair trade products.

In part, data on the size of the fair trade industry are difficult to assemble because there is disagreement over what counts. Probably the most widely used definition is found in the Charter of Fair Trade Principles: "Fair Trade is a trading partnership, based on dialogue, transparency and respect that seeks greater equity in international trade. It contributes to sustainable development by offering better trading conditions to, and securing the rights of, marginalized producers and workers—especially in the South. Fair Trade Organizations, backed by consumers, are engaged actively in supporting producers, awareness raising and in campaigning for changes in the rules and practice of conventional international trade."[57]

Note the prominence of rights discourse in this definition, including imagery of global equity and partnership. One could imagine, judging from the definition, a social movement in full "sixties style," with chanting, sign-holding street protesters, sit-ins, and hunger strikes, aimed at changing government policies. A little of this goes on, but it is not the centerpiece of the movement. Like many modern social movements, this one largely takes a highly organized form (and a rather dry one, as suggested by the certification criteria listed below). In the case of fair trade, product certifications, which incorporate elements of soft law and accounting, have become the central way to achieve the goal of increasing equity in international trade. Traditional social movement activities (e.g., letter writing campaigns and protests) are mainly intended to support and expand the organizational solution of product certification.

The gist of product certification is that retailers (and sometimes producers) hire independent third parties to verify that a product is created by a process that meets set criteria (e.g., that workers are paid a fair wage). Products typically then get a logo indicating that they pass a certain bar. Figure 4.5 shows some common product certification logos. In a survey of 24 developed countries, six in ten consumers recognized Fairtrade International's logo (shown in Figure 4.5, below).[58] Especially since the 1990s, product certification has been growing rapidly (see, for example, Figure 4.6 showing discussions of certification in forest and apparel trade journals). Some of the most visible groups advocating and implementing certification systems include Fair Trade USA, the Fair Trade Federation, the Fairtrade Foundation, and Fairtrade International.

To give a sense of why certification generates more complex organizations, consider the details of one of the largest fair trade certifications. Fairtrade USA

Figure 4.5. Fairtrade International Logo
Source: Fairtrade International website 2015.

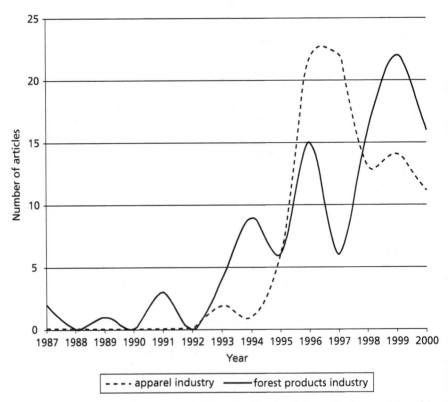

Figure 4.6. Distribution of Articles Mentioning Certification in Forest Products and Apparel Trade Journals, 1987–2000
Source: Bartley 2007: 303.

partners with the firm SCS Global Services (SCS) to evaluate producers. SCS provides this service to a number of clients, such as Safeway's Bright Green product line, Home Depot's Eco Options, and Starbucks's C.A.F.E. program for ethical sourcing. The process begins with a five-page application to get certified. It includes questions about existing certifications, audit practices, and producer characteristics (e.g., products, production volume, workforce size, target market).

To be eligible for Fairtrade USA's certification, producers must be legally incorporated entities. The very first step of certification is to take on the formal legal structure of an organization. Once the categorical shift is made, for example from a farm to a legal organization, the certification process can begin, generating further organizational elaboration.

The process, outlined in Figure 4.7, includes extensive legalized and contractual language that assumes a great deal about the producer's ability to understand and conform. For instance, one step reads, "Upon receipt of the signed documents and payment of the retainer fee, SCS initiates the audit planning process and sends the client an audit plan, along with a request for documents, in advance of the onsite audit. The client should confirm agreement with the plan in writing and send the requested documents via email in advance of the audit date." Respecting the producer's rights, the process is highly transparent and includes opportunities for recourse (through a Corrective Action Plan) before a final decision is rendered. The process is called an audit. It involves taking stock of a producer's formal and informal practices that relate to fair trade, assessing their value in the way a financial audit takes stock of a firm's books. The final approval or rejection illustrates the power of soft law, as it denotes inclusion (or exclusion) in the category of "fair trade producer."

During the audit phase, SCS evaluates producers in five general areas: (1) Empowerment, (2) Economic Development, (3) Social Responsibility, (4) Environmental Stewardship, and (5) Trade Requirements. The specific criteria differ by producer type (e.g., farm worker or independent smallholder), but over 200 items are used. Most of these items require organizational elaboration. For instance, from the Fair Trade USA Farm Workers Standard Version 1.1:[59]

- The company has carried out a needs assessment on the social and economic needs of all workers. The needs assessment should be based on surveys or primary data.
- All permanent workers have a legally binding, written contract that clearly describes the terms of hire and safeguards workers from loss of pay in the case of illness, disability or accident.... Temporary workers who are employed for a period of three months or more of uninterrupted service have a legally binding and signed contract with job description.

Application for Certification [year 0]	The client submits the completed application form to SCS, copying Fair Trade USA.
	SCS confirms receipt of the completed application form, reviews it, and sends client additional information requests or conformation of approval within 10 business days.
	SCS prepares a work order (quote) for the auditing service and certification decision (if applicable) and sends it, along with the SCS Assessment Services Agreement, to the client for authorization of work. Client signs and returns the work order and SCS Assessment Services Agreement. SCS issues retainer fee invoice for payment.
	Upon receipt of the signed documents and payment of retainer fee, SCS initiates the audit planning process and sends the client an audit plan, along with a request for documents, in advance of the onsite audit. The client should confirm agreement with the plan in writing and send the requested documents via email in advance of the audit date.
Evaluation and Re-evaluation Audit (years 0,3,6)	The SCS auditor will conduct on-site audit(s), which includes document review, worker interviews, and field observations. Initial findings are communicated during the closing meeting.
	Auditor completes the audit report with detailed findings and issues non-conformities (NCs), if applicable. SCS conducts an internal review of the submitted audit report. Audit report (including Non-Conformity Report [NCR]) is then sent to client within 20 business days from the day the auditor(s) returns to their office from the field audit.
	The client addresses any NCs by submitting a completed NCR with supporting Corrective Actions Plans (CAPs), typically within a timeframe of 30 days. The CAPs must include auditable timeframes and identify responsible parties to provide evidence that implementation of corrective actions has occurred.
Certification Decision (years 0,3,6)	SCS issues a certification decision based on the CAPs prepared by the client. Upon successful certification, a Fair Trade certification registration number, a certificate, and applicable certification label are provided. The reason(s) for a decision to deny certification will be explained in writing, at which point a client may decide to appeal.
Annual Surveillance Audit (years 1–2 and 4–5)	The annual surveillance audit process follows the process outlined above. Although Certification decisions are not applicable, CAPs are required if NCs are issued.
Suspension of Certification	If certification is suspend due to unsatisfactory responses to NCs from the annual surveillance audit, then, depending on the nature of the NCs, the certification process may need to be restarted with an evaluation or re-evaluation audit.

Figure 4.7. Overview of the Fair Trade Certification Process

Source: Fair Trade USA 2012: 5.

- The company has a written Fair Trade Implementation Plan. . . . At a minimum the plan includes: management goals, how to achieve the goals, how to measure achievement, timeframes, budgets. . . .
- The Fair Trade Implementation Plan is implemented and measures to reach compliance are reviewed annually by management. Annual review includes a progress check against past audit reports.
- Training on Fair Trade is provided at least annually for all levels, including workers and their representatives.
- A Fair Trade Committee, with representatives of the workers, has been created with equal representation of the work force. A written constitution defining the objectives, functioning, composition, means

and procedures of the Fair Trade Committee (in line with FTUSA Explanatory Document for Fair Trade Committees—section 4.3) is in place.

- CSR is part of the company's written mission or policy statement.
- The company has defined and documented a human resource policy, plan, and objective. Processes are in place to monitor and improve the implementation of HR policies and plans.
- A written grievance procedure is in place and communicated to workers verbally and in writing. A written grievance procedure is in place for cases of sexual harassment (and a committee is appointed to resolve cases).
- An internal employee suggestion system is in place.
- The company has carried out a needs assessment of migrant workers.... [It] should be based on surveys or primary data. The company has created and implemented a written development plan for migrant workers, based on the needs assessment.
- Access to primary education is ensured for all children of workers living on the farm property. Measures are in place and monitored within the Fair Trade Implementation Plan to improve education for all workers' children. Such measures may include the provision of scholarships, in-kind donations of educational materials and supplies, clothing, food or transport.
- Where children of the workers live on the farm, the company is responsible for providing access to day care facilities.

This list is just a selection of compliance points, mainly taken from the early part of the document, which runs on in this fashion for 22 pages. Drawing just on the points above, a producer would have to add the following written policies to its repertoire: a Fair Trade Implementation Plan, a mission statement, inclusion of CSR in its mission statement, job descriptions for all workers who will work more than three consecutive months, a constitution for a Fair Trade Committee, a human resource policy, a general grievance procedure and one for sexual harassment, and a plan for the development of migrant workers. The producer would also have to carry out the following activities: use surveys or primary data to conduct a needs assessment for all workers plus another for migrant workers, have meetings to review compliance and check progress, conduct fair trade training programs, and provide access to schooling and day care. These examples get at the essence of what we mean by organization. In adapting to these criteria, imposed by its wider environment, a small farm in Indonesia or Guatemala becomes an organization.

Poor farmers in the developing world are not the only ones who respond. Even large, rich corporations in the US adapt. In response to the pressures of certification, by 2011 Starbucks, the world's largest coffee chain, bought 86 percent of its total coffee—367 million pounds—through third-party verified or certified sources: Coffee and Farmer Equity Practices (Starbucks's own certification), Fair Trade (the certification offered by a licensing agreement with Fair Trade USA), or another externally audited system.[60] This is no small achievement, given the importance of coffee to the world economy (the second most valuable traded commodity after oil).[61]

Organizationally, Starbucks has developed its own internal certification process (with the standards developed in partnership with Conservancy International and audits carried out by SCS International): the company collects, compiles, and disseminates information about its practices, generating multiple documents including a website, fact sheets, and annual reports like the "Global Responsibility Report." To do all this, it has multiple management and staff roles that involve fair trade activities. Naturally, Starbucks's fair trade purchases do not necessarily lead to improved lives for coffee farmers around the world: abstract rules are often decoupled from functioning practices.[62]

Chapter summary

Organizational expansion is rooted in the rise and globalization of a culture celebrating scientific thinking and human empowerment, largely reflected in and spread by standardized education systems. This culture can shape local realities directly, but its consequences are further transmitted through authoritative structures—legal and accounting rules and all sorts of professionals—that reach into on-the-ground settings.

First, there are actual laws and law-like rules. These are categorical requirements—ways in which things must or must not be done based on considerations of law and propriety. Legal and proto-legal bodies carry them along. Every setting is surrounded by these pressures; they are experienced as things like environmental or human rights principles, or requirements for transparency. Second, there are value assessments. Accounting rules give a definition of worth that connects local settings to a broader context. Local quantification can run up to the global level, as with currencies or international educational rankings. There are also many less universalized countings and accountings—surveys of environmental greenness, of the quality of products or services, or of the best places to work. Any given entity faces value assessments on multiple fronts. Third, there are the professionals: lawyers and accountants, but also in substantive areas (like engineering or education, marketing or sales) and in general management. When actual capabilities for social control are unclear or minimal, professionals can provide advice on the best way to proceed. The social presumption is that these trained people have the needed competencies.

A mystery of contemporary action—that is it plausible to integrate vast numbers of people and activities into a single bounded entity called "an organization"?—is resolved by the myths of professional managerialism. Justified by social scientized rationalities, managers can coordinate activity with little exercise of imperative authority, and can make decisions with little substantive competence. In the extreme, they can make decisions based on abstract principles of science and human empowerment, removed from actual social realities or technical experience. As we shall see, these cultural abstractions enable contemporary social entities to sustain oddly incongruent elements.

▦ NOTES

1. Mörth 2004; Djelic & Sahlin-Andersson 2006; Bartley 2007; Schneiberg & Bartley 2008.
2. Espeland & Stevens 1998.
3. Wilensky 1964.
4. Beck 1992; Power 2007.
5. Meyer & Rowan 1978; Metz 1989; Hallett 2010.
6. Strang, David & Akhlaghpour (2014) discuss the "supply side" of organizational innovation as driven by consultants. For example, Ernst & Kieser (2002) describe the role of consultants in constructing organizational problems for their clients, generating additional demand for consulting services. Chabbott (2003) provides an in-depth study of the construction of education as a central problem in international development. Earlier, Spector & Kitsuse (1987) describes the collective construction of various social problems over time, describing the role of the American Psychiatric Association in problematizing homosexuality and "feeble-mindedness;" see also Hilgartner & Bosk 1988.
7. Czarniawska & Sevón 1996; Sahlin & Wedlin 2008.
8. Thornton 2013.
9. Strange 1996; Sassen 2006.
10. For example, for discussions of when entities are more or less likely to adhere to formal policies see (for countries) Cole 2005; Hafner-Burton & Tsutsui 2005; Schofer & Hironaka 2005, or (for organizations) Westphal & Zajac 2001; Hallett 2010; Sharkey & Bromley 2015.
11. Meyer, Frank, Hironaka et al 1997a; Frank 1999; Cole 2005; Wotipka & Ramirez 2008.
12. See Edelman 1992 for the case of compliance with the 1964 Civil Rights Act in the US.
13. Luca 2011.
14. Brunsson & Jacobsson 2000; Mattli & Büthe 2003; Hallström 2004; Mendel 2006.
15. Meyer et al. 1997.
16. Global Initiative to End All Corporal Punishment for Children website 2015a.

17. Global Initiative to End All Corporal Punishment for Children website 2015b. See also Bromley 2010 for a general overview of evaluation, research, and monitoring activities in international development.
18. Meyer 1996.
19. Ernst & Kieser 2002; Sahlin-Andersson & Engwall 2002; Strang, David, & Akhlaghpour 2014.
20. Ruef 2002. See also Rivera 2012; Binder 2014.
21. Abbott & Snidal 2000; Mörth 2004.
22. See Hallström 2004 for an analysis of the ISO.
23. Brunsson & Jacobsson 2000; Mattli & Büthe 2003; Hallström 2004.
24. Accounting standards are developing at the global level, mainly via the International Financial Reporting Standards (Wagenhofer 2009).
25. Meyer 1986.
26. Power 1997; Strathern 2000; Bartley 2007; Fombrun 2007.
27. Moeran & Strandgaard Pederson (2011) show how fairs, festivals and other competitive events serve as the location for "tournaments of values" where participants negotiate different cultural values to resolve economic issues.
28. Behn 2001.
29. See, for example, the many studies on PISA and Trends in International Mathematics and Science Study (TIMSS) tests (e.g., Schmidt et al. 2001; Simola 2005; Mullis et al. 2012), or on the Shanghai rankings for higher education (e.g., Dehon et al. 2010; Altbach & Salmi 2011), or studies of university rankings within the US (e.g., Espeland & Sauder 2007; Sauder & Espeland 2009).
30. Altbach 2004; Salmi 2009; Skvortsov et al. 2013.
31. Amato & Amato 2012.
32. Murray & Frenk 2010.
33. Godfrey & Zhou 1999.
34. Thrane & Hald 2006.
35. Strathern 2000.
36. Shin & Kehm 2013.
37. Strang & Meyer 1993.
38. Colyvas & Powell 2006.
39. The boundaries of the human person are negotiated in a similar way. Who counts as a person has expanded over time. And what parts of a person are sacrosanct and what parts can be patented, bought, and sold become socially negotiated through law and accounting mechanisms (e.g., Healy 2010).
40. Stark (2011) makes a similar point. As he describes, different "orders of worth" (Boltanski & Thévenot 2006) may make calculable actions possible, but ambiguity still remains. In Stark's formulation, this ambiguity or "sense of dissonance" provides space for innovation and entrepreneurs. We focus on the role of professionals and managers, who may indeed be very entrepreneurial, in balancing discordant pressures.
41. Larson 1977; Freidson 1994; Sullivan 1995; Evetts 2003; Faulconbridge & Muzio 2012; Abbott 2014.
42. Wilensky 1964.
43. Frank & Meyer 2007.

44. Sorensen & Sorensen 1974.

45. Edelman (1992) discusses, for example, the emphasis on process rather than outcomes in how firms responded to equal employment opportunity and affirmative action legislation in the wake of the civil rights movement in the US.

46. Larson 1977; Abbott 2014.

47. Edelman & Suchman 1997; Dobbin & Sutton 1998; Edelman, Uggen, & Erlanger 1999; Kelly & Dobbin 1999; Edelman, Fuller, & Mara-Drita 2001; Dobbin 2009.

48. Dobbin 2009.

49. Cyert & March 1963; March 1982.

50. Brunsson 1985, 2007; Luhmann 1993, 2005; March 1987, 1994; March & Olsen 1976.

51. Taylor 1911; Galbraith 1973; Veblen 1978.

52. Bartley 2003, 2007, 2010, 2011.

53. Bartley 2007.

54. The history of the fair trade industry is drawn largely from Ten Thousand Villages website (2013) and the Fair Trade Federation website (2013).

55. Kaplan 2011.

56. Fair Trade International 2012.

57. This definition of fair trade comes from the World Fair Trade Organization's Charter of Fair Trade Principles (2009).

58. Fair Trade International 2012.

59. Fair Trade USA 2013.

60. Starbucks website 2013.

61. Neal 2002; Global Exchange website 2013.

62. See Goffman (1959) for the same point about individuals' behaviors.

Part 2

The Dimensions of Organizational Actorhood: Non-Rational Integration

5 Organizations as actors

We turn now to discuss the characteristics that define and make up the contemporary organization. Older structures, such as firms under their owners, government bureaucracies under sovereigns, and charities infused with professional or religious authority, tend to become organizations with cadres of relatively standardized management—Chief Executive Officers, Chief Financial Officers, Chief Operating Officers, Chief Information Officers, Chief Privacy Officers, managers for sustainability, human resources, community relations, and so on. Modern individuals have unprecedented levels of empowerment and hugely expanded assigned capacities. These people construct organizations that are similarly empowered and have similarly attributed capacities for rational, autonomous, responsible action. This is indeed an institutionalized vision of a possible global stateless social order. Thus, the essential defining feature of contemporary organization—one that distinguishes it from alternatives such as bureaucracy—is its construction as legitimate, autonomous *social actor*.[1]

The term "actor" once had a primary meaning diametrically opposed to its present social-scientific one. An actor was, and in some usages still is, a person playing a role according to a script written by someone else. Such an actor did not produce what we now mean by action; rather, an actor *enacted* a role. If we shift to a more collective level, a classic bureaucracy, professional organization, or family firm was legitimated as an enactor of the will of an external sovereign state, profession, or owner. And if the modern globalizing world were primarily built around a strong central state or imperial collectivities, the dominant social structures might look like bureaucracies enacting the will of their globally dominant principals. There might be more top-down control and less of the managerial, "shared power", or "networked" forms of governance we now observe because there would be less empowered autonomy, and fewer legitimate, empowered stakeholder groups.[2]

In contemporary society, the term actor has acquired a dramatically new meaning in the social sciences. It now connotes rational action, responsibility, autonomy, and sovereignty, rather than more passive conformity to authoritative scripts. Causal accounts in modern organizational theories increasingly privilege the role of actors over the cultural and institutional contexts that construct them.[3] For example, use of the term "actor" itself increases sharply in the social sciences, as shown in Figures 5.1 to 5.3.

"Actors" can refer to individuals or organizations (or nation-states)—the essence of actorhood lies in its properties, not in a particular unit of analysis.

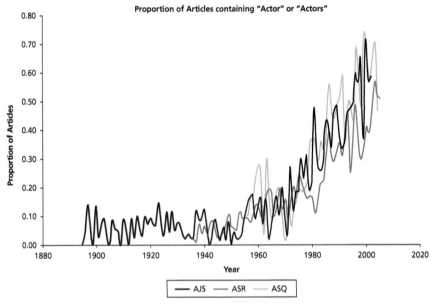

Figure 5.1. Proportion of Articles Containing "Actor" or "Actors" in the *American Journal of Sociology, American Sociological Review,* and *Administrative Science Quarterly*
Source: Hwang & Colyvas 2013.

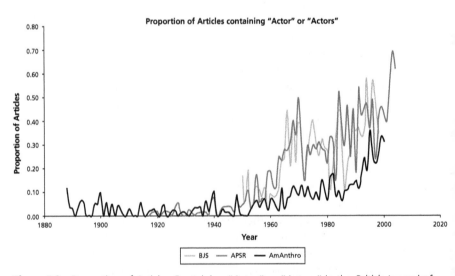

Figure 5.2. Proportion of Articles Containing "Actor" or "Actors" in the *British Journal of Sociology, American Political Science Review,* and *American Anthropologist*
Source: Hwang & Colyvas 2013.

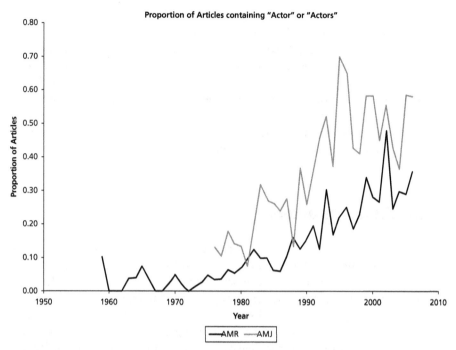

Figure 5.3. Proportion of Articles Containing "Actor" or "Actors" in the *Academy of Management Journal* and *Academy of Management Review*
Source: Hwang & Colyvas 2013.

The qualities of actors are often taken for granted in research, as though actorhood were a natural status independent of any context.[4] Seen in historical and comparative perspective, however, the characteristics of contemporary actors are clearly derived from their cultural context.[5] In today's dominant context, people and their social structures are constructed as strong actors: in earlier and alternative social forms, people were seen as more embedded in society and culture, rather than legitimated autonomous carriers of their own interest.[6]

Actorhood is a constructed role, and carries the posture of voluntarism, activity, and agency. Thus, contemporary actors are not structured as passive enactors of their institutional environment, but are equipped with socially legitimated agency. In some views they are seen as natural entities, though with bounded autonomy: that is, they are real actors navigating constraints from their environments.[7] Our view differs in that we see actorhood itself as constructed, in addition to the institutional opportunities and constraints that actors negotiate.[8] This reconstruction of people and social structures as actors is at the heart of organizational expansion and elaboration. And because both contemporary individuals and organizations posture in the role of actors, a great many claims are built into their identities and structures far in excess of what is functionally necessary or manageable. Much contemporary organizational differentiation can be seen as hyper-organization, involving the display of rationalization as ritualized assertion over and above effective coordination: exaggerated claims about actorhood are essential to the maintenance of a whole stateless global polity. Just as national-states, in the high period before World War I and II, maintained over-the-top claims of their functioning and its roots in national identity, contemporary individuals and organizations are depicted (and depict themselves) in very unrealistic ways—as actors in the central dramas of now-global social life.

Individuals as actors

In the same way that earlier modern legal and social scientific conceptions shifted their model of the person from embedded peasant to the early modern individual,[9] contemporary social-scientific usage remakes the older term "actor" to describe the contemporary version. The obedient citizens subject to the authority of a centralized state in a society of the high nationalist period (e.g., before World War II), or the traditional peasants of a pre-Enlightenment world now left for the anthropologists, are quite removed from the agentic and schooled individual persons envisioned in contemporary global culture. Individuals today are empowered and responsible, and their choices are supposed to determine the social world in nearly all domains—economy,[10] polity,[11] even family and religion.[12] Further, these individuals are theorized to have a good deal of internal differentiation: on an axis of goal-orientation, preferences lead to choices which lead to actions. On an axis of internal integration, differentiation also follows: displayed decisions are claimed to, and supposed to, respond to experience and control behavior.

From the economy to politics, from family life to religion, a universalistic cosmology asserting an underlying commonality of individual rights and powers is on the rise, in theory and ideology if not in practice. This individual empowerment not only enables us to build organizations but also shapes internal organizational dynamics. Each person should respect the choices and capacities of others because we and they are entitled by a common cultural frame. Choices and actions in specific daily settings are more likely to be legitimate when formulated in terms of these abstract principles. For instance, if students miss deadlines, it is hard for them to protest a grade reduction if their teacher invokes the principle of fairness to other students. At the same time, if another student needs extra time for assignments on the grounds of a disability accommodation, classmates are unlikely to protest.

These ideologies of individualism routinely unfold in contemporary workplaces as well. Within a firm, for example, employees can organize legitimate social mini-movements to incorporate their external commitments to the natural world or human rights in any given occupational setting, generating labels like "tempered radicals"[13] and "social intrapreneurs."[14] A *Forbes* report says:

It's no surprise that Millennials, raised as digital natives in a world where social movements are pervasive, have brought a sensibility of social change to the workplace. Rather than checking their values at the door, they follow in the footsteps of a previous generation of tempered radicals—not as lone wolves, but as a movement seeking to make the corporate world more humane, more just, and more sustainable, from the inside out.... We've met dozens of these social intrapreneurs who use the opportunities provided by corporate settings to create initiatives ranging from a corporate Peace Corps at IBM, to a fair trade marketplace at eBay, to an ambitious global human rights code at Ford, to a new store bringing healthy foods to an economically distressed city at Whole Foods.[15]

Note that universalistic principles do not resolve inconsistencies. They can be invoked to justify either the resistance of "green" policies in the name of efficiency or their adoption in the name of rights; or to provide a rationale for both timely and late assignments. A core argument (developed in Chapter 6) is that the expansion of individual rights and scientized capacities generates many possibilities for inconsistency. At the same time, decisions linked to universalistic principles of rights and science generate less overt conflict than those framed as the arbitrary execution of power or raw pursuit of self-interest. Consequently, modern actors can incorporate many inconsistencies with surprisingly few clashes between contradictory elements.

Contemporary actors posture as autonomous creatures whose choices, when rooted in the principles of science and rights, legitimately rule the now-globalized world. The term "actor" denotes autonomy, sovereignty, decision-making authority, and technical action capability.[16] A central quality attributed to contemporary actors is the ability to generate and pursue purposes in the world: constructing means–ends relations in quasi-scientific fashion. Elaborate displays of differentiation follow. Proper individual actors have goals, plans to achieve them, and technical capacities for pursuing the plans; in optimal cases they also have the resources to back up the required technical actions. Control and decision structures integrate these elements. This model of individual actorhood naturally assumes a high level of information about and control over the environment from which the resources are to be assembled, and in which the purposes are to be pursued. Regardless of actual proficiency, the proper individual actor is assumed to be able to make sovereign and autonomous decisions, to implement these decisions, to maintain information on activities and their effects, and to legitimate activity in the wider social environment: obviously, a great deal of role-differentiation is involved.

Of course, we are discussing matters of cultural definition. These are always at variance with local realities, and decoupling is routine and extreme.

Traditional peasants in fact often undertook individual and collective activities of high rationality. More recent citizen-persons were often unable to conform to the limited expectations of early modernity, on the one hand: on the other hand, others among them demanded the rights now attached to contemporary "actors." Displays of rational decision-making are central to modern identities, but few people in the contemporary world can effectively make the inflated choices (in polity, economy, and culture) that are in principle their birthrights. For example, modern individuals might develop distinctive long-term life plans for family and career, but it takes Herculean effort and enormous luck to have things unfold as planned: it is easier if the individuals simply copy standard plans. People have limited capability to implement long-term plans, engage in the required self-control, and effectively perceive and manage relations with the environments within which goals are achieved and cooperation maintained. Much social support is required, and actual autonomy is far less than prevailing ideologies of individualism depict.

Further, dramatic inconsistencies are built into contemporary models of the individual as actor. The requirements of practical action are likely to be inconsistent with the exigencies of properly carried-out decision-making, and much decoupling is inevitable. Nils Brunsson emphasizes the point that the proper modern actor is something of a hypocrite, whose inflated identity claims (e.g., as "decision-maker") are inevitably inconsistent with the urgent demands of immediate activity.[17] Classic time-use studies of managers and executives reinforce this vision.[18] From multiple analyses, we see that the central daily activities of managers are reactive, largely consisting of trouble-shooting and responding to others' initiatives, and subject to constant interruption. If we look at how leaders really spend their time, the notion of managers as strategists and planners, methodically controlling the direction of an organization far into the future, is often unrealistic. In practice, plans and decisions change rapidly and opportunistically in response to idiosyncratic and often unpredictable events.

Even ordinary individuals in social life are unlikely to be able to effectively conform to the vision of rational purposiveness and internal integration. Indeed, normal human socialization through families and communities is thought inadequate to provide proper preparation for the demands of exaggerated modern individualism. Almost always, throughout the world, it is understood that formal education is needed—and usually becomes compulsory.[19]

Individuals routinely express the features of their actorhood: much of this is ritualized assertion, reflecting the extraordinary value placed on effective, controlled, purposive actorhood. For example, people prominently display educational successes on their résumés (in contrast, family background rarely shows up). In social life, similar qualities appear. Surveyed respondents opine on religion, politics, and culture,[20] and routinely mobilize around issues related to their identity but removed from immediate goals and interests. There are increasing choices to be made in terms of personal identity: traditional gender, racial, ethnic, and religious categories can be selected to a greater extent than in earlier times.[21] People often put a great deal of effort into selecting and displaying a chosen identity. In fact, being a proper person—an actor—in the contemporary world takes up a great deal of time and energy, and the displays involved can greatly detract from purposive action capability.[22] Academics, for instance, could spend all their time maintaining websites and blogs; networking with colleagues; responding to various department and university requests to get involved in events and activities like improving campus engagement, greenness, or research ethics oversight; or filling out reporting requirements for departments—or for accreditation and ratings agencies. Although these ancillary activities can constitute a full-time job, none is directly focused on the research or teaching thought to be the central aims of the enterprise. Taking on too many such things interferes with the core purposes of academia, but taking on too few leads to criticism and weakens external legitimacy. As we will observe, exactly the same tensions arise as modern social structures become "organized actors." Seeking to maintain this delicate balance is a core challenge facing contemporary individuals and organizations, a point to which we return in Chapters 6 and 7.

Organizations as actors

Historically, formal social organization was understood to be created and legitimated by sovereign collective actors: states, religious structures, sometimes distinctive professions. Only after the Enlightenment did individuals slowly start to be seen as capable of building organizations. Even into the late nineteenth century, the legitimacy of private organization was questioned. For one thing, it seemed obvious that managers and employees would steal everything from owners. For another, private organizations were viewed as criminally suspect conspiracies and illicit monopolies. In the early periods, private organizations were sanctioned to exist only for particular special purposes, and required approval from states. Only later and in liberal contexts did legal norms permit the general incorporation of organizations for a broad range of purposes.[23]

Now all this has changed. Worldwide, individuals can and do establish formal organizations and engage in an array of organizing activities, often globally, and often with minimal state control. People, empowered under common principles, and engaging in action in an increasingly scientized and lawful environment, are seen as naturally able to come together in common association and capable of systematically accomplishing goals. This is the legitimating theory of modern organizations, and living up to it creates a great deal of ritualized hyper-organization. At the extreme, religious organizations are now seen as built and changed by individuals. So are organizations in economic life. In an odd reversal, even states—once rooted in history, religion, tradition, and dynastic authority—are now seen as organizations built and operated by the choices and decisions of individual persons:[24] this principle is built into their founding constitutional documents everywhere.

Organizations, built up and populated by individuals seen as actors, are thus constructed collectives with all the properties of actorhood. This is the central defining feature of the contemporary concept of organizations. Like the modern individual, an organization has its own legitimate purposes, not simply those of its external sovereign. It is accountable to various "stakeholders," but it is also responsible for defining its mission, likely to be put forward on a universalistic basis. An organization makes means–ends decisions about how to accomplish its purposes, using the defined resources it possesses. All this occurs through an organization's decision-making processes, based on a theory of command over its internal components and external relations, and based on systems of information and self-control.

To demonstrate their status as contemporary actors, organizations are pressed by their environments to make displays of their agentic capacities—often beyond reasonable limits of actual control. Elaborate structural differentiation may reflect the symbolic expression of actorhood rather than effectively coordinated action. For instance, the Carbon Disclosure Project (CDP), one of the largest and best-known global emissions watchdogs, pushes firms to generate reports on emissions targets decades into the future, a task that obviously requires enormous assumptions about firm growth, macro-economic trends, technological developments, and so on. The CDP is "an international, not-for-profit organization providing the only global system for companies and cities to measure, disclose, manage and share vital environmental information."[25] In its 2013 assessment of carbon disclosure practices among Standard and Poor's 500 Index (S&P 500) companies, the CDP reports that 75 percent of respondents set short-term emissions targets, but it criticizes the firms for not projecting and planning further into the future. The report states, "Despite progress on setting near-term targets, only 62 of the 252 that set targets do so to 2020 or beyond, with just 8 companies setting targets beyond 2020."[26] To put this admonishment in context, in 2012 the average life span of a firm listed on the S&P 500 was 15 years,[27] meaning that companies are being pressed to set emissions targets into a future where about half of them will no longer exist. Thus, for a firm to be a proper organizational actor, it must produce displays of decision-making and control that stretch the limits of its actual ability.

To achieve the autonomy required of actors, boundaries distinguishing organizations from their environments are set out sharply in internal rules and external legal and accounting principles. As in a traditional bureaucracy, lines are drawn between the participants in their roles as organizational members and the other roles in their lives; it is sometimes unethical, if not illegal, to allow these worlds to merge. Clear specifications delineate between the resources that belong to the organization and external resources. Unlike a bureaucracy, however, in an organization these differentiated elements reflect a range of social and cultural concerns and not just structural efficiency or the whims of a sovereign. Organizations are constituted by their adherence to external pressures and, in part, structural distinctions that show conformity affirm the existence of the organization. Additional displays of actorhood and identity are routine—from offices that could be featured in *Architectural Digest* to logos and brands.[28] Organizational actorhood, just as with individual actorhood, is demanding in terms of its overhead costs, and it can take much time and resource.[29] Just as modern individuals rely on their supporters (therapists, legal advisors, occupational advisors, coaches, and so on), modern organizations are often propped up by waves of consultants: indeed, consulting has become a major component of the global economy, as we discussed in Chapter 4.

Actorhood, both individual and organizational, is a core ontological component of the contemporary world. It takes precedence over many other and older social forms. A contemporary school is less a school and more an organization than it was formerly, and it is thus more likely to have decision-making management, statements of purpose, and accounting and information systems. The same transformations occur in every social sector, from religion to private business to government agencies. An enormous variety of social functions is now absorbed in the general category of non-profit organizations. Many management and administrative roles can be common to any sort of organization in the whole category, as well as to government agencies and firms. Organization, in short, becomes a category in its own right, and it is highly respectable to get professional training in management, including organization theory, without any specification of the substance of activity that is to be managed.

The theory of modern organization is that information and control systems are expected to replace the substantive (often tacit, experience-based) knowledge formerly held by heads of schools and businesses. Statistical reports, performance evaluations, outcomes assessments, and so on provide bases for decision-making. One can study the structure of a firm without really understanding what it produces or sells. Unlike the old days, the manager of a produce company is likely to have an MBA and a sophisticated system for gathering and analyzing information, but may not know much about vegetables. Similarly, the modern manager of a school or university may be uninformed about the substance of teaching and research, but must certainly have a grasp of the school *qua* organization. Practical religious, educational, medical, industrial, commercial, and governmental activities go on underneath the umbrella of organizational forms. Organization, in the contemporary system, takes on a life of its own.

In becoming legitimate actors, organizations assume a different and broader role in society than the traditional substantively specialized structures did. Just as modern individuals take on broad citizenship rights and responsibilities, organizational actors become something like collective citizens in contemporary national and global society. In the absence of a supra-national state, in fact, individual personhood and organizational actorhood serve as dominant theories of how global coordination is possible. In the US the trend toward corporate citizenship is reflected in Supreme Court cases assigning the rights and responsibilities of personhood to organizations. But, as we emphasize, their social standing as actors extends beyond the law.[30]

Organizational actors as responsible citizens of global society

Individual persons become modern actors, often via formal education, and assume broader rights and responsibilities in every sector of society. In the same way, social structures that become organized actors come under expanded expectations. They are to pursue their goals, certainly, but to do so with all the forms of good citizenship in a now-global society. This, in fact, is a core liberal and now neoliberal theory of global social order.

Proper organizations should manage their staffs according to norms established by hard and soft law, including broad visions of human rights. They should also maintain proper relations with customers, suppliers, surrounding communities, stockholders, legal bodies, and the public in general. And they should attend to their impact on the natural world, appearing to be the appropriate shade of "green." Finally, all these dimensions of the organization's business are to be conducted with an almost-Calvinist transparency, open to inspection by a wide range of stakeholders.

Current notions of social responsibility capture the essence of corporate citizenship. They define a broad agenda for the proper organization, no matter what its original specific purposes were. Dozens of associations, worldwide, create hard and soft laws specifying organizational responsibilities. Typical large organizations belong to these, attempting to behave correctly (and/or produce the right reports). Figure 5.4 shows the expansion of CSR guides and initiatives over time. The Global Reporting Initiative (GRI) is one particularly important effort. It is recognized as a leader among CR performance programs.[31] The GRI is "a non-profit organization

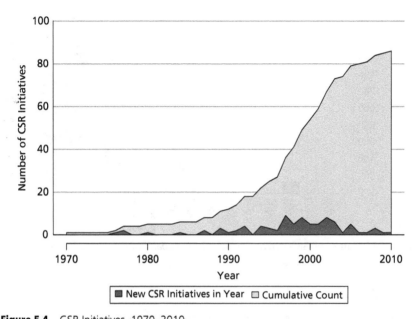

Figure 5.4. CSR Initiatives, 1970–2010

Source: Meyer, Pope, & Isaacson 2015; Visser, 2010.
Note: One initiative started in 1948, but the next initiative is not established until 1976. The timeframe starts in 1970 to ease visual representation.

that promotes economic, environmental, and social sustainability. GRI provides all companies and organizations with a comprehensive sustainability reporting framework that is widely used around the world."[32] Figure 5.5 shows the adoption of GRI guidelines by companies around the world between 1999 and 2010.

The GRI's core supporters are known as "Organizational Stakeholders." These participants contribute their name to GRI's mission, provide expertise and financial contributions, and play a role in governance. They come from a wide array of industries and countries. For example, the first ten businesses listed alphabetically on the GRI website include (headquarter location and industry in parentheses): ABB Asea Brown Boveri Ltd (Switzerland, Equipment), Abertis (Spain, Other), Abu Dhabi National Oil Company (United Arab Emirates, Energy), Access Bank PLC (Nigeria, Financial Services), AFNOR Competencies (France, Commercial Services), AGEMA Corporation (Italy, Media), Al Jazeera International Catering LLC (United Arab Emirates, Food and Beverage Products), Alive2Green (South Africa, Media), Alliander (Netherlands, Energy Utilities), and AMATA S.A (Brazil, Forest and Paper Products). Public agencies, such as A Coruña Port Authority in Spain, and non-profit organizations, such as the Institution of Occupational Safety and

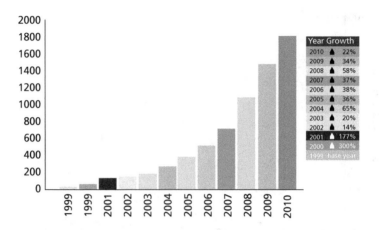

Figure 5.5. Uptake of GRI Guiding Principles by Companies Worldwide, 1999–2010
Source: Global Reporting Initiative 2010/11: 7.

Health in the UK are also stakeholders; labor organizations, universities, and IGOs participate in this role as well.[33]

Guiding principles provided by the GRI suggest the range of responsibilities a proper organizational actor should assume. They include: Strategy and Analysis, Organizational Profile, Identified Material Aspects and Boundaries, Stakeholder Engagement, Governance, and Ethics and Integrity, plus indicators for economic, environmental, and social performance (including labor practices and decent work, human rights, and society). The principles are spelled out in a 94-page document outlining "Reporting Principles and Standard Disclosures." We provide the Table of Contents in Figure 5.6. As with our earlier discussion of fair trade certification, this sustainability reporting is highly scientized. It involves a cycle of data collection to produce measures, followed by reporting and responding to the GRI.

Notions of responsibility and accountability are broad. In addition to the social dimensions, firms are obligated to maximize shareholder value.[34] In parallel, in the public domain government agencies and non-profits increasingly must demonstrate accountability and responsibility to their donors and clients using measures of efficiency and effectiveness.[35] Akin to the process of establishing common methods for valuing assets and liabilities, methods emerge to measure social returns on investment, or more general performance indicators and evaluation metrics for public purposes. The core point is that organizations are responsible to many stakeholders on many dimensions and must document their accountability in relatively scientific ways for external and internal purposes.

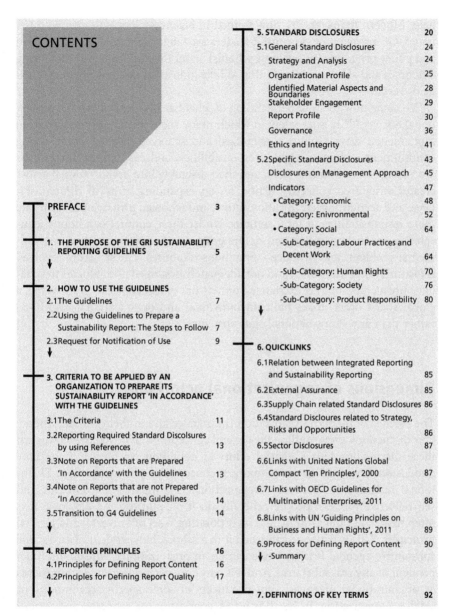

CONTENTS

Figure 5.6. Table of Contents for the Guiding Principles of the Global Reporting Initiative
Source: Global Reporting Initiative 2013: 2.

Of course, it is difficult to conform to so many requirements. Organizations often hire specialists and create departments to do the work: such people, as professionals, belong to the emerging professional associations, which help determine what must be done. And they often turn to external consultants to help. Modern managers are now trained in business schools to deal with CR issues. Government or non-profit leaders are taught in public administration and policy programs (or business schools) about the importance of measuring outcomes and about ways to do this. Whole industries and new organizational fields result.

We come now to an understanding of what has been called the "Organizational Society."[36] It is a society in which many social structures are altered in fundamental ways around a scientized and schooled culture and a strong commitment to human rights, responsibilities, and capabilities. Individuals are strong actors in this system, and their assembly into organizational actors creates structured collective action on an expanding array of dimensions. Legal and accounting specifications grow, and schooled professionals translate these responsibilities in local settings. Under these cultural conditions, educated individuals perceive and define great numbers of social and environmental problems and produce voluminous responses. The structure involved is distinctly organizational, and not adequately described by analogies to state-like bureaucracy, market exchanges, or network or associational ties. Overall, a global social order arises built on individual and organizational actorhood rather than any supra-national state structure.

Dimensions of organizational actorhood

The essence of modern organization (in practice and in theory) is actorhood. Our discussions above outline the general conceptions involved. Here, we turn these discussions into a central effort at definition, spelling out the core dimensions involved in contemporary conceptions of organization. Definitional tasks matter because "organization" is a highly self-conscious and self-reflective process: people generally do it on purpose. As ideology, it is often treated as built around, and incorporating, a set of universal and general principles. This is why one can teach it in a school, independent of any actual substantive agenda. It is why one can be an organizational consultant, independent of any real substance. And it is why core personnel can see themselves as organizational managers, not producers of some specific commodity or service. Organization, in short, is a folk concept in the schooled and rationalized society—imagined as a coherent phenomenon, independent of practice. Whatever practical or functional structure is built into an organization's structure may be overridden by differentiated structures taking the organization's statement as an integrated goal-oriented project. Similarly, the entities constructed under this concept are structurally depicted as coherent and sharply bounded from the society around them: they are distinct, have names (and logos), and claim a special social, legal, and ontological status.

The independence from practice can be quite dramatic. The managed and self-conceived organizational structure is often far removed from the substance of actual activity. Decoupling is intrinsic to the field, precisely because of the sweeping universalism of concepts of organizations themselves. A university conceived as an organization is likely to be highly decoupled, compared with a university thought of only as a university. The decoupling involved can include gaps between formal policies and practices and also the incorporation of a range of inconsistent activities that are pressed in by the wider culture, rather than the specific requirements of teaching and learning.[37]

The core meaning of "organization," in contemporary usage, has two broad components. First, there is the organization as a purposive collective enterprise, taking rational *action* toward clear ends: this is ordinarily spelled out in a differentiated formal structure, the components of which are set in a claimed means–ends relation to each other. Second, there is the organization as an entity—a unified *actor* as a matter of identity—that legitimately possesses the goals and acts on them in a coordinated and controlled way, as a member of society. In the organizational drama, social construction consists of displays of purposive action and of identity—above and beyond the minimum requirements for coordinating action. We review these two dimensions of organizational actorhood in turn. The discussion is summarized in Table 5.1.

Means–ends relations: structuring the action: a central feature of life in an organization is the articulation of purposive action. Activity tends to be built into a clearly differentiated structure reflecting a causal model of means–ends relationships. An association to enhance a community, for instance, may have vague goals, and may be more a part of the community than an actor accomplishing goals within the community. But when the association becomes an organization, a sharper boundary is constructed between the entity and the environment from which it draws resources and in which it pursues its goals. Purposes are likely to be stated clearly, activities are likely to be carried out around them, and environmental resources and constraints are likely to be clearly defined. Similarly, when a school becomes an organization, broad notions of learning are likely to become specific educational goals such as test scores. Articulated means–ends relations are central to modern conceptions of organization, and one can assess the degree to which a social entity has become an organization by examining their specification. Since organization is highly valued—a preferred social form—in the modern system, it follows that the differentiated structuring of rational purposive action is often overdone and overstated. It has, that is, ritual value and standing and is likely to be dramatized beyond realistic practice. In the same ways that modern individuals display their actorhood, organizations do too.

Decision-making and managers: A central mystery in the construction of organizations as actors is the location of purpose and choice. People today are more or less seen as born with legitimate purposiveness, attributed to them by

Table 5.1 Dimensions and Indicators of Organizational Actorhood

Identity: Constructing the Actor	Means–Ends Relations: Structuring the Action
Boundaries: Clear legal, accounting, and symbolic demarcations of the organization from the environment. Internal roles sharply distinguished from external linkages. • e.g., names, acronyms, branding; claims to organizational culture.	**Decision-making and Managers:** Depictions of clear and rationalized means–ends decisions and processes, typically located in management. **Goals and Plans:** Written goals, mission statements, and planning documents to achieve production outcomes; often at multiple levels with opaque relation to each other.
Citizenship: Establishing organizational policies, roles, structures, or routines to fill role of corporate "citizen;" recognize actorhood of internal components and other organizations and individuals. • e.g., demonstrating attention to workplace diversity, work–life balance, extended benefits, philanthropic efforts, environmental care, public and community relations, and ethical governance; feedback mechanisms in these areas. Obtaining certifications, such as Leadership in Energy and Environmental Design (LEED) recognition for buildings; tracking external trends in the media or among peers.	• e.g., formal goals for individual positions and/or departments, as well as entire organization; monthly or quarterly plans, annual plans, long-range plans. **Defining Means–Ends Relations:** Progress towards goals monitored internally and externally through professional, legal, and/or accounting indicators: elaborate depictions and accounts of technical steps in producing outputs. • e.g., seeking out and tracking rankings or ratings; meeting benchmarks; conducting evaluations; studies of consumer, or client satisfaction; maintaining memberships in various professional associations.
Autonomy and Sovereignty: Displays of the organization as an autonomous, responsible, rights-bearing entity. **Central Authority:** Clear specification of a central unified node of a sovereign authority and responsibility. **Integration:** Elaborated control and information systems linking peripheries to the center. Extended displays of data on activities and personnel.	**Resource Specifications:** Detailed accounting, tracking, and allocating resources as source of effectiveness and of technical activities. Inputs and outputs explicitly defined. • e.g., use of financial and management accounting, elaborate accounting for cost of employee time to numerous projects; detailed information on human resources. **Monitoring and Evaluation Formally Differentiated**

contemporary culture. With organizations, one must specify a locus of decision-making (and, thus, of actorhood). The solution lies in a conception of rational management with the authority and capacity to make decisions and set goals. As social entities become organizations, they display elaborate and often ritualized decision-making processes, centered on management. Managers are the central location of organizational action, and leaders are lionized in contemporary management theory. Good leaders are heroic figures who are thought to steer an organization, determining its purposes, and strategically charting a course using the tools of rational planning and decision-making.

Proper decision-making has to take into account that both the participants in organizations and external audiences are modern, often highly schooled, people. They are actors themselves, and often one aim of organization is to involve their preferences and commitments in the structure itself through, for example, attention to various forms of incentivizing employees and managers to work on the organization's behalf. Proper management is often accompanied by systems for participatory decision-making and closely monitoring the internal and external environment.

Goals and Plans: one indicator that an entity has become more of an organization is the production of statements of its goals, vision, and mission. Further, controlling behavior toward goals involves planning. Goals and plans are rationally specified in terms of differentiated means–ends relations; thus they may be operationalized in terms of targets, benchmarks, or other indicators of success. A university might want to move up in some rankings or a business to move toward the front of its industry. Like decision-making, goal-setting and planning processes can be inclusive, incorporating and recognizing the actorhood of employees and other stakeholders. Organizations develop multiple goals and subgoals, as well as long-term and short-term plans, on several dimensions reflecting inconsistent and manifold arenas—CR, greenness, employee and consumer satisfaction, efficiency and profit, and so on. As goals and plans are highly valued cultural symbols under contemporary conditions, they are often put forward in unrealistic ways: organizational plans are commonly and notoriously unfulfilled.[38]

Defining means-ends relations: a central element of organizing is explicitly articulating the steps that will lead to the accomplishment of goals. The causal chain may involve technological matters, as in a classic production process. It may also involve functional differentiation, as when distinct sales and marketing departments are created. As organization expands as a social form in the contemporary order, these means–ends relations are rarely fixed and self-evident, as they might be in a more traditional assembly line. Instead, professionals theorize about causal relationships to support planning. In the non-profit world, phrases like "theories of change" and "logic models" are in vogue.[39] The reactivity between organizations and their environments further complicates definitively establishing means and ends. Today's well-established causal theories and relations can be gone tomorrow, and actions that seem superfluous today can become linked to core purposes over time. For instance, a few decades ago a firm's efforts to reduce pollution were little related to its share price, but today investors (and others) may penalize high polluters. As the environment becomes more complex and populated with more actors, socially constructed causal chains expand and become more complex. Thus, organizations dedicate enormous work to establishing and spelling out the causal chains that are built into their differentiated formal structures.

Resource specifications: rational planning, decision-making, and goal-setting require the clear differentiation and specification of necessary resources—material, human, and cultural. For example, for a religious congregation resource definitions might involve spelling out the uses of space, funds, and volunteer commitments for worship and non-worship activities. Cultural dimensions might include the required social and legal approvals. And it is now standard to include professional qualities and status of employees in an account of resources.

Monitoring and evaluation: to bring goal-setting and planning full circle, proper organizations should assess their effectiveness and efficiency in their environments, both internally and across their boundaries. In theory, these assessments feed back into daily decision-making for a cycle of continuous improvement. They can also, theoretically, be used to improve goal-setting, means–ends calculations, and resource allocation. In practice, however, it is well-known that information often goes unused, and in many settings it is unclear how to evaluate outcomes.[40]

Formal differentiation: a critical manifestation of the organizational processes and components discussed above is formal differentiation. Decision-making becomes a distinct social process that can be studied or applied as a core activity unto itself, as can planning, resource allocation, and evaluation. A group of commonly committed people may be an association, but they are not necessarily an organization. They become more organized when their commitments are expressed as distinct elements.

Identity: constructing the actor: organizations are not natural actors: they are built and changed, and maintaining their construction is a principal focus of their self-reflective behavior. An organization is an organization because it and surrounding parties say it is an organization.[41] For instance, in many legal systems organizations have standing to sue or be sued, and to possess assets and liabilities. Some thinking about modern organizations deconstructs this essential element, conceiving of organizations as a "nexus of contracts,"[42] "legal fictions,"[43] or collections of individuals.[44] These descriptions can be realistic descriptions of activities and relationships, but they miss the core construction of self-conscious (and commonly established by legal and accounting rules) organizational identity.

The importance, and the problematic character, of the construction of organizations as legitimated actors in the world leads to a great deal of formal structuration. Elements that might be handled casually and informally in some settings (e.g., dispute resolution within a family) must be elaborated in explicitly formalized and differentiated ways in organizations. This means that much contemporary organizational structure is in a sense artificial from the point of view of the actual function of activities being carried out. Disputes can be resolved without formal structure, but in an organization the process must be spelled out. Moreover, what gets spelled out may be more elaborate than what will actually be done in practice. Thus decoupling is increasingly likely as the contemporary organization takes on more of an identity, requiring formal articulation on more dimensions.[45]

Boundaries: organizations, compared with other social structures, more clearly specify which material, human, and cultural elements are internal to them, and which are part of an environment. A school principal, for instance, may have diffuse authority over the young people in a small town: as the school becomes an organization, the boundaries of this authority are sharpened and made explicit: the principal is both empowered and constrained in the process. Legal and accounting principles are central here, defining what resources and responsibilities lie with the organization, and which are external. Similarly, occupational and professional role specifications define which activities lie under the jurisdiction of the organization, and which are external. In all cases—but especially with professionalization—there may be a good deal of ambiguity, and elaborate structuration results, often accompanied by extended conflicts.

Citizenship: boundaries imply both internal and external structuration. Organizations are differentiated from their environments, but then construct links with them—offices, departments, policies, and programs for relationships with surrounding communities, official bodies, customers, suppliers, labor, researchers, consultants, and so on. Organizations elaborate depictions and structures establishing their legitimate standing in the community: legal forms, public relations activities, and differentiated organizational structures relating to the environment, seen as external (but also, commonly, as stakeholders).

Autonomy and sovereignty: to be an organization is to be an actor capable of autonomous action. This implies social and legal accountability and responsibility, and thus the related capacity for choice and decision. A core issue in the rise of organization is the source of legitimated sovereign autonomy. Classically, bureaucratic structures derived sovereignty, and some measure of autonomy, from states and religious structures, both of which claimed roots in a transcendental world. With the contemporary weakening of the special charisma of these sources, the bureaucracies dependent on them tend to lose authority. Indeed, both states and religious bodies now derive much of their authority from their people, seen as individual actors, not from their gods.

Thus in practice contemporary organizations derive their authority from some set of empowered and choosing individual actors who join together in creating and participating in them. These various participants—shareholders, stakeholders, voters, parishioners, and so on—bring their actorhood, through one or another legitimated process, together in organization-building. The particular processes involved have considerable ritual significance, as they carry empowered actorhood to the created structures, and they tend to be prominently displayed in organizational charters and constitutions. The result is crucial: the organization must be unified and seen as capable of coordinated action. This implies both some structural center and some sort of control system linking peripheries to this center.

Authority: choice and action require at least the depiction of chooser and actor. Organization requires some models integrating disparate elements in a choice–decision process. This ordinarily involves a clear hierarchical structure of roles, though contemporary organizations—filled with people who are themselves professionalized actors—often build central authority up out of the organized process of expanded participation. That is, extreme hierarchy, in the world of contemporary organizations, tends to be moderated by principles of participation. This means that explicit and formalized processes of establishing both central authority and the decisions it makes are necessary. Overall, in one way or another, authority relations must be defined, and hierarchy (along with formalized procedure) is central to the way it is generally done.

Integration: internally, organization means elaborated control systems to turn decisions into activity, to create coordination, to avoid deviation, and so on. Related, organization means systems of information and reporting and inspection. In both cases the effort is to link center and periphery of the internal structure. The construction of systems for participation, noted above, also has obvious functions for building organizational identities. Processes of integration are important in maintaining an organizational boundary. Central integrating forces rest in legal and accounting rules. Social mechanisms also integrate the people involved, creating a sense of loyalty and shared experience. Physical boundaries define organizational location, mapping out geographic areas that count as internal and external. Symbols also play this role: organizational names, brands, histories, websites, slogans, and so on.[46]

Chapter summary

The defining feature of the modern organization is that it is a rationalized and differentiated, but unified, actor. Actors have sprawling responsibilities and commitments, but incorporate integrated theories of action and identity. Deriving from the actorhood of modern individuals (rather than, for example, states and churches), the organization becomes a unitary legal and moral entity, endowed with its own sovereignty, purposes, and identity, while simultaneously accountable to other actors in its environment. Its construction is undergirded by the expansion of scientific and rights-based cultural principles. Paralleling the modern individual, the core features of organizations are their assembly around clear purposes and goals, and their integration of (often inconsistent) activities into unitary identities. In constructing activity around goals, they generate and depend on large numbers of causal theories working from resources to goal-achievement. In doing so, they construct identities that integrate many domains of human life within a common boundary and create links from inside their boundaries to their elaborate and complex environments.

NOTES

1. Brunsson & Sahlin-Andersson 2000; Krücken & Meier 2006; King, Felin, & Whetten 2010; Hwang & Colyvas 2011.
2. Jones, Hesterly, & Borgatti 1997; Crosby & Bryson 2005; Sørensen & Torfing 2005; Osborne 2006, 2010; Provan & Kenis 2008.
3. Scharpf 1997; Ingram & Clay 2000; Lawrence & Suddaby 2006; Jackson 2010; King, Felin, & Whetten 2010; Lawrence, Suddaby, & Leca 2011; Meyer 2010; Hwang & Colyvas 2013. For the non-profit sector, Prakash & Gugerty (2010b: xv) note, "We begin with the premise that since advocacy is a collective endeavor, advocacy NGOs should be viewed as actors pursuing collective action."
4. Meyer & Jepperson 2000: 101; Suddaby et al. 2010.
5. Hwang & Colyvas 2011.
6. In the current world, societies have experienced the construction of both individual and organizational actorhood quite unequally. As we show in Chapter 2, for example, data from several available sources indicate that the extent of the organizational revolution is lower in the Middle East and North Africa. Religious and traditional familial sources of cultural authority are stronger there, and the doctrines of individual empowerment that we argue drive organization and hyperorganization are weaker. Specific settings within contemporary developed societies also vary in the extent to which they are influenced by principles of science and individual empowerment, and thus vary in the extent to which they are susceptible to organizational expansion. For example, centralized entities with accountability only to a leader at the top of a hierarchy (i.e., a bureaucracy) are likely to be less densely organized than decentralized entities with multiple accountabilities. Cultural conditions, however, have changed on a very broad scale, and so have the prospects for both individual and organizational actorhood.
7. Hedström & Swedberg 1998; Thornton, Ocasio, & Lounsbury 2012; Westphal & Zajac 2013.
8. Meyer & Jepperson 2000.
9. Stinchcombe 1965.
10. For example, the contemporary economy is, in dominant liberal and neoliberal ideologies, to be driven by the choices of individuals: consumers, investors, producers, inventors, and entrepreneurs in vast markets for labor, consumption, and productive resources (Read 2009: see Fridman 2010 for an example of the diffusion of the *homo economicus* model to Argentina). Ideas of utility maximization and competition are, implicitly and explicitly, baked into much contemporary thinking, despite well-known critiques about the boundaries of human rationality (Simon 1972, 1982, 1991; March 1978). The rise of *homo economicus* is one well-known dimension of the rise of society based on models of empowered, rational individuals, but it is certainly not the only one (See Ng & Tseng 2008 for a discussion of the social construction of *homo economicus* and this model's convergence with *homo sociologicus.*)
11. For example, in a world where democracy is a highly legitimate form of political structure, the choices and rights of rational individuals are expected to drive

government action. This invocation of democratic discourse is "practically universal by political regimes" (Held 2006: 230). Even the constitutions of authoritarian and repressive regimes espouse commitment to these principles (Hafner-Burton, Tsutsui, & Meyer 2008; Beck, Drori, & Meyer 2012). For example, North Korea declares its commitment to elections (Article 66) and a system of petitioning complaints (Article 69) (Democratic People's Republic of Korea's Socialist Constitution 1995). It further pledges freedom of speech (Article 67), freedom of religion (Article 68), and gender equality (Article 77). Contemporary governments of all stripes are expected to serve their people, and citizens are depicted as empowered individuals with rights and decision-making capabilities.

12. The same philosophies of individual empowerment and choice even appear in widespread contemporary models of family life (Thornton 2013). Individuals now are to choose to build and sustain families: marriage, family, and kinship are less authoritative than they used to be. And children are increasingly socialized to have preferences and make choices; at the extreme, in some places parental emancipation is a possibility. Likewise, the choices of entitled individuals characterize modern culture and religion: today's individuals can decide who God is, as very few countries substantially establish a religion defining a god who decides who the individual is. Individuals can decide which belief system to follow, and change their spiritual practices and beliefs at will (for instance, to decide that there is no god).

13. Meyerson 2001.

14. Mair & Marti 2006.

15. Davis & White 2012.

16. Meyer & Jepperson 2000.

17. Brunsson 1985, 1989.

18. Mintzberg 1973, 1975; Kurke & Aldrich 1983. For a review see Hales 1986.

19. Further, education is central to stratification systems everywhere: individual education and occupational certifications based on schooling are central measures of social prestige in countries around the world. This in itself indicates the enormous value placed on the rights and capabilities of actorhood.

20. Jepperson 2002.

21. Frank & Meyer 2002.

22. Brunsson 1985.

23. For accounts of the history of incorporation and the transformation of corporations into legitimate social actors see Coleman 1982, 1990; Creighton 1990; Dobbin 1994; Kaufman 2008; King, Felin, & Whetten 2010.

24. Bendix 1980.

25. CDP website 2015.

26. CDP 2013: 17.

27. Gittleson 2012.

28. Drori, Delmestri, & Oberg 2013.

29. Brunsson 1989.

30. King, Felin, & Whetten 2010.

31. Brown, de Jong, & Lessidrenska 2007.

32. Global Reporting Initiative website 2013.

33. Global Reporting Initiative website 2014.
34. See Lazonick & O'Sullivan 2000 for a discussion of the rise of shareholder value ideology.
35. For examples in the non-profit sector see Bagnoli & Megali 2009; Barman & MacIndoe 2012; MacIndoe & Barman 2012; in education see Colyvas 2012; in government see Carter, Day, & Klein 1992 or Heinrich 2002.
36. Coleman 1982; Zald & McCarthy 1987; Perrow 2002.
37. Bromley & Powell 2012.
38. Mintzberg 1994.
39. Carman 2010; Knowlton & Phillips 2012.
40. Feldman & March 1981.
41. Whetten, Felin, & King 2010.
42. Alchian & Demsetz 1972; Jensen & Meckling 1976; Demsetz 1988.
43. Fama 1980.
44. Clegg & Hardy 1996; Weick 1995, 1998.
45. Meyer & Rowan 1977; Bromley & Powell 2012.
46. Glynn 2000; Drori et al. 2013.

6 Dialectics: non-rational integration

Cultural transformations (described in Chapter 3) transmitted into local settings (Chapter 4) drive the expansive reconstruction of organization, and build the new model of organizational actorhood (Chapter 5). Expansion is especially striking in areas distantly removed from core purposes and clear functional linkages, or what we have called hyper-organization. Becoming a proper actor means developing ties to an expanded variety of human and social environments, and ritualized demonstrations of rationality.

The transformation of informal associations or hierarchical bureaucracies into contemporary organizations generates a wide range of inconsistencies. Just as with the modern individual, the modern organization, as it assumes more responsibilities on more dimensions, expands beyond its actual capacity for autonomous and integrated action.[1] Law-like pressures come in from all directions, but nothing (except the imagined capacity for choice and decision-making) makes them coherent, consistent with each other or with basic goals, or capable of effectively producing the intended outcomes. Accounting processes and professionals work to produce stories about how new and necessary programs contribute as "investments" or "costs" or even "efficient strategies," but they ratify the situation after the fact and provide an organization with little guidance for balancing all the externally supported arrangements.

Thus organizational expansion takes on a non-rational or hyper-organizational character, growing far beyond the requirements of technical coordination and beyond the needs of political power and authority. Naturally, some organizational structures serve obvious coordination or power-based functions, but wide ranges of organized activity cannot be justified in these terms. The breadth of cultural rationalization and the accompanying organizational expansion creates two over-riding dialectics.

First, organizational structures become rife with inconsistencies and tensions incorporated from increasingly complex rationalized environments. They are expected to accomplish ends, but also to satisfy a growing array of stakeholders. In responding to expanding external pressures, organizations acquire more and more responsibilities. They incorporate dimensions that are inconsistent—or at least distinct enough so that it is impossible to definitively assess values in terms of core goals. Thus, organizations incorporate elements with indeterminate value, even in the absence of direct competition: firms pursue CR, non-profits adopt risk management procedures, and government agencies implement performance measurement. At the same time, organizations are legitimated as coherent entities—as unified, empowered, and responsible actors—and must display this unity to legal and social environments.

Second, in practice organizational autonomy is constrained: boundaries are porous, and externally structured organizational and professional elements are incorporated internally: the modern organization is in part a composite of introjected organizational and professional structures. It is filled with people who are schooled to see themselves as empowered or "professionalized" actors, and with whole departments with similar external empowerment. But as an identity matter, organizations depict themselves as bounded and autonomous, and they are painted this way in legal, accounting, and colloquial discourses allocating responsibilities and liabilities. Doctrines of science and empowerment drive organizations to show that they are rationally controlling a wide range of issues beyond their actual capacity. Activities that denote autonomy and control, such as planning, decision-making, and risk assessment, grow rapidly, but organizations are deeply interconnected with and dependent on their environment for definitions on how to integrate these activities (e.g., what a proper plan, and planning department, look like). In an ironic twist, organizations dramatize their proactive doings on the issues where they are most penetrated by their environment and therefore have the least actual independence. In this way, they parallel the tendencies to conformism for which the modern, nominally free, individual is notorious. Beyond meeting the environment at its boundaries, the contemporary organization incorporates much of it internally.

We can put these two points together with an illustration briefly sketched in Chapter 4. If we wanted to establish a sporting or recreational activity, the modern system provides a plethora of structures, some available as helpful options and others as mandatory requirements. There can be coaches, with training technologies, rules, and procedures for improved performance. There may also be leagues and associations of similar groups, with administrators and rules, such as standards of fair competition. Medicine and safety, including special protections for children, are likely to be involved. The natural world must be accounted for as well. In cities, sports are often limited to designated fields or a certain amount of use, to protect the grass from too much damage. Entities are scrutinized, in terms of not only their own goals and activities but also the collateral dimensions of other rationalized domains. This creates internal inconsistency, our first point above.[2]

But then our second point applies: to deal with all the external standards and pressures, our sporting organization would be likely to incorporate representatives of these external standards within its own structure. It might employ the relevant specialist professionals. It might simply accept that its own participants pursue their own externally legitimated goals. In either case, the supposedly autonomous organization is likely to be very constrained.

In the sections below we discuss these organizational inconsistencies and dependencies and consider the main alternative interpretations of them.

Inconsistent or incomparable rationalities

The expansion of rationalized culture drives organizations to adopt concerns weakly linked to their own purposes. In essence, this phenomenon comes up in older discussions of loose coupling and decoupling.[3] But in its contemporary form, decoupling penetrates far more deeply into organizational structures and, as we discuss below, even characterizes individual roles. In this extreme form, sometimes characterized as "means–ends decoupling" rather than the buffering process of "policy–practice decoupling," entire causal chains of how an organization achieves its own goals become reconstructed by outside interests (e.g., in the evolution of the "business case" for human rights or green policies).[4]

In responding to these cultural changes, contemporary organizations incorporate an expanded array of considerations that are neither naturally integrated nor the outcome of coherent internal analyses and actions intended to promote either efficiency or control.

First, expanded organizations are certainly likely to have internal inconsistencies at many points. How is a manufacturing firm to balance its desire to maximize shareholder value with moral (and increasingly legal) concerns for the health and safety of overseas workers? How is a non-profit that supports the homeless to provide the full range of necessary services while simultaneously protecting the clients' privacy rights? How is a state agency to efficiently manage its work while maintaining an elaborate secrecy regime? In instances like these the optimally rational response is unclear. In each of these cases, contemporary organizations build internal structures to manage externally legitimated claims: this turns the conflicting claims into inconsistencies.

Second, regardless of whether organizational components are ultimately inconsistent, they are often incomparable. The internal organizational elements that deal with one set of issues—say human resources—cannot be easily assessed against the considerations of effective production. For example, how does the proper resolution of a student problem or conflict through a Dean of Student Services contribute to teaching and learning? How does an executive choose which philanthropic activities, if any, will maximize shareholder value or employee commitment and morale? How does the government decide what level of protection it should have for technology systems in case of an emergency? There is no natural solution for the way in which an organization should manage such situations. Main efforts come through the putative expertise of managers whose core function is to take on decision-making about uncertainties and balance inconsistent or incommensurable pressures.

Thus the construction of the contemporary organization as a bounded social actor has a non-rational character. Diverse elements are incorporated as a matter of identity—for instance, they are legally required or normatively drawn in. The relative values of diverse elements are set by accountings reflecting entirely external "markets," which themselves use much culturally constructed material to determine prices.[5] Their internal workings are frequently created by professionals reflecting external standards of activity. So we can learn the proper way to resolve a personnel issue from human resource professionals, and these professionals have a value in the form of their salaries. But the link between these functions and other organizational activities is determined by external legal and accounting rules rather than by functional integration or a definitive contribution to any bottom line.

Systemic effects: all these tendencies are built into the construction of the modern organization as actor. But they are intensified by the expansion of organization in contemporary society as a whole. Overall, the organized density of the entire system increases the degree of organization of any given structure, by elaborating the effective environmental pressures on it— organizational expansion is a general characteristic of contemporary society. The hypothetical sporting or recreational organization we described above is surrounded, and pressed, by many other organized structures in a modern society. It does not stand alone. Each contemporary organization exists in relation to an expanding set of other organizations, and these reflect a wide variety of interests and goals, from the environment, to legal accountability and transparency, to human rights. Stakeholders—themselves now commonly organized—abound. In fact, expanding science, human empowerment ideologies, and education help to explain the observation that organizations, public and private, have increasing numbers of stakeholders or operate in increasingly plural and complex environments.[6]

It is important to qualify this general point. Contemporary societies are not necessarily more complex than earlier modern forms, though that may be true in some ways (depending on definitions of the slippery term "complexity"). But complexity in contemporary society is of a particular form: it is explicitly differentiated and structurally articulated. Participants themselves become rationalized and differentiated actors. A romantic vision that individuals and organizations in an earlier period were more real and potent—and that the modern versions are emasculated and tamed—is too simple. But it captures the sense that the modern organization (and individual) is embedded in a dense network of rationalized pressures, constraints, and directed opportunities that incorporates an expanding array of social goods, from economic commodities to human personal satisfactions, to the health of the planet. Faced with this, the proper organized actor is supposed to pose as an empowered and effective decision-maker: indeed, that assumption underlies the whole structure.

As this society expands, any given organization is confronted by more organized actors at its boundaries and is likely to have to expand its structure to deal with them. Perhaps it expands by constructing new differentiated components to relate to the particular organized environmental bodies. Or perhaps existing components or roles expand. In either case, it becomes more complex, incorporating its social context on more fronts in a manner akin to Mead's "generalized other."[7] By internalizing the proper elements required by the environment, organizations lose functional coherence and the ability to autonomously pursue the interests of single master, or to be their own master.

Thus we arrive at twin propositions. As an entity becomes more of an organized actor (i.e., a bounded, autonomous entity with an identity, goals, and responsibilities), the resulting structure tends to become filled with inconsistencies and farther from any calculable rationality. In parallel, as the social field around it becomes filled with more organization, the resulting structure tends to become more complex, inconsistent, and non-rational.

Internalized interdependence

The densely structured and rationalized character of contemporary society generates a second dialectical source of non-rationality for any specific organization. The environment is not simply a context—its elements become components of organizations themselves. Roles, programs, and policies are developed in external society, rooted in principles of science and rights, and then brought in to organizations. Organizations do not grow naturally and their structures do not usually reflect some fixed law of nature that reflects efficiency pressures. The environment–organization relationship goes further than passive mimicry or the active navigation of the outside world. This relationship is constitutive, one of continuous interpenetration. Every contemporary organization is an assembly of actual or potential organizations— each with external legitimation and support. At the base are the schooled and professionalized individuals, each a sort of mini-organization. These can readily assemble into organized groups, legitimized by external linkages and definitions. And the larger organization itself, by incorporating externally defined programs and departments, in effect encourages and validates the employment of external authority claims.

The dependencies involved can be seen clearly when we look at professionals and professionalized programs. To resolve any internal or external problem, the contemporary organization is likely to employ relevant experts.

Sometimes they are contracted temporarily, but often their roles are more permanently built in: whole departments are built up out of externally constructed professionalization. As all these experts function internally, they carry their external professional identities, responsibilities, goals, and standards with them. As outside professional standards change, the professionals' advice is expected to change too, independent of any local organizational authority, decision, or requirements. Top executives rely on the expertise of these people. They follow recommendations from marketing, human resources, and community relations people in good faith that their guidance is, if not directly linked to improved performance, at least necessary by cultural (and sometimes legal) rule. And the marketing and human resources people, in turn, are now highly professionalized and march to tunes set in their environmental communities.

In area after area, professionalized conceptions and activities, changing in the environment, are incorporated within organizations. In a school or university, curricula are likely to change to reflect external legal or professional rules regardless of the characteristics of the local student body or features of leadership.[8] Similarly, hospital administrators may shape some elements of medical practice, but a great deal of medical administration is rooted in changing professional standards.[9] In a firm, many issues are settled exogenously and brought into the local setting by professionalized people who know about safety, the environment, human resource and rights principles, fashionable production technologies, community relations, marketing necessities, or sales strategies.[10]

In Chapter 4, we distinguish four general types of professionals: substantive experts of core work processes (e.g., engineers, chemists, teachers, software developers); substantive experts of processes from the environment (e.g., sustainability officers, community and public relations people); lawyers and accountants who maintain an organization's status as such by defining boundaries and monitoring resources; and professionalized managers (e.g., administrative professionals, planning and strategy experts).

In all these cases, organizational leaders have limited ability (and often little inclination) to exercise much of the imperative authority of the old bureaucracy. The theoretical sovereignty of the "decision-maker" and of "leadership" is eviscerated—what really goes on is better captured in the term "management." Of course, professionals and managers are capable of making decisions or behaving strategically—in fact, they are expected to do these things in culturally appropriate ways. Contemporary society does not produce the proverbial "cultural dopes"[11]—it produces empowered and responsible actors. But proper contemporary decision-making and strategizing lack true autonomy; they are highly participatory and often rely on the support of many types of expertise. They are done under conditions of great uncertainty and conflicting demands, often appearing more to be a system of best guesses rather than best practices.[12]

Organizations are built up, in good part, of exogenously produced professionals, who are themselves proto-organizations attributed with expanded actorhood and action capability. Today, this principle extends far beyond just the cases of particular occupational categories. The contemporary cultural system turns an enormous number of people into quasi-professionals.[13] The expansion of education, incorporating scientism and human rights and responsibilities, creates professionalism everywhere. And a feature of organization, compared, for instance, with bureaucracy, is that it is often made up of these professionalized people at all levels, regardless of their occupational roles.

These contemporary organizational participants bring greatly expanded powers and responsibilities to their positions. They are not supposed to simply obey orders, but to understand and interpret and create order. As properly empowered individuals, endowed with quasi-scientific thinking and many rights and capacities, they can and should bring all sorts of norms from the rationalized society into organizational life: human rights standards, transparency, environmentalism, technical competence, and so on. In many cases, they have an obligation to do so. A central participant in violations of human rights cannot properly mount a defense as "just obeying orders."[14] Nor can a central participant in violations of environmental standards, fraud, money laundering, discrimination, or other contemporary standards.

Sometimes, modern people bring such standards into play on their own. As schooled and professionalized citizens of society they are empowered to act across a wide spectrum. So, nearly any organizational participants can legitimately be concerned about recycling and energy efficiency, privacy rights, workplace discrimination, or participatory decision-making. They can organize on these dimensions within their employing organization regardless of their particular job description or the organization's goals. At the extreme, organizations encourage employee organizing around principles of self-expression. Google, for example, touts its employee networks, claiming that "Diversity is a core part of our business and who we are.... [Our Employee Resource Groups] bring the community together and, most importantly, help make Google a place where you can bring your whole self to work."[15] A news report describes the resulting groups:

Google has 19 "Employee Resource Groups" or ERGs, employee-initiated entities that receive financial support from the company and represent social, cultural, or minority groups, including the Gayglers (for lesbian and gay employees), the Greyglers (for older employees), the Hispanic Googler Network, Google Women Engineers, VetNet for military veterans, and the Black Googlers Network, or BGN. But there are literally tens of thousands of special-interest groups that can range in size from two to more than 1,000 members and cover topics from wine to hiking to quilting to Dungeons & Dragons. There are the Gleeglers (who sing a cappella); the Dooglers, who bring their dogs to work; the Snowglers (skiers); and the Skeptics (who question everything). There are groups for pilots, expectant moms, and photographers, and a group for

Googlers who like flea markets. There's even a group for former startup employees whose companies were bought by Google and who may struggle to navigate a company where they must be both entrepreneurs and employees.

Any employee can start a group—in fact, employees are encouraged to, said Stacy Sullivan, Google's chief culture officer, a title bestowed by the founders.... The very idea of taking it upon yourself to launch a group is an example of a basic tenet at Google: Ideas are supposed to bubble up from the grass roots. Managers are supposed to be enablers, not dictate from the top down.[16]

Google is not alone. The consulting firm McKinsey notes that it has had a lesbian, gay, bisexual, transgender (LGBT) employee network group, "GLAM," since 1994.[17] Similarly, universities have long encouraged various types of associations, but lists of all these clubs have expanded greatly (Stanford University's directory lists about 550). Some causal stories propose links between such groups and the bottom line, emphasizing positive effects on retention, morale, and productivity. In reality, evidence of the functional contribution of any particular group, or a set of groups, is weak. But regardless of any causal link between self-expression and productivity or innovation, the connection seems highly dependent on the contemporary context. In historical or comparative contexts where widespread individual empowerment is unknown or delegitimated, outcomes would be unlikely to depend on expanded self-expression.

Thus, contemporary organizations are built up of schooled individual persons, themselves possessing expanded capacities and entitlements. A core feature of modern organized life is that it should recognize the generally sacralized status of persons and therefore be participatory.[18] Contemporary people and groups are supposed to bring their own messages to the table of decision-making and to respect the views of others. So, in addition to specific professional roles (e.g., for a certified diversity officer to promote diversity), any individual member of a contemporary organization might legitimately bring in principles about animal rights, gender equality, transparency, or proper waste management.

Formal structures have always been subject to the potential mobilization of internal groups. The distinctive feature of the contemporary organized actor is that the internal groups can themselves be mini-organizations incorporated within the larger entity, but reflecting external concerns. These groups can carry much legitimacy inside and outside the organization, and can form around a mind-boggling expanse of topics. The legitimate incorporation of outside domains feeds the structuring of inconsistencies, described in the previous section, but it also hampers the autonomy of a robust leader to unapologetically make unilateral decisions, or to be viewed as doing so. Instead the contemporary leader has to balance many preferences, work for "buy-in," and rely on experts for making decisions on an expansive list of domains, all while taking external and internal audiences into account. If the safety people say a facility is unsafe, following various professional standards, for example, what manager can legitimately override them? Or if human resource professionals recommend particular diversity practices, with the potential for legal or reputational censure looming, what top executive can confidently reject their advice?

Overall, our discussion here leads to simple propositions: organizational expansion, and the expansion of organization in the surrounding social arena, produce the internalization of environmental elements—professionalism, and the extension of it to individual participants. This helps legitimate organizations in their environments, but lowers their autonomy and increases internal inconsistency.

Resolutions

The two dialectic points of our argument are these: expanded modern organizations are depicted as coherent, autonomous, and rational actors, but routinely (1) incorporate responses to multiple inconsistent or incommensurate claims, and (2) rely on the internalization of external criteria and structures for sustaining the appearances of actorhood. This means that these entities have increasing inconsistencies, with internal components that reflect external requirements on multiple dimensions. These inconsistencies are problematic from a view that assumes organizations are efficient production machines or vehicles for wielding power, but from an institutional view the tensions and contradictions are inherent and provide cultural legitimacy. How is the myth of the autonomous and integrated organization sustained in these circumstances?

To a considerable extent, the social forces that transmit broad cultural pressures down to concrete organizing situations, as discussed in Chapter 4, tend to mitigate some of the tensions.[19] Hard and soft laws that require organizing may also define appropriate (and perhaps arbitrary) standards to which organizations can safely conform. Accounting principles that facilitate the organizing also produce by fiat assertions of its value (e.g., the market price of a Chief Sustainability Officer). Professionals who carry out organizational functioning also bring standards of proper conduct in their arenas. In all these cases, an organization may be seen as performing satisfactorily no matter what the substantive outcome of its work. And in all these cases, ineffectiveness and conflict may be concealed by ritualized conformity.

The mechanisms above can render the inconsistencies of organizational life partially invisible as specific elements or practices become taken for granted. But a further problem is the maintenance of the myth of unity of the organization as an empowered and responsible actor. Two resolutions are most apparent as aiding in the display of actorhood. One strategy is to absorb inconsistencies into the central professionalized decision-making roles, which we discuss below as the "mystery of management." Professional managers are created, and endowed with the authority to manage tensions and integrate decisions. A second resolution to organizational inconsistencies involves the oft-observed phenomenon of "decoupling."[20] In both cases, these solutions are incomplete and artificial. They allow activities to continue, but the overall coherence and functional rationality of the organization are diminished. And, from time to time, the weaknesses of these solutions are exposed as great scandals. For example, in *The Audit Society: Rituals of Verification* management scholar Michael Power describes how societal expectations of auditing to prevent and detect fraud outpace the capabilities of auditing to do so.[21]

The mystery of management: a dominant worldwide solution has the invention of the professionalized manager as carrying actorhood—an expert on abstract organizational functioning and on the making of "decisions." Business schools have expanded worldwide, at even greater rates than the general growth in higher education, as shown in Chapter 3. Their expansion is closely related to the development of rationalized—often mathematicized— notions of management and decision-making. Managerial roles and ideas take on special prominence under expanded organizational conditions with maximal organizational interdependence and interpenetration. Managerial experts absorb inconsistencies into their professional roles, specifying an appropriate course of action under unclear conditions.[22]

The mystique centers on endowing these professionals with the ability to make putatively rational causal determinations when causality is in fact unclear. The resolution occurs because subsequent organizational decisions and action may continue as if the truth had been revealed; the initial uncertainty is concealed or ignored. Definitively establishing the best course of action using causal social science methods is rarely plausible. The relevant research is often prohibitively expensive and time consuming. Thus, management experts and professionals rely on their culturally and educationally endowed capacity for quasi-scientific thought to produce answers. For example, people with training in general management ideologies create enormous numbers of recommendations and case studies that share "best practices." The phrase "best practice" implies that there are multiple feasible alternatives, but experts have studied the matter and determined the optimal solution. Executives turn to these "best practices" and to consultants because something is unclear, involving complex trade-offs between multiple, conflicting goals. If the appropriate course of action were obvious, an expert would not be required to determine the way.

Many decisions are legitimated by devices like cost-benefit analyses, return-on-investment estimates, input-output models, and the like. The assumptions required to generate specific calculations, for instance of the value added by a new construction project, are heroic. But modern cultural requirements require a rationalized basis for decision-making, and so professionals are endowed with the authority to decide on the causal relations that underpin such models, and then processes go on as though the assumptions are correct. Flaws or omissions in these models may never be revealed, as we cannot observe counterfactuals. But sometimes dramatic failures appear, as in the largely unpredicted devastation to the US and global economies in 2008 when it became clear that trillions of dollars in financial investments were based on the incorrect assumption that housing prices would not decline.

In another example, recently professionals have gone to great lengths to make the "business case" for CR. This is an effort to redefine the causal chain that leads to profits. In contemporary literature the evidence is mixed. Some assert that CR leads to increased profits.[23] Others decry these efforts as detracting from efficiency, or point to very mixed empirical evidence.[24] Regardless, an important point is that the cultural embeddedness of organizations can change prior causal relationships, not only in perception, but also in reality. Certainly, CR was not linked to profits in the 1800s—the concept did not exist. But it is plausible that in time the reputational sanctions facing irresponsible corporations will become so heavy that it would become a clear financial mistake to be a poor corporate citizen.

In the non-profit sector, rationalized terms like "social return on investment," "theory of change," and "logic model" are becoming commonplace. Formal evaluations of programs are now standard. We know that these models and measures fail to capture many of the relevant components: this is often lamented by non-profit scholars.[25] Some are concerned about the destruction of expressive capacity in society created by over-rationalization and professionalization.[26] Others emphasize that rationalized types of accounting push organizations to focus on measurable outcomes at the expense of long-term or poorly measured goals.[27] Despite these fears, a rationalized environment calls for accountability to an array of stakeholders and a systematic, scientific approach to doing so.

The professionals granted the authority to develop these stories of causality often acknowledge their limitations. The resolution occurs not because the solutions are correct in an absolute sense, but because they represent the best available alternatives as determined by organizational experts. It is very unclear how best to protect the environment, or motivate employees, or protect human rights, and there may not be any best solutions. But in order to move forward, authority to make decisions is conferred on the appropriate professionals. Thus the uncertainties and inconsistencies that are generated by the expansion of formal organizational actorhood are partially resolved.

Decoupling: a second organizational response is captured in the concept of decoupling with its multiple dimensions.[28] One common form is buffering between internal components,[29] such as when human resource departments and policies are only weakly linked to production regimes. If different dimensions of an organization, each linked to distinct environments, in fact have little functional interdependence, they can maintain inconsistent policies. Only modest amounts of buffering may be required. So an organization may maintain quite elaborate policies for diversity in employment in the human resources department, with little transformation in policy in other components, if information flows are constricted. Tight linkages to disparate environments generate inconsistencies: separating and bounding the relevant components helps resolve them.

Another common form of decoupling occurs when policies and structures are weakly linked to practice, in what organizational theorist Nils Brunsson calls hypocrisy.[30] As he notes, maintaining the picture of an organization as a unified entity linked to multiple and complex environments requires elaborated forms of management and nominal "decision-making." Practical considerations may dictate simpler and different resolutions. Thus elaborate formal rules protecting worker safety or the environment may seem in practice to make little sense, and to impede effective local action. One set of rules, in other words, applies to maintaining an organization's identity as a proper actor; while another set may apply to effective action. Buffering is needed, of course, to maintain some distance between the level of organizational structure and decision, and the levels at which work goes on.

A traditional literature discusses these issues under the heading of "differentiation," meaning that different dimensions of organizational life are structured in distinct elements and then integrated by their functional interdependencies (or by imperative authority from above).[31] In contrast, as we emphasize, the contemporary organization is expanded far beyond the clear functional interdependencies that are incorporated. The functional relations among its components cannot be clearly defined or set in a common frame. The same traditional literature, imbued with much faith in the prospects for effective integrated action, treats decoupling as a social problem to be resolved: there are many discussions of effective devices for integrating structure and policy with practice. Some of these involve the resocialization of practitioners to conform to policy norms, while others involve tighter information and inspection systems, and more rewarding or coercive control systems. Similarly, lateral decoupling between distinct components of organizations, related to distinct environments, is usually analyzed in the literature as problematic and as requiring more effective integration.

From our point of view, decoupling is as much solution as problem. As more and more complex pressures are built up in the rationalized and scientized society and transmitted down to organizational (and individual) actors, it is inevitable that these actors assume multiple and inconsistent roles (or in the organizational case, departments and programs). And it is similarly inevitable that they will decouple these various roles from each other, and find mechanisms to buffer the inconsistencies involved. Complex identities of personhood are the result at the individual level. Decoupled organizational structures—but with integrated claims to abstract identity and responsibility— are natural solutions at the more collective levels.

A general point in our discussion of organizational dialectics follows: as a descriptive assertion, or one depicting cross-sectional relationships, organizations with real functional coherence are less likely than others to need much management. And those that have a great deal of management are less likely than others to be substantively coherent. This is not a matter of direct causal relationships: there is no reason to argue that management creates incoherence, or that incoherence creates management. It is rather an outcome of the macro-social processes, discussed in Part 1 of this book, that produce expanded organization and hyper-organization. The expansion of organization into so many opaque domains leads both to more management and to conditions under which real integrated authority and coherent function are unlikely. As "non-profits," for instance, become organizations, the pressures for managerialization are extreme, and are likely to be reinforced by funding and other environments.[32]

As a similarly descriptive matter, organizations with highly structured processes for decision-making are likely to be those with little capacity for actual independent decisions. The expansion of organization into unlikely domains produces both consequences. Organizations where autonomous decisions can legitimately happen may dispense with much of the formal structure that can accompany decision-making (e.g., soliciting participation). The processes that produce formal displays of decision-making are precisely those that indicate real decision-making authority is weak.

Cultural rationalization also limits the arbitrary and autonomous execution of power by requiring scientized action in expanding domains, even in those with little hope of developing a real scientific knowledge base. This helps explain the ritualization of management that appears at the core of contemporary organizations.[33] Drawing on vaguely scientific principles, management experts, consultants, and managers are granted the authority to make causal claims in opaque settings. Top executives are treated as great centers of success and failure. For instance, CEO status is lionized through huge salaries and perks like private jets, but pay is weakly tied to performance.[34] Managerial decision-making, much of which is constrained by context, is treated as the pivotal center of life for organizations and organizing activities—from great multi-national firms down to the individual person making career and life choices.[35]

A main basis for contemporary social order (and structure) rests on the assumption that organizations and individuals are fairly rational actors making informed choices (including an assessment of how other stakeholders will react to their choices). But where the rituals of decision and management are strongest, actual room to control outcomes and maneuver is likely to be quite small.

Alternative accounts of intra-organizational inconsistency

It is useful to contrast our view with other approaches to explaining the dialectics we note, which are sometimes seen as pathologies. The explanatory problem arises especially because of the endemic nature of organizational inconsistency. The main alternative lines of thought are economic and power-based theories. A third alternative, found in versions of institutional theory, has some complementarity with our arguments, although there are also points of divergence.

Economic: economists are certainly aware of inconsistencies in organizations, but tend to depict these tensions as the optimal outcome of compromises required to balance the competing interests of principals and agents. Organizations, in other words, are machines for achieving clearly defined goals, and their structures represent the "least possible dysfunction" solution in a series of cost-benefit trade-offs.[36] This view is difficult to support. First, it is naïve to imagine that reasonable cost-benefit analyses can be determined for many organizational structures. As a vast literature attests, it is implausible to definitively establish the costs and benefits of particular structures, or of the relative cost of having such a structure inside or outside an organization.[37] Certainly, particular calculation methods can be used, but they are based on a series of fundamental (and often questionable) assumptions. Second, distinguishing principals from agents is difficult. This was a smaller problem when large corporations could be thought of as bureaucracies, serving the interests of a sovereign. But today professionalized individuals carry some sovereignty, and organizations have many external and internalized masters with legitimate claims.

Finally, a vision of the interests of principals or agents as self-evident and a priori ignores the vast body of work illustrating the socially constructed and culturally embedded nature of these definitions. There is no single truth to the problem of optimal organizational design: solutions depend on the time and place in which an organization operates. Plausibly, today or in the future, CR programs could contribute to the bottom line, but this depends on changes in the external environment. There is no inherent necessity for CR in a lean production machine: the causal chain that leads to perceived optimal efficiency relies, instead, on cultural definitions.

Political: central intellectual figures who emphasize power-based elements of organization include Charles Perrow and James Coleman. In his article "A Society of Organizations," Perrow says, "Organizations are above all devices for controlling and coordinating the activities of many more or less willing employees."[38] That is, organizations are less about efficiency (as in economic interpretations) and more about control and power. Large organizations gave elites a tool for amassing unprecedented power in society. One challenge in this approach is that it endows elites with an extraordinary ability to covertly orchestrate oppression, like super villains in a world without super heroes. These elites are charged with bringing other elements of society into organizations (e.g., family, church, community) in order to weaken the authority of these other institutions and to strengthen their own control through indirect and unobtrusive means because that is a less costly strategy than direct controls. Certainly, organizations are the main loci of inequality in society, but the view of elites as all-powerful ignores the influence of social movements—and their own resulting organizations—that have made headway in changing practices around issues like civil rights, environmental practices, and women's rights. A second challenge is that Perrow's observations focus on the US, but the trend toward increased organizing occurs worldwide, in countries with vastly different class and inequality structures. As globalization proceeds, even egalitarian countries like Finland have increasingly complex and inconsistent firms and draw on a fairly standardized set of management practices.[39] Culturally legitimated organizational expansion now reflects the widest array of interests in contemporary society, not simply those of elites. Last, Perrow focuses on large organizations, especially firms. But we see elaboration across the board, even in very small or non-profit organizations far from any elite standing.[40]

Unlike Perrow, Coleman roots the rise of organization more broadly in the "rational reconstruction of society" rather than in the narrow interests of elites.[41] Coleman argues that industrialization and the French Revolution played pivotal roles in eroding primordial social institutions (e.g., the tribe, clan, and family) and contributed to the rise of societies where "purposively constructed social organization" is the main form of social structure.[42] We generally concur with his historical description, though not with his implied causal analysis. In any case, we diverge in that our central focus is on the rapid expansion and globalization of management and organization that occurred mainly after World War II.

Another point of divergence is our view of the consequences of organizational expansion for society. In *The Asymmetric Society*, Coleman lays out his view that corporate entities are becoming disturbingly powerful relative to individuals.[43] This imbalance, he argues, is a main source of inequality. In contrast, we emphasize that organizations are constituted and constrained by their environments. Certainly in some instances corporations may seem to possess unlimited autonomy and hold vast ability to pursue their interests independently, but in many other cases even powerful organizations conform to extensive mandatory and voluntary social controls. Organizations arise around the interests of the rich and powerful, but also around every other interest that arises in contemporary society. Moreover, most organizations are small and relatively weak: only a privileged few might come close to Coleman's depiction. Although his views may accurately capture the dynamics in particular instances, they fall short of accounting for our main concerns: the worldwide and cross-sectoral organizational explosion and the common presence of contradictory features that seem to do little to promote the interests of elites or powerful corporations themselves.

Institutional: a third perspective on organizational inconsistencies is rooted in the institutional tradition. Especially since the 1990s, institutional scholars have become more focused on the growing complexity of organizations and institutions, often using the frame of "institutional logics" or "institutional complexity." Given its proximity to our arguments, we discuss this literature in more detail. Some of the inconsistencies we describe here could be described, to use common phrases, as "multiple logics," "conflicting logics," or "competing logics," or they could be tied to the development of forms of "hybrid" organizations and "blurring" between sectoral boundaries.[44] An emergent body of literature on institutional complexity and pluralism is rooted in the internal tensions that are attributed to competing demands from different logics.[45] The language employed in this literature can vividly describe conflicts faced by organizational participants in the contemporary system.

This literature does not reach to analyses of the origins and change in institutional settings—the core of our arguments. In *The Institutional Logics Perspective: A New Approach to Culture, Structure, and Process*, sociologists Patricia Thornton, William Ocasio, and Michael Lounsbury identify six institutional orders—family, religion, state, market, profession, and corporation. This pre-existing and fixed set of "institutional orders" forms the basis for complexity and inconsistency. Our core argument is that cultural rationalization has radically created and changed the structured institutional complexities involved, and operates to create frameworks that force the construction and expansion of organization.

The emphasis on a fixed set of institutional orders creates an ongoing challenge in the institutional logics literature. It comes from the difficulty of linking specific settings to the larger institutional orders and their changes. In a discussion of misconceptions about logics, Patricia Thornton and William Ocasio say, "Most studies of institutional logics do not in some way tie their analyses back to the institutional orders of the inter-institutional system."[46] Without a link between research settings and logics, it is difficult to explain change processes. That is, it is unclear why actors begin to prefer one kind of logic to another or why and how logics come into conflict. Researchers struggle with this question because it is difficult to tell which logic or order many phenomena belong to, and many more empirical realities seem to span multiple logics and orders. For instance, many of the changes we discuss appear in associational life—now the non-profit sphere. But it is unclear which of the six logics associations, voluntary groups, and non-profits are tied to: there are many possible options. In contrast, we posit an undetermined but increasing number of cultural domains that can generate internal inconsistencies. In our view, any setting that comes to be rationalized has the potential to become influential in the environment. Thus, changing logics are dependent variables in a macro-social analysis.

Another important difference with our arguments is that the institutional logics literature emphasizes the autonomy and capacity of individuals as robust and natural actors. In this sense, it has much in common with other new institutionalisms that focus on "microfoundations," "institutional entrepreneurs," and "institutional work."[47] This work depicts people as largely autonomous, within some institutional constraints—more akin to the depiction of individuals in economic and power-based conceptions. In contrast, we maintain a more phenomenological view,[48] emphasizing the constructed and environmentally dependent nature of individuals and organizations. Actors do not simply operate within environmental constraints, they are defined by them, as with the sweeping schooled professionalism of the contemporary order. At the micro-level, our view of individuals is aligned with the social psychology of Goffman and Mead: people enact roles that reflect societal frames and expectations.[49] Related, in lines of thought emphasized by James March, managers faced with multiple objectives and expectations have limited ability to know how best to balance alternatives or achieve outcomes.[50] In particular, as we emphasized in Chapter 5, the specification of individuals as empowered and rights-bearing actors is a social construction. People today certainly make strategic decisions, and seek to control their outcomes by planning and being attentive to the natural environment (e.g., by recycling or respecting others' human rights), but these actions reflect a role conferred by cultural rationalization that varies over time and across national and other contexts.

In some ways the institutional logics literature simply has a distinct focus: the idea of an institutional logic focuses on the persistent elements of these structures over time, whereas we emphasize how many structures change in response to rationalization. For example, as we have noted throughout the book, contemporary professionalism has a new, managerial character. The state, religion, families, and family firms are all also transformed. Thus, we analyze how logics or orders are altered by cultural rationalization. In our account, the persistence of traditional structures would be stronger in settings where authority is more centralized (e.g., France or Germany versus the US) and settings with alternative sources of authority (e.g., the charismatic basis of religious organizations or older professions) than in newly constructed arenas (e.g., to protect the environment). More generally, organizational expansion is likely to be slower in settings where the cultural underpinnings of science, empowerment, and education (discussed in Chapter 3) and legal, accounting, and professional vehicles for transmitting culture (discussed in Chapter 4) are weaker.

Finally, in the logics perspective, the question of whether, why, and how organizations expand and become increasingly elaborate and inconsistent over time is not central. We focus on these points, arguing that cultural rationalization creates inconsistencies in the environment and that accounting, law, and professionalization transmit them to organizations. Cultural rationalization could be seen as cutting across all logics, bringing contradictions inside each entity. So religious groups adopt practices of evaluation and customer satisfaction surveys as religion becomes culturally rationalized. Or firms adopt "green" policies and practices when the natural world becomes more rationalized. Generally, as an institutional order is rationalized, it is more likely to become structurally interpenetrated with other orders, creating complexity and inconsistency. A similar speculation from the logics perspective is that "particularly in pluralistic societies, individuals and organizations typically assume multiple roles and identities, which often create conflicting pressures."[51]

An illustration: presentation of self in annual reports

As an example of organizational dialectics, we discuss changes in how firms present themselves in reports, the amount of reporting that goes on, and the types of reports generated. Reporting is useful because it indicates the array of issues where firms seek to display responsibility and attentiveness. It is precisely this responsiveness to multiple pressures in the external environment that generates internal inconsistencies and tensions. A coherent, integrated firm would be likely to minimize reporting and focus on production and profit. A firm that is interpenetrated with an increasingly complex environment is likely to demonstrate attentiveness to many dimensions of responsibility and management beyond its core production. Drawing on the points from the discussion above, we outline trends in reporting, drawing on published studies and a new dataset consisting of a random sample of 80 firms listed on S&P 500 between 1960 and 2010.[52]

To begin with, the amount of reporting has increased over time. In US firms, the length of an annual report in our sample has grown from an average

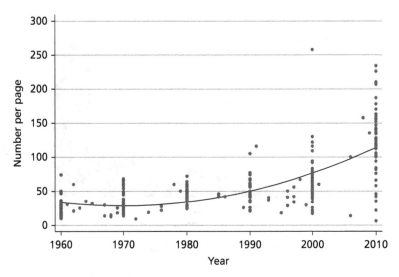

Figure 6.1. Length of Annual Reports in US Firms, 1960–2010

of 27 pages in the 1960s to more than 120 pages in the 2000s, as shown in Figure 6.1. This expansion is net of firm size. A firm in 1960 had far fewer things to report on annually than a firm of equal size in 2010, precisely as our analyses suggest.

The lengthening of annual reports is only the beginning when it comes to the expansion of reporting: more reports of different types are also created. The percentage of firms that state in their annual report that they produce additional reports or policies related to some element of CR has increased from zero in the 1960s to 44 percent in the 2000s, as shown in Figure 6.2. Additional reports (many firms produce more than one) have such titles as "Health, Environment, and Safety Report," "Code of Conduct," or "Quarterly Report on Annual Giving."

The Coca-Cola Company, for instance, keeps an online archive of "Annual and Other Reports."[53] This includes its Annual Report (which also serves as the legal Form 10-K filing and Annual Report to Shareholders), its Annual Review (which highlights major achievements of the year, such as in 2012 winning an award for "Creative Marketer of the Year" and receiving more than 1.3 million tweets per quarter), and dozens of Sustainability Reports. The Sustainability Reports include the company's annual filing to the GRI, discussed earlier. Coca-Cola has shared reports since 2008; excluding translations, the total count includes ten firm-wide reports, eight for Eurasia and Africa, five for North America, twenty-six for Europe, thirteen for Latin America, and nine reports for the Pacific. Nine reports are about water (e.g., conservation, watershed restoration, and community partnerships),

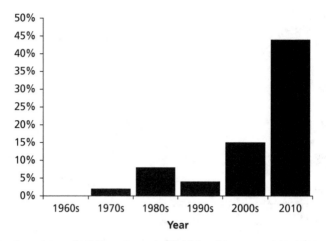

Figure 6.2. Percentage of US Firms Reporting Additional Reports, 1960–2010

and there is one external report. This produces a grand total of 81 sustainability reports. These are listed in Figure 6.3.

In a series of surveys on CR starting in 1993, the consulting firm KPMG has tracked the rise of reporting, as shown in Figure 6.4. In 2011 it analyzed the reports of more than 3,400 companies globally, including the world's 250 largest companies, and found that 95 percent of the 250 largest companies in the world (G250 companies) and 64 percent of the largest 100 companies in each country in their sample (N100) now report on their CR activities.

Two additional findings of the KPMG study are relevant to our arguments. First, the reporting phenomenon is not dominated by the US. Two-thirds of non-reporters are American-based firms, and the prevalence of CSR reporting is highest in Europe. Despite the dominance of American firms and American-style management in the world economy, the conception of a firm as subject to contradictory external pressures is worldwide, and US firms are under pressure from this universal conception rather than simply being leaders of it. Second, reporting is highest among publicly traded companies and lower among family-owned enterprises, cooperatives, and companies owned by professional investors. Of the 100 largest firms in each country (N100 companies in Figure 6.4), 69 percent of publicly traded companies conduct CR reporting, compared to just 36 percent of family-owned enterprises and close to 45 percent for both cooperatives and companies owned by professional investors, such as private equity firms. In line with our arguments, family firms and other structures that are linked to alternative bases of authority are likely to be less susceptible to rationalized pressures in the environment.

Company Reports
- Sustainability at Coca-Cola
- 2011/2012 Sustainability Report
- 2011/2012 Global Reporting Initiative (GRI) Report
- 2011 The Coca-Cola Company Annual Review
- 2010/2011 Sustainability Report
- 2010/2011 Global Reporting Initiative (GRI) Report
- 2010 The Coca-Cola Company Annual Review
- 2009 The Coca-Cola Company Annual Review
- 2009/2010 The Coca-Cola Company Sustainability Review
- 2008/2009 The Coca-Cola Company Sustainability Review

Water Reports
- 2012 The Water Stewardship and Replenish Report
- 2011 The Coca-Cola Company and World Wildlife Fund "A Transformative Partnership to Conserve Water"
- 2011 Coca-Cola Europe Water Footprint Sustainability Assessment
- 2011 The Water Stewardship and Replenish Report
- 2010 Product Water Footprint Assessments
- 2010 Quantifying Replenish Benefits in Community Water Partnership Projects
- 2009 Quantifying Water Access Benefits in Community Water Projects
- 2009 Quantifying Watershed Restoration Benefits in Community Water Projects
- 2009 Coca-Cola Europe Water Report
- 2010 Coca-Cola Japan Sustainability Report – English
- 2010 Coca-Cola Japan Sustainability Report – Japanese
- 2010 Coca-Cola Korea Environment Report – English
- 2010 Coca-Cola Korea Environment Report – Korean
- 2009 Swire Beverages Sustainable Development Report English
- 2009 Swire Beverages Sustainable Development Report Mandarin
- 2008 Coca-Cola Amatil New Zealand Environmental Report

Europe
- 2012 Netherlands Responsibility & Sustainability Report (in 2011)
- 2011–2012 Coca-Cola Great Britain Corporate Responsibility & Sustainability Summary
- 2011–2012 Coca-Cola Enterprises Corporate Responsibility & Sustainability Report
- 2011–2012 Coca-Cola Norway Corporate Responsibility Report
- 2011–2012 Coca-Cola Sweden Corporate Responsibility Report
- 2011 Coca-Cola Benelux Corporate Responsibility Report
- 2011 Coca-Cola Germany Corporate Responsibility Report
- 2011 Coca-Cola HBC Italia Responsibility Report
- 2011 Coca-Cola HBC Switzerland Sustainability Report – English
- 2011 Coca-Cola HBC Switzerland Sustainability Report – French
- 2011 Coca-Cola HBC Switzerland Sustainability Report – German
- 2011 Coca-Cola Hellenic Social Responsibility Report
- 2010–2011 Coca-Cola Europe Environment Review
- 2010 FEMSA Social Responsibility website – English, Portuguese and Spanish
- 2009 Coca-Cola Brasil Relatório de Sustentabilidade – Portuguese 2009 Coca-Cola Central Latin Reporte de Sostenibilidad – Spanish
- 2009 Coca-Cola Central Latin Sustainability Report - English
- 2009 FEMSA Informe de Responsabilidad Social – Spanish
- 2008 Coca-Cola Mexico Sustainability Executive Summary - English
- 2008 Coca-Cola Mexico Informe de Responsabilidad Social y Sustentabilidad – Spanish

External Reports
- IRRC Institute and the Sustainable Investments Institute

Eurasia & Africa
- 2011 Eurasia & Africa Group Sustainability Review
- 2011 Coca-Cola Içecek Corporate Social Responsibility Report
- 2011 Coca-Cola Sabco Sustainability Review
- 2010 SAB Miller Sustainable Development Report
- 2009 Coca-Cola Hellenic Sustainability Report
- 2009 Coca-Cola Sabco Sustainability Review
- 2008–2009 Coca-Cola Içecek Corporate Social Responsibility Report
- 2008–2009 Coca-Cola India Environment Report

North America
- 2011–2012 North American Sustainability Report
- 2010–2011 Coca-Cola Refreshments Sustainability Report
- 2010–2011 Coca-Cola Enterprises Corporate Responsibility & Sustainability Report
- 2009 Coca-Cola Enterprises Corporate Responsibility & Sustainability Report
- 2007–2008 Coca-Cola Canada Sustainability Report

Pacific
- 2012 Coca-Cola Korea Environment Report
- 2011 Coca-Cola Amatil Corporate Responsibility Report
- 2011 CSR Coca-Cola Vietnam – Vietnamese
- 2010 Coca-Cola Amatil Corporate Responsibility Report
- 2010 Coca-Cola China Sustainability Report – English
- 2010 Coca-Cola China Sustainability Report – Mandarin
- Coca-Cola Europe Environment 2020 Commitments and Performance Update
- 2010–2011 Coca-Cola Enterprises Corporate Responsibility & Sustainability Report
- 2010–2011 Coca-Cola France Corporate Social Responsibility Report – French
- 2010–2011 Great Britain Corporate Social Responsibility Report
- 2010–2011 Coca-Cola Netherlands Corporate Responsibility Report
- 2010–2011 Coca-Cola Norway Sustainability Report
- 2010 Coca-Cola Germany Sustainability Report Update – German
- 2010 Coca-Cola Hellenic Social Responsibility Report
- 2009–2010 Coca-Cola Europe Environment Review
- 2009 Coca-Cola Europe Environment Review
- 2009 Coca-Cola France Corporate Social Responsibility Report – French
- 2009 Coca-Cola HBC Austria GmbH Römerquelle Sustainability Report – German
- 2009 Coca-Cola Hellenic Social Responsibility Report

Latin America
- 2011 ARCA Social Responsibility Report
- 2011 FEMSA Sustainability Report
- 2011 Coca-Cola México Informe de Responsabilidad Social y Sustentabilidad – Spanish
- 2010 ARCA Informe de Responsabilidad Social – Spanish
- 2010 FEMSA Informe de Responsabilidad Social – English
- 2010 FEMSA Informe de Responsabilidad Social – Spanish

Figure 6.3. Coca-Cola Company Sustainability Reports, 2008–12

Source: Coca-Cola Company Sustainability Reports. Accessed on August 29, 2013: <http://www.coca-colacompany.com/stories/sustainability-reports>.

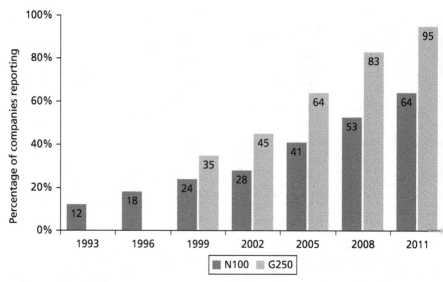

Figure 6.4. International Survey of Corporate Responsibility Reporting, 1993–2011

Source: KPMG International Survey of Corporate Responsibility Reporting 2011: 7.

Notes: "G250=largest firms in world; N100=largest firms in each sampled country." Survey results for the years 1993 to 2002 represent separate CR reports only. Due to the increasing trend in integrated reporting the figures published after 2005 represent total reports.

Separate CR reporting is increasing dramatically worldwide, indicating the multiple pressures that firms face. But perhaps even more telling, within annual reports themselves, the content is changing. For example, the proportion of the report that focuses on production has decreased over time. In the 1950s, 43 percent of a firm's annual report was dedicated to discussing products, production processes, operations, and market segments. In the 2000s, just 19 percent of a firm's report focused on these issues. The proportion of a report dedicated to CR is on the rise, but only slightly, probably masked by the explosion of alternative reports discussed above. Most strikingly, and tied to our example of financialization in Chapter 3, the proportion dedicated to financial reporting has increased sharply. Figure 6.5 shows these trends over time. A similar trend emerges in the pictorial images in the report. From 1960 to 1970, 60–65 percent of the images in a report were related to production (e.g., pictures of facilities, products, assembly lines), but by the 1990s and through 2010 this share drops to just over 50 percent of pictures. The proportion of CR–related images increased from 2 percent in the 1950s to 4 percent in later periods.

Although some CR policies may be entirely without substance, it is now well documented that many firms do dedicate substantial resources to these issues.[54] Twenty-eight percent of the firms in our sample of US reports

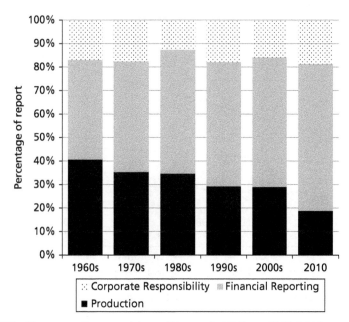

Figure 6.5. Changes to Content of Annual Reports in US Firms, 1960–2010

indicate specific resources allocated to socially responsible issues (e.g., donations of dollars, hours, or products).

Social responsibility is increasingly framed as part of the causal chain of
economic success: a "business case" responsibility reflects its institutionalization. Reports like the "State of Corporate Citizenship" produced by Boston
College claim: "It doesn't just make firms look good and employees feel good.
It helps to achieve business goals such as increasing market share and managing risk."[55] In annual reports, the financial reporting section is most clearly
related to assessing profit and loss, a firm's central goal. Assessing the extent to
which CR and citizenship issues have become incorporated into financial
reporting speaks to the extent to which these issues are fundamentally reshap-
ing the nature of for-profit work. Figure 6.6 shows the proportion of a firm's
financial reporting section that overlaps with issues in the corporate citizenship realm: discussions of employees, environmental protection or damage,
corporate ethics, and legal compliance or ongoing lawsuits. The overall
amount of financial reporting has increased, but even after adjusting for this
growth (by measuring the average number of paragraphs of CR–related topics
per financial reporting page), corporate citizenship issues are substantially
integrated into a firm's technical profit and loss core.

As shown in Figure 6.7, the language used in the reports has also changed.[56]
For instance, two phrases centrally related to a firm's core goals, "profit" and

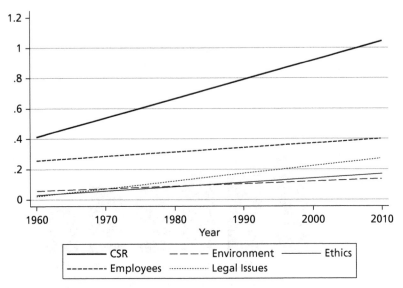

Figure 6.6. Changes to Content of Financial Reporting Section in US Firms, 1960–2010

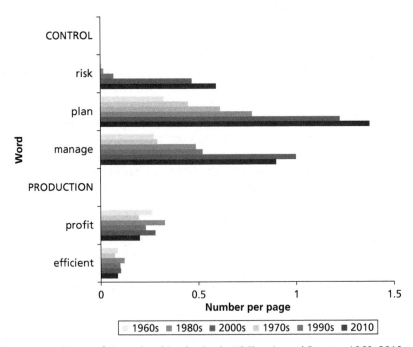

Figure 6.7. Phrases of Control and Production in US Firm Annual Reports, 1960–2010

"efficiency," have remained in use at about the same rate over time, "profit" showing up on about two out of every ten pages and "efficiency" on one in ten pages. But words related to demonstrations of control, such as "plan," "risk," and "manage," are increasing sharply. By 2010 the word "manage" showed up, on average, once on every page of a report (compared to three out of ten pages in the 1960s). Similarly, by 2010 the word "plan" appeared 1.4 times per page on average (compared to four out of ten pages in the 1950s).

Chapter summary

Broad cultural rationalization produces organizations that are internally inconsistent and have limited autonomy. First, broad cultural trends create a growing number of domains in an organization's external environment that require attention. Internal organizational elaboration and complexity result, and the model of a structure tightly integrated around core goals weakens. This change, linked to the increased emphasis on the actorhood and responsibility of organizations, poses striking problems. As new rationalized domains emerge, they support new organizations and reshape existing social structures. Any given structure, once rationalized, becomes less coherent and integrated than previously because it is incorporating external demands that are likely to be loosely related or unrelated to its primary focus.

Second, organizational elaboration in a "society of organizations" and professions involves the internalization of many environmental elements. Organizational professionals—a category that now includes large numbers of participants—bring their externally created organized identities into any given structure. Their programs and policies change with changes in these external identities, constraining possibilities for choice and action in any given focal organization. Similarly, the generally empowered actorhood of the schooled modern person creates fluid possibilities for legitimate organizing within any given organizational structure. Subgroups can and do legitimately mobilize, potentially bringing their own environmentally supported considerations into play. The contemporary organization is filled, thus, with highly legitimated actors, but these may be both participants and destabilizers.

In response to these inconsistencies and tensions, the contemporary organization is infused with managerialism, built on doctrines of rationalized decision-making. And it experiences a great deal of decoupling. There is vertical decoupling, so that extraordinarily smooth displays of financial reporting and formalized structure are uncertainly linked to practical activities. And there is horizontal decoupling, so that articulated accounts of the causal process by which outcomes are produced link elements together rhetorically that may be unrelated or in fact are in conflict.

▨ NOTES

1. In the case of the modern individual, causal analyses run in both directions. Some see the modern conscious individual as the product of social differentiation and complexity (Simmel 1903 is the *locus classicus*): individual actorhood, both as a cultural and as an experiential matter, arises to integrate the institutional conflicts and inconsistencies of modernity. In the line of argument we develop here, we focus on causality in the other direction: the structural differentiation of modernity arises around an imagined society of individuals empowered with choices in expanding domains. Both processes operate, so the matter can never be permanently resolved.

2. Very generally, one strand of neo-institutional literature emphasized variability across organizations in response to broader pressures (e.g., DiMaggio & Powell 1983; Fligstein 1990; Kellogg 2009). More recently, an emergent body of work looks at internal variation in response to external pressures (e.g., Binder 2007; Battilana & Dorado 2010; Gray & Silbey 2014).

3. Weick 1976; Meyer & Rowan 1977.

4. Bromley & Powell 2012.

5. Zajac & Westphal 2004; MacKenzie, Muniesa, & Siu 2007; Smelser & Swedberg 2010.

6. Pierson 2000; Osborne 2006; Greenwood et al. 2011. The rise of a stakeholder theory of the corporation is also a reflection of the increasing cultural relevance of multiple constituents for organizations (see Freeman 1984 for an initial development of stakeholder theory: more recently see Freeman, Harrison, Wicks, Parmar, & Colle 2010).

7. The term "generalized other" refers to the perspective an actor takes when imagining what others expect of him/her, and accounting for these expectations in subsequent action. Thus, behavior is guided by one's own perception of how words and actions will be viewed by external audiences. This perspective provides the foundation for the relationship between self and other in a shared social system.

8. Frank & Gabler 2006; Suárez & Bromley 2012.

9. Ruef & Scott 1998.

10. Edelman 1992; Dobbin 2009.

11. Garfinkel 1967.

12. Kalev, Dobbin, & Kelly 2006.

13. Wilensky 1964.

14. For a legal discussion see, for example, Minow 2007.

15. Google website 2014.

16. Swift 2011.

17. "As a management consulting firm, McKinsey relies on the knowledge and skills of its employees, and prides itself on attracting the world's top talent regardless of sexual orientation, gender identity, or any other markers of diversity. McKinsey's LGBT employee network group, "GLBT at McKinsey" (GLAM), was established in 1994. This self-governing, self-selecting global group convenes as a full diversity

network in person every 12 to 18 months, with regular communication and programming occurring in between these conferences through a combination of meetings, receptions, videoconferences, and teleconferences among a subset of the network." (McKinsey website 2014a; see also McKinsey website 2014b.)

18. Elliott 2007.
19. Edelman et al. (2011) describes how the law is also endogenous to organizations, whereby the diffusion of organizational structures and policies come to constitute legal compliance. The authors describe how "legal endogeneity theory calls attention to the constitutive sources of cyclicality, as institutionalized organizational structures are gradually incorporated into legal doctrine" (p. 892).
20. Meyer & Rowan 1977; Orton & Weick 1990; Bromley & Powell 2012.
21. Power 1997.
22. Battilana & Dorado 2010; Jay 2013.
23. For example, Posnikoff (1997) finds a positive link between CSR and financial performance in the case of disinvestment from South Africa during the apartheid era.
24. For example, Wright & Ferris (1997) observe a negative association between CSR and performance. McWilliams & Siegel (2000) give an overview of the mixed empirical evidence.
25. Newcomer (1997) and Fine, Thayer, & Coghlan (2000) outline many of the challenges involved. See also Frumkin 2002.
26. Frumkin 2002.
27. Poister 2008; Bromley & Powell 2012.
28. For reviews see Orton & Weick (1990) and Bromley & Powell (2012).
29. Weick 1976.
30. Brunsson 1989.
31. Luhmann 1982; Alexander & Colomy 1990.
32. Hwang & Powell 2009.
33. See, for example, a discussion of the ritualization of strategy workshops in organizations by Johnson, Prashantham, Floyd, & Bourque (2010).
34. In a meta-analysis of empirical studies linking CEO pay and performance, Tosi, Werner, Katz, & Gomez-Mejia (2000) find performance accounts for just 5 percent of the variance. Related, Staw & Epstein (2000) find that CEO pay is higher when companies adopt new management fads related to quality, empowerment, and teams, even though the adoption of such fads is unrelated to firm performance.
35. A wealth of management studies on decision-making considers things like the relative authority of executives versus boards of directors in making strategic decisions (e.g., Carpenter & Westphal 2001), the types of knowledge CEOs draw on for decision-making (Brockmann & Simmonds 1997), or how conflict influences decisions in top management teams (Amason 1996). For a more phenomenological view of decision-making see Brunsson (2007).
36. Fisman & Sullivan 2013: 4.
37. See, for example, Ghoshal & Moran (1996). In a meta-analysis of transaction cost economics studies David & Han (2004) find weak empirical support.

38. Perrow 1991: 728.
39. Morgan, Kristensen, & Whitley 2001.
40. Hwang & Powell 2009.
41. Coleman 1993: 14.
42. Coleman 1993: 2. For a more detailed discussion of this social transformation see Coleman 1990.
43. Coleman 1982.
44. See, for example, Friedland & Alford 1991; Evers, 2005; Binder, 2007; Billis, 2010; Pache & Santos, 2010a, b; Thornton et al. 2012.
45. Glynn 2000; Kraatz & Block 2008; Greenwood et al. 2011.
46. Thornton & Ocasio 2008: 120.
47. Fligstein 1997; Powell & Colyvas 2006; Garud, Hardy, & Maguire 2007; Battilana & D'aunno 2009; Lawrence et al. 2009.
48. Berger & Luckmann 1967.
49. Mead 1934; Goffman 1959.
50. See, for example, Cohen, March, & Olsen 1972; March & Olsen 1975.
51. Thornton et al. 2012: 57.
52. These data come from Bromley & Sharkey (2014). The S&P 500 consists roughly of the 500 largest firms in the US by market capitalization, although selection is by committee and takes additional criteria into account. It has a more diverse range of firms than other large indices (e.g., the Nasdaq or Dow Jones Industrial Average) and is one of the best indicators of trends in the US economy overall. The sample here consists of 278 annual reports collected from 72 distinct firms over the period 1950–2010. The firms were chosen randomly from the S&P 500, with a third being listed over the entire period, a third listed at the exchange's opening but exiting before 2010, and a third listed in 2010 but entering sometime after 1957. The Index opened in 1957, but we selected reports from anytime in 1950 based on availability (not every firm had a report available for 1957). More details are available from the authors.
53. Coca-Cola website 2013.
54. Waddock & Graves 1997; Lamberti & Lettieri 2009; Santos 2011.
55. Center for Corporate Citizenship website 2013.
56. Key word searches were done electronically using optical recognition software of pdf documents. The searches include all variations of a word (e.g., plan, planned, planning, plans; manage, manager, managed, manages, managers, managing, management).

7 Conclusions

Organizational expansion is extreme, stretching across institutional sectors and national societies. Every social arena around the contemporary world comes to be a locus for organizing and organization. The proliferation of organization is so extensive that traditional functional theories locating it in particular demands for economic efficiency or political control cannot effectively explain it. Over and above these theories, we put forward a cultural account for the massive, worldwide reconstruction of distinct structures of government, business, charity, and so on into densely organized post-modern, post-bureaucratic systems. As a final matter we reflect on the normative concerns that commonly arise in conversations about the rise of our organized and organizing society, as well as the implications we envision for management professionals, society, and the future. Before turning to these issues we briefly review our account of the worldwide expansion and elaboration of organization.

Overview

In our view, the hyper-expansion of organization arises in the post-war liberal and neoliberal era, with a stateless global order built on the rapidly growing principles of science and human empowerment. These two cultural pillars are brought together in formal education, which has exploded around the world. Schooled people, by and large, are the creators and inhabitants of contemporary organization and its world. They turn older forms of bureaucracy and association into contemporary organized *actors*, with accountability, responsibility, and sovereignty. Schooled people are socialized to be empowered and to collectively construct these purposive rationalized structures, and they do so in a world rendered (in principle) expansively predictable and analyzable by a scientization that is global in character. The result is a worldwide wave of organizing, and hyper-organizational extensions of this organizing to domains where it is more rhetorical than real or required. For instance, elaborate structures for human resource management, organizational planning and strategizing, or relations with physical and social environments come to be routine.

Global and universalistic cultural changes are instantiated in specific locales through law and law-like institutions, and through principles of monetary and non-monetary accounting that render formerly obscure functions visible, definable, and countable. Legal and accounting functions are internalized in contemporary organizations by the incorporation of the appropriate professionals. But the global explosion of education generates professionalism far beyond existing functions, and every new task of the firm or agency, from executive management to janitorial work, can now be managed by professionals. Experts are brought in to tame uncertainties, often on matters that have an opaque relation to the supposed goals and outputs of an organization. A university can have its economic course taught by an adjunct for a few thousand dollars, or a Nobel prizewinner for a hundred thousand. It is very unclear which solution makes sense because it is not obvious or visible how the credentials are linked to learning or other intended outcomes. Similarly, a local congregation can devote its resources to a grand new building, or a program for local poverty reduction, or schooling for spiritual enhancement. Even a hard-headed business manager must contemplate spending resources for a new ISO certification, or an improved personnel selection process, or better community relations. In each case, leaders must consider how high-powered and expensive the needed professionals should be: in no case is there a clear relation to the bottom-line.

In the expansion of organization perhaps the most striking shifts occur in the components of society often described as existing between states and markets. Large parts of what were once called community and society are now structured as non-profit organizations. Schooling, medical care, and many dimensions of family life come under the scrutiny of such formal organizations, with linkages and reporting mechanisms—and sometimes authority—reaching up to the global level. The enrollment of a child in a school is now reported to international organizations, and it is a serious matter to do so. Children have a globally defined right to be educated by their country: nation-states sign the relevant international treaties, and many local, national, and international organizations (both governmental and non-governmental) are responsible to see that states fulfill their obligations. Similarly, conditions of health and disease are reported and brought under control efforts worldwide. So are some central features of family life, such as reproduction, marriage, divorce, and aspects of abuse.

Governments, with their uniquely recognized claims over citizens and control over law, represent a special case. Nonetheless, parallel changes also occur in public agencies worldwide. Nation-states do not simply become organizations, but they expand structurally on the same sorts of dimensions as firms and non-profits, shifting from the hierarchical bureaucracies of high modernity to the flatter structures of the contemporary system. Libraries come to measure return on investment, state agencies adopt "green" strategies, and all of them have human resource departments. Overall, doctrines like the New Public Management or those emphasizing multiple forms of power and accountability transform traditional public structures into entities that look more like the modern organizational model. Thus public institutions such as contemporary school systems are likely to be more elaborated structures than in previous periods. Alternative explanations for why organization exists and expands, predominantly rooted in demands for technical coordination or desires for power, fail to explain why we see such similar changes in social structures throughout the economy, society, and political life.

Because cultural rationalization affects many social domains, organizational expansion takes on a curiously non-rational character, growing beyond the requirements of technical coordination and beyond the needs of political power and authority. Some organizations and organized activities serve coordination or power-based functions, but wide swathes of activity cannot be justified in these terms: we can call the result hyper-organization. "Getting organized" means collective structures are imagined, often very unrealistically, as bounded and agentic, in colloquial, identity, legal, and accounting terms. Social forms like firms, hospitals, schools, and charities become actors. But to be legitimate organizational actors they must also incorporate a multitude of inconsistent purposes and activities from their environments, respecting a wide range of entitlements of others. Myths of managerial capability for integration combined with extensive decoupling can help solve or conceal the inconsistencies. Related, the abstract principles of law and accounting can often take multiple forms when translated into practical reality; professionalism can provide similar protections.

The relatively recent social construction of the idea of the professional manager makes possible much organizational expansion that seems unreasonable on obvious functional grounds. Managers hold together organizational structure, covering disparate functions and domains, by drawing on myths about their ability to rationally employ *information* and reach *decisions*. Much of the decision-making involves the creation of theories about how various organizational add-ons (including the justification of professional salaries) relate to the bottom line; for instance, how a new marketing or publicity strategy will lead to increases in a university department's rank or a firm's sales.

The expansion of organization creates structures designed to make responsible and legitimate decisions on a wide variety of matters—this is how the contemporary liberal society is supposed to work. But the same processes that assign the responsibility for social outcomes to rational decision-makers also tightly constrain the decision-making process to fit within exogenous social structures. The most elemental choice of whether or not to respond to external pressures is rarely plausible and the range of feasible alternatives for any given decision are heavily censored by the growing domains of rationalized culture—and dense organizational life in both external and internal environments. A great irony ensues: wherever, in the contemporary world, decision-making is organized, there are probably fewer core decisions that can be made.[1] Contemporary organization inherently constrains absolute autonomy.

Figure 7.1 depicts the overall argument of this book. It captures our conceptions of the cultural roots of the contemporary organizational explosion,

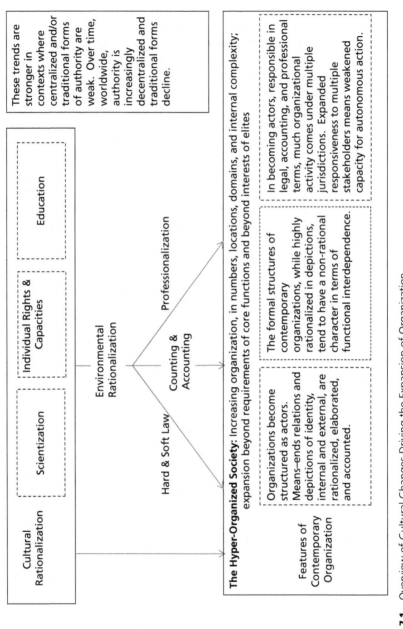

Figure 7.1. Overview of Cultural Changes Driving the Expansion of Organization

the processes that mediate the transmission of these cultural frames, and the consequences for organizational expansion that result. It also captures our arguments that the cultural basis of expansion results in hyper-organization: non-rational structures incorporating inconsistent and incommensurable dimensions.

Normative issues

The integration of expanding amounts of rationalized cultural material inside organizations in the "society of organizations" has some benefits for sociocultural order. It provides a clear picture of how a world of socially legitimated and responsible actors can produce large-scale and even worldwide coordination without an overarching state and legal order—governmentality underpinned by global cultural shifts rather than a centralized state.[2] At the same time, it is by no means certain that the system of social controls involved actually works, or operates to solve the range of problems of national and global society.

As new interdependencies or social problems are discovered or defined, they can be interpreted as new powers and responsibilities for the organized actors involved. In this way, cultural ideologies can explain how an expanding variety of human rights and needs are to be dealt with, or expanding environmental problems, or extreme asymmetries of power and resources. In the abstract, everything can be seen as brought under control, which allows for collective action in any arena.

Overall, however, the rationalization of liberal society generates embedded actors of a non-rational sort. Collective structures arise, but it is difficult to assess them on a rationality–irrationality dimension, since the core reality is that they are in large part cultural artifacts. The central content of the organizing society rests in cultural frames of science and human empowerment, and, like many forms of culture, it may make little sense to seek to assess it on grounds of instrumental rationality. If a social entity is not coherent and integrated and autonomous (i.e., the structure is not solely a means to instrumental ends), it is hard to calculate whether or not it is rational or effective. The "knowledge society" is open-ended, and sustains visions of coming disaster as well as dreams of sustainable order and growth.

Regardless of whether organizations, and the organizational society, achieve their depicted goals, their expansion generates two main critical reactions. First is the criticism that massive organizing around the world produces a great concentration of poorly controlled power. Second is the criticism that the dominance of organizational roles over other aspects of life is alienating and standardizing, suppressing the diverse identities of people and their cultures. In both cases, the criticisms are difficult to assess if we look at overall social trends—the morality of organization depends on what perspective one employs.[3] Critiques typically rest on pictures of a past golden age, imagined alternatives in some distant Shangri-La, or more benign future possibilities. They rely on unrealistic ideas that the modern system is controlled by a particular sector (perhaps especially the economy in liberal democracies), particularly powerful organizations (e.g., large firms), or elites (the "one per cent"): depictions of an entire *society* populated and woven globally by complex organizations in multiple domains are left out.

Organization and the concentration of power: in obvious ways, the rise of the organizational society involves the concentration of power; a common criticism in the literature on the society of organizations.[4] The creation of organization is indeed intended to control activity, sometimes on massive scales. Global flows of people, resources, ideas, and rules are facilitated by the contemporary expansion of rationalized organization. The question is who or what controls and/or gains from these flows.

The concept of power is notoriously problematic and usually heavily ideological,[5] partly because of normative attempts to locate individual or collective actors who "have power." Critiques of the concept usually end up disavowing any notion of a power-holding actor, which makes the notion of power very obscure. In fact, decisions are embedded in institutionalized non-decisions and in taken-for-granted cultural assumptions about authority and responsibility. Decision-makers can be depicted as powerful, or as burdened by obligations and responsibilities—or, in our analyses, as scripted enactors rather than actors. In any event, decisions and decision-making roles are highly constructed (and thus constrained).

If we think in institutional terms rather than in terms of powerful individuals, answers are clearer. Organizations of all kinds gain in the contemporary world. Older collective social forms and communal groups lose out. The authority of the family weakens, as do traditional communities, old-style professions and their corporate associations, and traditional religious structures. The nation-state also loses a good deal of its charismatic authority, and becomes more like a set of service organizations with multiple accountabilities. In tandem, individual roles linked to organizations gain influence and resources, and those linked to the more traditional structures lose authority. The traditional father, priest, landowner, owner of the family firm, and head of nation-state lose out. Their authority is in good part replaced by organizations. Today, the old priest is embedded in, participates in, and is partly controlled by organization, as is the old professor or head of a political structure.

Individuals gain as they acquire organizational status. Centrally, this involves education and its credentials, which become core in the contemporary stratification system: occupational prestige hierarchies uniformly put the schooled people at the top.[6] Education produces enhanced prospects for organizational formation, entry, and status. Thus, schooled people occupy positions of organized authority in the contemporary world, and can be seen as the holders of power: even those with wealth and power make sure their children are heavily schooled. The power involved is constrained, however, by the elaborated systems of rules making up organizations, and under which these organizations function. Thus critics of the concentrated power in society most frequently emphasize instances in which the rules are violated by participants acting in raw self-interest: gross instances of corruption, illicit political contributions, exercises of monopoly power, or direct violence. These critics do not focus on the ways in which organization is, and facilitates, social control. One can criticize Nike for exploiting overseas workers: but Nike is a much easier target for mobilization and organization than the dispersed networks of small operators and middle-men that existed in an older world.

In practice, the expanded power of organization generates expanded organization among competitors and stakeholders in reaction. Even advocates of control over organizational power quite sensibly organize themselves, perhaps as social movement organizations or proponents of thicker regulatory structures. It is difficult, in fact, to find serious believers in returns to a social system dominated by older arrangements like monarchy and the church. The people promoting the rights of indigenous people organize on a global scale, as do the supporters of sustainable agricultural production, fair trade, or good governance techniques. From many points of view, more organization is the path to equality and social justice. Although critics of the organized society tend to employ images of a past golden age of more equitable relations among people and groups, comparisons with earlier societies as a whole do not often suggest favorable contrasts.

Nevertheless, the dominant culture of the organizational society generates a penumbra of sentimental oppositions—visions of cooperative order without great bone-crushing organization. The organized university competing for status as a world-class university generates imagery of an older innocent ivory tower. Giant hospitals and health care facilities generate pictures of the old country doctor with whom patients could interact, supposedly on more equal terms. Large school systems trying to teach abstract skills like critical thinking are set against more tailored forms of education providing concrete training in an actual occupation. Enormous public firms trying to maximize shareholder value are contrasted with old-style craft production and with "company town" manufacturing firms. In all these cases, a good deal of nostalgia, and much unrealism about the broader social context of the time, can be involved.

The organized society can, as these examples illustrate, be set against an idyllic past. They can also be set against a more benign future. Visions of more flexible and creative futures are routine cultural themes. Some hope for a world of flexible production, network relationships, and socially mobile workforces. Beyond contrasts with these imagined benevolent pasts and futures, the organized society can be criticized relative to other types of societies. Sometimes the romanticized alternatives are politically rooted—communism in Cuba or Nicaragua, social democracy in Sweden, or even personal freedom in the egalitarian US. Sometimes they are simply pastoral, as in the celebration of small town life, or mountain cultures, or tribal solidarities.

In practice, the organized society has some defenses. Regardless of how efficiently or effectively outcomes are achieved, huge numbers of organizations arise against actual and potential disorders—extreme injustice, great inequalities, and social and environmental destruction. However artificial and constructed, organizing looks good to people, in contrast with doing nothing in the face of waves of genocide, rampant cronyism, or toxic pollution. Standardized and organized welfare arrangements look impressive when contrasted with huge pockets of rural poverty protected by archaic religious arrangements. Mass production by huge organizations outcompetes old-style craftwork: few contemporary people would want to risk depending on a single local shoemaker of uncertain competence and sobriety for all the shoes they would ever wear. The inefficiency and uncertainty of an older world clearly violate present-day conceptions of equality, efficiency, order, and justice; the act of organizing has massive cultural value in itself.

Organization and the loss of identity: a second criticism is that the standardizing pressure of the organizing society involves a loss of identity for people (and groups), and is thus alienating. Unquestionably, contemporary people—particularly the increasing numbers of schooled ones—play more and more elaborated standardized and rationalized roles. They function in organizations, whose hallmarks include differentiation, rationalization, and standardization. A long tradition in social thought sees this as disconnecting people from their more natural settings. The term "lifeworlds" is sometimes employed—and modern lives are seen as colonized by economic and political structures.[7] The implied, and sometimes explicit, contrast is with an earlier, supposedly more "natural," identity, as if in a social world without a role structure.

Contemporary alienation is described in two main forms. First, in the organized society, roles are specialized and differentiated, so that each one comprehends only part of a whole structure. Second, the roles are generally structured, only partly around the life of the individual, but in terms of great social institutions. The contemporary individual, thus, is (a) relatively meaningless and powerless and (b) part of a great machine (as Chaplin in *Modern Times*).[8] Ideologies and practices of returns to community (and/or nature), rediscovering the self, and similar themes are common in contemporary society, as reactions to rationalization.

This criticism, a common thread in Weber's work, applies more to the bureaucratic form than to contemporary organized actors. The structure, purposes, and activities of organizations are quite distinct from traditional Weberian bureaucracies (including early corporations, which were understood to have the characteristics of bureaucracies). The traditional bureaucracy was not a responsible *member* of society, but a specialized instrument—by some accounts to produce efficient collective action and by other accounts to effectively serve the interests of an elite. It did not have the inconsistencies and manifold responsibilities of an actor, but carried the authority of its sovereign down into practical activity.

At the top, the bureaucracy had its head, carrying imperative authority from the sovereign, sometimes mixed with more arbitrary authority of its own. Whatever happened in actuality, theory was clear, and the boss was the boss. There still are many old-style family firms whose heads do not call themselves managers. There are still classic bureaucrats who might be insulted by the term "manager." Traditional doyens of these sorts may still exert imperative authority, commonly derived from an external sovereign. They are less managers of issues made urgent by the external environment, less likely to use the rationalized and ritualized procedures evoked by the term decision-making (e.g., cost-benefit analyses or surveys of stakeholders), and therefore more free to pursue an independent course of action.

In contrast, in organizations decisions are to be made from outside-in or sometimes even bottom-up rather than top-down. The contemporary system celebrates the rights and capacities of the individual person, and many of its institutions are focused on enhancing these rights: the market economy, the democratic polity, the elaborate educational and medical systems, the free religious and cultural norms, family systems built on individual choice, and so on. In some analyses, these are responses to alienation and organized power: in others, they are seen as historical developments in their own right. In our own analyses, expanded individualism is a source of, more than a response to, the organized society.

In an organization, unlike in a bureaucracy, a wide variety of issues can and should be brought into a decision process—often a participatory one—and the process should be infused with technical competence and expertise as much as political or economic clout. Notions of managers as expertly integrating and balancing diffuse interests rise in the twentieth century, and especially its last half, alongside generalized liberal or neoliberal notions of societal (and often global) order. As principles of management spread worldwide, they provide a legitimate and ordered basis for collective activity globally. Cooperation across borders becomes more feasible under shared cultural principles, and within national societies structures come to have more in common even without direct international ties.

In practice, thus, individual persons, perhaps entrapped in narrow specialized roles, are entitled and likely to pursue multiple roles in organizational structures. Many of these roles accommodate diverse facets of individual preferences, from work–family policies to encouraging employees to "take initiative" on things in the workplace that interest and challenge them. The modern organizational society facilitates this integration: the culture of contemporary individualism encourages it, providing many recipes for solving life problems through more, not less, organizing.

Much of the organizational structure of contemporary society, in fact, is built around stabilizing and normalizing the life course of the individual: creating a world that is to make sense from the point of view of that individual. Thus contemporary child-rearing is designed, and partly organized, to be child-centered. Schooling is designed, less to impose high collective truths, but to be sequenced in terms of student development.[9] Similarly, linkages between schooling and work are institutionalized, as are career-development processes, and those leading to retirement. In short, the organizational system may be as much colonized by the ideologies of the individual life course as it colonizes them.

Professionals and management

Given the expansion of organizational structures into domains little related to their core goals, how are structures to be coordinated and integrated? Professionals are the main answer. Some have substantive expertise, but many are professional managers—an abstract concept, role, and profession unrelated to any specific problems or tasks to be managed. A central implication of our arguments, in contrast to much management literature, is that the most important task of managers is to integrate disparate pressures within organizations. It is not to monitor or incentivize employees, nor is it to pass along directives from some higher up. It is not even to ensure efficient and effective production.

Many elements of contemporary organization are distant from concrete tasks, activities, and outputs—one can often describe large swathes of an organization without mentioning its core purpose. The manager, itself an abstract role, carries a set of procedures for management that can be applied nearly anywhere, and may be especially useful if nothing clear is to be coordinated. If it is required that some unclear activities be done (e.g., planning, branding, improving an entity's culture, risk management, public relations), it is better that certified professionals with rational procedures be hired to do them. Structuring the uncertain requires the skills of a certified and trained manager, whose expertise renders the intangible concrete and the invisible apparent.

Thus, the development of management training, and theories of management, tend to emphasize abstract functions and activities, in contrast to empirical studies that show that actual managers devote their time to concrete and messy immediate problems.[10] At the center of the focus, and the core of management, is the decision. Decisions are seen in very abstract terms, ideally capable of formulation in terms of abstract models and principles.[11] The organizational revolution arises in close conjunction with the development of management as a rationalized and professionalized concept. Indeed, having professionally trained management is one of the core indicators of the extent to which a social structure has become a proper organizational actor.[12]

Management and "the decision" are central concepts in the contemporary world. In a liberal, and globally stateless, world society, human actors are understood to legitimately drive history and progress. Aggregated to more collective levels, they form organizations which are also proper actors. The decisions people and their organizations produce have to make sense in rather universalistic terms if we are to understand this kind of world as an orderly, stable, and progressive case. Governmentality is central to the culture of the system, and managed organizational actors are central to its production.

Implications for world society

The society of organizations is, as we have stressed, built on universalistic and rationalistic principles of science and human empowerment. The cultural claims involved in theory apply everywhere, and organizational actors in fact grow in the widest set of arenas. Science, human rights and empowerment, and education create a cultural system that undercuts traditional differentiation in the world: the norms involved apply everywhere and press for much isomorphism. Local cultural practices can be analyzed as violating scientific principles, human rights standards, or standards of social transparency. What was once culture can now be called corruption, or human rights violations, or irrational technical practices—and rated on global scales. As cultural principles do, the rationalized ideologies of science and human rights impose standardizing social controls everywhere they spread. But they also make possible organized actorhood everywhere they touch: in this sense, they are empowering and enable action.

A further consequence, which we noted at the outset of this book, is that organization reaching to a global scale now becomes routine: the expanding bases of a common rationalized culture make possible organizations cutting across every national and regional boundary. INGOs and IGOs and multinational firms appear everywhere and reach down into all national societies. One can see this as reflecting the rise of a global society. One can also see it as reflecting the construction of a transnational elite, with a global concentration of power.

The expansion of educational systems—which struggle for, and claim, isomorphism with each other—creates local stratification systems built on education. These are readily integrated with each other: curricula are quite homogeneous, and degrees and certificates are increasingly given common meaning. So the local stratification systems merge into a global one, built on education. Global scientization and human empowerment is instantiated in what amounts to a global educational system, and a stratification system built on it: global organizational structures in society, economy, and public life then concretize this hierarchical order.

The underlying cultural commonalities account for the fluidity with which local orders can now be integrated into great supra-national and global orders. It is, for instance, easy for managers from different countries to join together in supra-national economic or social organizations—they are trained in the same business schools, or schools aggressively copying each other, and thus share in a common managerial culture. The same thing characterizes almost every other rationalized and scientized (or social scientized) profession. Even something so local as a university admissions process can be professionalized with organizations and discourse operating at the global level.

There is no real reason to imagine that the globalized culture and organizational system in fact resolve the obvious problems of world society. They shift consensus to supra-national levels. But they also aggregate conflicts to higher levels. Social movements in world society—conflictful or consensual—organize on global bases, now. One can find organized world movements of many sorts: on behalf of children, in favor of technical standardization, or in defense of rights for gays and lesbians. Even indigenous peoples, defined by their distance from the great civilizations, can now organize on a world scale. The organized world, built on great and common principles, is not necessarily a peaceful one.

The globalized stratification system, and the organizational systems it helps create, produce a considerable global integration and centralization of status, power, and income in world society. It is easy for people to see a "democratic deficit" in Europe, and even easier to see it in the world. And around the world we can observe many populist reactions to the society of organizations and the educational stratification system on which it is based. These may legitimate themselves with reference to religion, ethnicity, race, poverty, or cultural distinctions. In the current world, if the critics acquire a modicum of schooling and rationalization, they can try to construct global conflicts.

Reflections on future developments

We see the contemporary system, filled with organizations in every domain and society, as driven into place by a post-war cultural complex. Expanded interdependence, in a stateless world society, creates liberal models of society built on strong actors functioning in rationalized environments. Given that culture, a frenetic period of organization-building has come into place, with individual actors constructing collective ones at a great pace. Further, organizations are distinct from the traditional structures producing clear economic outputs and political controls. They reflect cultural changes that may be distant from immediate functional pressures: ideologies of human resources, issues about the natural environment, and faith in managerialism built on constructed decision-making, accounting, and information systems.

The authority of the culture involved has perhaps been declining in recent years, following on and creating disorder in economies and polities worldwide. It is difficult to believe that the myths of the market economy, the democratic polity, and high individualism continue to have the authority they did a decade or two ago. Even science comes under suspicion, challenged by international trends like rising religious fundamentalism.

If the elaborated organization-as-actor depends on these cultural bases, and if these cultural bases continue to lose some authority, the question arises: what happens to all the hyper-organizational structure that depends on it? Can we envision a slowdown in the expansion of higher education and the associated "professionalism of everybody"? Will the expansion of business schools and the particular professionalization of abstract management decline? Will rates of organization-building decline?

Answers to such questions depend on what ideologies and models come to the fore, replacing in part the scripts of liberal individualism and scientization. In the brief period of the 1980s, for example, Japanese success in the world economy led to whole literatures celebrating more corporatist Japanese organizational forms (and secondary, though not higher, education): this experiment collapsed, along with the Japanese economy, in the early 1990s. A future world involving China at the center will obviously emphasize different models than a German-dominated one would: though in both cases, national and state organizational structures would play a stronger role, and autonomous actors-as-organizations a weaker one.

But over and above new models reflecting changing centrality in world society, the organizational world we have depicted has internal dynamics that generate change. So much of this system depends on faith in liberal cultural assumptions, reinforced by competitive and mimetic processes, that it all seems rather inflationary in character. An organization adopts an information system, or a decision-making system, or planning, because it is fashionable to do so, and because competitors do: as we have stressed, many components of contemporary organizations are in no way known to be internally functional. One can easily envision that much of the business is an inflationary bubble, susceptible to collapse.[13] The sense that this is likely pervades the system throughout its modern history. For example, critics both fear and hope that the exorbitant claims for education and its credentials will collapse in the face of practical realities.[14]

In our view, the expanded identities of contemporary individuals and their organizations generate responsibilities and expectations that far exceed what is plausible. Both individuals and organizations (including state agencies) can be seen as continually falling short on multiple fronts. Given exorbitant contemporary expectations, almost every national state could be portrayed, now, as a "failed state." On the one hand, actors require constant education and reform from a host of therapeutic and educational "others" who prop them up.[15] On the other hand, all these "others" now themselves organize, often as non-profit organizations. The result is a set of organized actors with surrounding actors themselves organized in interconnected webs: the stakeholders have stakeholders, and these also have dense organizational structures behind them. One can think of this social system as the "knowledge society." Or one can consider it an inflationary bubble.

▩ NOTES

1. Brunsson 1985, 2007; March 1987.
2. Foucault 1978; Miller 7 Rose 1990; Rose, O'Malley, & Valverde 2006.
3. Boli 2006.
4. Coleman 1982; Perrow 2002.
5. Dahl 1957; March 1966; Lukes 1974; Gaventa 1980.
6. Ganzeboom, de Graaf, & Treiman 1992; Ganzeboom & Treiman 1996.
7. Habermas 1984, 1987.
8. These themes are common in classics by Marx, Weber, and Durkheim. See Seeman (1959) for a review.
9. Bromley, Meyer, & Ramirez 2011.
10. Mintzberg 1973, 1975; Kurke & Aldrich 1983; Hales 1986.
11. March 1987, 1994.
12. Hwang & Powell 2009.
13. For the educational parallel see Collins (1979).
14. See, for example, discussions of over-education by economists (e.g., Sicherman 1991 or Hartog 2000) and sociologists (e.g., Burris 1983), as well as historical perspectives on the fear of over-education in the late nineteenth century in England (Middleton 2005).
15. Brunsson 1989; Brunsson & Olsen 1993; Brunsson 2009.

■ LIST OF SOURCES

AACSB website (2013). "Total Enrollment." Retrieved 12/3/2013 at: <http://www.aacsb.edu/dataandresearch/dataglance/enrollment_total.html>.

Abbott, A. (2014). *The system of professions: An essay on the division of expert labor*. Chicago, IL: University of Chicago Press.

Abbott, K. W. and Snidal, D. (2000). "Hard and soft law in international governance". *International Organization* 54(3), 421–56.

Ahrne, G. and Brunsson N. (2008). *Meta-organizations*. Cheltenham: Edward Elgar.

Ahrne, G. and Brunsson, N. (2009). Complete and incomplete organization. (Score Reports 2009: 2). *Stockholm: University*. Retrieved on 1/27/2015 from <http://www.score.su.se/polopoly_fs/1.26609.1320939802!/20092.pdf>.

Ahrne, G. and Brunsson N. (2011). "Organization outside organizations: The significance of partial organization". *Organization* 18, 83–104.

Albert, S. and Whetten, D. A. (1985). "Organizational identity". *Research in Organizational Behavior* 7, 263–95.

Alchian, A. A. and Demsetz, H. (1972). "Production, information costs, and economic organization". *The American Economic Review* 62(5), 777–95.

Aldrich, H. E. (1999). *Organizations evolving*. Thousand Oaks, CA: Sage.

Alexander, C. R., Bauguess, S.W., Bernile, G., Lee, Y.A., and Marietta-Westberg, J. (2013). "Economics effects of SOX Section 404 compliance: A corporate insider perspective". *Journal of Accounting and Economics* 56, 2–3, 267–90.

Alexander, J. C., and Colomy, P. B. (Eds). (1990). *Differentiation theory and social change: Comparative and historical perspectives*. New York City, NY: Columbia University Press.

Alexander, J., Brudney, J. L., and Yang, K. (2010). "Introduction to the symposium: Accountability and performance measurement: The evolving role of nonprofits in the hollow state". *Nonprofit and Voluntary Sector Quarterly* 39(4), 565–70.

Altbach, P. G. (2004). "Globalisation and the university: Myths and realities in an unequal world". *Tertiary Education and Management* 10(1), 3–25.

Altbach, P. G., and Salmi, J. (Eds). (2011). *The road to academic excellence: The making of world-class research universities*. Washington, DC: World Bank Publications.

Amason, A. C. (1996). "Distinguishing the effects of functional and dysfunctional conflict on strategic decision making: Resolving a paradox for top management teams". *Academy of Management Journal* 39(1), 123–48.

Amato, L. H., and Amato, C. H. (2012). "Environmental policy, rankings and stock values". *Business Strategy and the Environment* 21(5), 317–25.

Anderson, B. (2006). *Imagined communities: Reflections on the origin and spread of nationalism*. Brooklyn, NY: Verso Books.

Anderson, R. M., and Funnell, M. M. (2005). "Patient empowerment: Reflections on the challenge of fostering the adoption of a new paradigm". *Patient Education and Counseling* 57(2), 153–7.

Anheier, H., and Salamon, L. (2006). "The nonprofit sector in comparative perspective". Pp. 89–117 in W. Powell, and R. Steinberg, (Eds), *The Non-Profit Sector: A Research Handbook*. New Haven, CT: Yale University Press.

Anteby, M. (2013). *Manufacturing morals: The values of silence in business school education*. Chicago, IL: University of Chicago Press.

Apollo Group website. (2015). *University of Phoenix*. Accessed 6/22/2015 at: <http://www.apollo.edu/learning-platforms/university-of-phoenix>.

Ariès, P. (1960). *L'enfant et la vie familiale sous l'Ancien Régime*. Paris: Plon.

Aucoin, P., and Peter, A. (1995). *The new public management: Canada in comparative perspective*. Montreal: Institute for Research on Public Policy.

Bagnoli, L., and Megali, C. (2009). "Measuring performance in social enterprises". *Nonprofit and Voluntary Sector Quarterly* 40(1), 149–65.

Baker, D. (2014). *The schooled society: Education and the transformation of global culture*. Stanford: Stanford University Press.

Bail, C. A. (2014). "The cultural environment: Measuring culture with big data". *Theory and Society* 43(3–4), 465–82.

Bandiera, O., Barankay, I., and Rasul, I. (2005). "Social preferences and the response to incentives: Evidence from personnel data". *Quarterly Journal of Economics* 120(3), 917–62.

Bandiera, O., Barankay, I., and Rasul, I. (2010). "Social incentives in the workplace". *Review of Economic Studies* 77(2), 417–58.

Barber, W. J. (2010). *A history of economic thought*. Middletown, CT: Wesleyan University Press.

Barker III, V. L., and Mueller, G. C. (2002). "CEO characteristics and firm R&D spending". *Management Science* 48(6), 782–801.

Barman, E., and MacIndoe, H. (2012). "Institutional pressures and organizational capacity: The case of outcome measurement". *Sociological Forum* 27(1), 70–93.

Barr, A., Fafchamps, M., and Owens, T. (2005). "The governance of non-governmental organizations in Uganda". *World Development* 33(4), 657–79.

Bartel, A., Ichniowski, C., and Shaw, K. (2007). "How does information technology affect productivity? Plant-level comparisons of product innovation, process improvement, and worker skills". *Quarterly Journal of Economics* 122(4), 1721–58.

Bartley, T. (2003). "Certifying forests and factories: States, social movements, and the rise of private regulation in the apparel and forest products fields". *Politics and Society* 31(3), 433–64.

Bartley, T. (2007). "Institutional emergence in an era of globalization: The rise of transnational private regulation of labor and environmental conditions". *American Journal of Sociology* 113(2), 297–351.

Bartley, T. (2010). "Transnational private regulation in practice: The limits of forest and labor standards certification in Indonesia". *Business and Politics* 12(3).

Bartley, T. (2011). "Certification as a mode of social regulation". In the *Handbook on the Politics of Regulation*. Cheltenham, UK: Edward Elgar Publishing, pp. 441–52.

Bartley, T. and Child, C. (2014). "Shaming the corporation: The social production of targets and the anti-sweatshop movement". *American Sociological Review* 79(4), 653–79.

Barzelay, M. (2001). *The new public management: Improving research and policy dialogue*. Berkeley, CA: Univ of California Press.

Battilana, J., and D'Aunno, T. (2009). "Institutional work and the paradox of embedded agency". In T. Lawrence, R. Suddaby, and B. Leca (Eds), *Institutional Work: Actors and Agency in Institutional Studies of Organizations*. Cambridge, UK: Cambridge University Press, pp. 31–58.

Battilana, J., and Dorado, S. (2010). "Building sustainable hybrid organizations: The case of commercial microfinance organizations". *Academy of Management Journal* 53(6), 1419–40.

Beck, C. J., Drori, G. S., and Meyer, J. W. (2012). "World influences on human rights language in constitutions: A cross-national study". *International Sociology* 27(4), 483–501.

Beck, U. (1992). *Risk society: Towards a new modernity*. London, UK: Sage.

Becker, B.D., and Huselid, M.A. (1998). "High performance systems and firm performance: A synthesis of research and managerial implications". *Research in Personnel and Human Resources Journal* 16(1), 53–101.

Beckfield, Jason. (2010). "The social structure of the world polity". *American Journal of Sociology* 115(4), 1018–68.

Behn, R. D. (2001). *Rethinking democratic accountability*. Washington, DC: Brookings Institution Press.

Bell, D. (1976, May). "The coming of the post-industrial society". *The Educational Forum* 40(4), 574–79). Taylor and Francis Group.

Bell, P. F. (2008). "The Asian economic crisis and capitalist restructuring: Two approaches". *Critical Asian Studies* 40(2), 317–22.

Benavot, A., and Riddle, P. (1988). "The expansion of primary education, 1870–1940: Trends and issues". *Sociology of Education* 61(3), 191–210.

Bendix, R. (1980). *Kings or people: Power and the mandate to rule*. Oakland, CA: University of California Press.

Bendix, Reinhard. (1964). *Nation-building and citizenship*. New York, NY: Wiley.

Berger, P. L., and T. Luckmann. 1967. *The social construction of reality*. Garden City, NY: Anchor.

Berle, A. A., and Means, G. G. C. (1991). *The modern corporation and private property*. Brunswick, NJ: Transaction Publishers.

Berman, S. (1997). "Civil society and the collapse of the Weimar Republic". *World Politics* 49(3), 401–29.

Berry, F. S. (1994). "Innovation in public management: The adoption of strategic planning". *Public Administration Review* 54, 4: 322–30.

Bertrand, M., and Schoar, A. (2003). "Managing with style: The effect of managers on firm policies". *The Quarterly Journal of Economics* 118(4), 1169–1208.

Bies, A. L. (2010). "Evolution of nonprofit self-regulation in Europe". *Nonprofit and Voluntary Sector Quarterly* 39(6), 1057–86.

Billis, D. (Ed.). (2010). *Hybrid organizations and the third sector: Challenges for practice, theory and policy*. London: Palgrave Macmillan.

Binder, A. (2007). "For love and money: Organizations' creative responses to multiple environmental logics". *Theory and Society* 36(6), 547–71.

Binder, A. (2014). "Why are Harvard grads still flocking to Wall Street?" *Washington Monthly*. Retrieved on 1/28/2015 from <http://www.washingtonmonthly.com/magazine/sep temberoctober_2014/features/why_are_harvard_grads_still_fl051758.php>.

Birdi, K., Clegg, C., Patterson, M., Robinson, A., Stride, C. B., Wall, T. D., and Wood, S. J. (2008). "The impact of human resource and operational management practices on company productivity: A longitudinal study". *Personnel Psychology* 61(3), 467–501.

Black, S. E., and Lynch, L. M. (2001). "How to compete: The impact of workplace practices and information technology on productivity". *Review of Economics and Statistics* 83(3), 434–45.

Bloom, Nicholas, and Van Reenen, J. (2007). "Measuring and explaining management practices across firms and countries". *Quarterly Journal of Economics* 122(4), 1351–408.

Bloom, N., Genakos, C., Sadun, R., and Van Reenen, J. (2012). "Management practices across firms and countries". *National Bureau of Economic Research Working Paper 17850.* Cambridge, MA: National Bureau of Economic Research.

Bloom, Nick, Tobias Kretschmer, and John Van Reenen. (2011). "Are family-friendly workplace practices a valuable firm resource?." *Strategic Management Journal* 32(4), 343–67.

Bloom, N., Sadun R., and Van Reenen, J. (2012). "Americans do IT better: US multinationals and the productivity miracle: Dataset". *American Economic Review* 102(1), 167–201.

Boli, J. (2006). "The rationalization of virtue and virtuosity in world society". In Djelic, M. L., and Sahlin-Andersson, K. (Eds). *Transnational Governance: Institutional Dynamics of Regulation.* Cambridge, UK: Cambridge University Press, pp. 95–118.

Boli, J., Ramirez, F. O., and Meyer, J. W. (1985). "Explaining the origins and expansion of mass education". *Comparative Education Review* 29(2), 145–70.

Boli, J., and Thomas, G. M. (1997). "World culture in the world polity: A century of international non-governmental organization". *American Sociological Review* 62(2), 171–90.

Boli, J., and Thomas, G. M. (1999). *Constructing world culture: International nongovernmental organizations since 1875.* Stanford CA: Stanford University Press.

Boli-Bennett, J., and Meyer, J. W. (1978). "The ideology of childhood and the state: Rules distinguishing children in national constitutions, 1870–1970". *American Sociological Review* 43(6), 797–812.

Boltanski, L., and Thévenot, L. (2006). *On justification: Economies of worth.* Princeton, NJ: Princeton University Press.

Boris, E. T., and Steuerle, C. E. (Eds). (2006). *Nonprofits and government: Collaboration and conflict.* Washington DC: The Urban Institute.

Boston, J., Martin, J., Pallot, J., and Walsh, P. (1996). *Public management: The New Zealand model.* Melbourne: Oxford University Press.

Bovens, M. (2007). "Analysing and assessing accountability: A conceptual framework". *European Law Journal* 13(4), 447–68.

Bovens, M. (2010). "Two concepts of accountability: Accountability as a virtue and as a mechanism". *West European Politics* 33(5), 946–67.

Boxenbaum, E., and Jonsson, S. (2008). "Isomorphism, diffusion and decoupling". In Greenwood, R., Oliver, C., Suddaby, R., and Sahlin-Andersson, K. (Eds). (2008). *The Sage Handbook of Organizational Institutionalism.* London: Sage, pp. 78–98.

Brickson, S. L. (2005). "Organizational identity orientation: Forging a link between organizational identity and organizations' relations with stakeholders". *Administrative Science Quarterly* 50(4), 576–609.

Briscoe, F., and Safford, S. (2008). "The Nixon-in-China effect: Activism, imitation, and the institutionalization of contentious practices". *Administrative Science Quarterly* 53(3), 460–91.

Brockmann, E. N., and Simmonds, P. G. (1997). "Strategic decision making: The influence of CEO experience and use of tacit knowledge". *Journal of Managerial Issues* 9(4), 454–67.

Bromley, P. 2010. "The rationalization of educational development: Scientific activities among international non-governmental organizations". *Comparative Education Review* 54(4): 577–601.

Bromley, P., Meyer, J. W., and Ramirez, F. O. (2011). "Student-centeredness in social science textbooks, 1970–2008: A cross-national study". *Social Forces* 90(2), 1–24.

Bromley, P., and Russell, S. G. (2010). "The Holocaust as history and human rights: A cross-national analysis of Holocaust education in social science textbooks, 1970–2008". *Prospects* 40(1), 153–73.

Bromley, P., and Powell, W. W. (2012). "From smoke and mirrors to walking the talk: Decoupling in the contemporary world". *Academy of Management Annals* 6(1), 483–530.

Bromley, P., Hwang, H., and Powell, W. W. (2012). "Decoupling revisited: Common pressures, divergent strategies in the US nonprofit sector". *M@n@gement* 15(5), 468–501.

Bromley, P., and Sharkey, A. J. (2014). *Annual Report data.* Unpublished original data collection. Chicago, IL.

Brown, H., de Jong, M., and T. Lessidrenska. 2007. "The rise of the Global Reporting Initiative (GRI) as a case of institutional entrepreneurship". *Corporate Social Responsibility Initiative, Working Paper No. 36.* Cambridge, MA: John F. Kennedy School of Government, Harvard University. Retrieved on 1/28/2015 at: <http://www.hks.harvard.edu/m-rcbg/CSRI/publications/workingpaper_36_brown.pdf>.

Brunsson, N. (1985). *The irrational organization: Irrationality as a basis for organizational action and change.* Chichester: Wiley.

Brunsson, N. (1989). *The organization of hypocrisy: Talk, decisions and actions in organizations.* Chichester: Wiley.

Brunsson, N. (2007). *The consequences of decision-making.* Oxford: Oxford University Press.

Brunsson, N. (2009). *Reform as routine: Organizational change and stability in the modern world.* Oxford: Oxford University Press.

Brunsson, N., Jacobsson, B., and associates. (2000). *A world of standards.* Oxford: Oxford University Press.

Brunsson, N., and Olsen, J. P. (1993). *The reforming organization.* London: Routledge.

Brunsson, N., and Sahlin-Andersson, K. (2000). "Constructing organizations: The example of public sector reform". *Organization Studies* 21(4), 721–46.

Bryson, J. M. (2011). *Strategic planning for public and nonprofit organizations: A guide to strengthening and sustaining organizational achievement.* San Francisco, CA: John Wiley and Sons.

Burman, E. (1996). "Local, global or globalized? Child development and international child rights legislation". *Childhood* 3(1), 45–66.

Burris, V. (1983). "The social and political consequences of overeducation". *American Sociological Review* 48(4), 454–67.

Cameron, D. M. (Ed.). (1978). Power and responsibility in the public service/Pouvoir et respopnsabilité dans la fonction publique. Toronto, ON: Institute of Public Administration of Canada.

Caporaso, J. A. (1996). "The European Union and forms of state: Westphalian, regulatory or post-modern?" *JCMS: Journal of Common Market Studies* 34(1), 29–52.

Carman, J. G. (2010). "The accountability movement: What's wrong with this theory of change?" *Nonprofit and Voluntary Sector Quarterly* 39(2), 256–74.

Carpenter, M. A., and Westphal, J. D. (2001). "The strategic context of external network ties: Examining the impact of director appointments on board involvement in strategic decision making". *Academy of Management Journal* 44(4), 639–60.

Carter, N., Klein, R., and Day, P. (1992). *How organisations measure success: The use of performance indicators in government*. New York, NY: Routledge.

CDP. 2013. "S&P 500 climate report." Retrieved 1/28/2015 at: <https://www.cdproject.net/CDPResults/CDP-SP500-climate-report-2013.pdf>.

CDP website. 2015. Retrieved 1/28/2015 at: <https://www.cdproject.net/en-US/Pages/HomePage.aspx>.

Center for Corporate Citizenship website 2013. "The state of corporate citizenship 2012." Accessed on August 27, 2013 at: <http://www.bcccc.net/index.cfm?pageId=2043>.

Chabbott, C. (2003). *Constructing education for development: International organizations and education for all*. New York, NY: Routledge.

Chambers, S., and Kymlicka, W. (Eds). (2002). *Alternative conceptions of civil society*. Princeton, NJ: Princeton University Press.

Chan, Y. C. (2004). "Performance measurement and adoption of balanced scorecards: A survey of municipal governments in the USA and Canada". *International Journal of Public Sector Management* 17(3), 204–21.

Chandler, A. (1977). *The visible hand*. Cambridge, MA: Harvard University Press.

Cheney, G. (1991). *Rhetoric in an organizational society: Managing multiple identities*. Columbia, S.C.: University of South Carolina Press.

Child, J., and Rodrigues, S. (1996). "The role of social identity in the international transfer of knowledge through joint ventures". *The Politics of Management Knowledge* 46(68), 133–39.

Chreim, S. (2005). "The continuity–change duality in narrative texts of organizational identity". *Journal of Management Studies* 42(3), 567–93.

Christensen, T., and Lægreid, P. (2006). "Agencification and regulatory reforms". In Christensen, T., and Lægreid, P. (Eds). *Autonomy and Regulation: Coping with Agencies in the Modern State*. Northampton, MA: Edward Elgar, pp. 8–52.

Clegg, S. R., and Hardy, C. (1996). "Introduction: Organizations, organization and organizing". In S. Clegg, C. Hardy, and W. Nord (Eds), *Handbook of Organization Studies*. London, UK: Sage Publications, pp. 1–28.

Clegg, S. R., Rhodes, C., and Kornberger, M. (2007). "Desperately seeking legitimacy: Organizational identity and emerging industries". *Organization Studies* 28(4), 495–513.

Coase, R. H. (1937). "The nature of the firm". *Economica* 4(16), 386–405.

Coase, R. H. (1984). "The new institutional economics". *Zeitschrift für die gesamte Staatswissenschaft/Journal of Institutional and Theoretical Economics*, 229–31.

Coca-Cola website. (2013). "Annual and Other Reports." Accessed on August 29, 2013 at: <http://www.coca-colacompany.com/investors/annual-other-reports>.

Cohen, M. D., March, J. G., and Olsen, J. P. (1972). "A garbage can model of organizational choice". *Administrative Science Quarterly* 17(1), 1–25.

Cole, W. M. (2005). "Sovereignty relinquished? Explaining commitment to the international human rights covenants, 1966–1999". *American Sociological Review* 70(3), 472–95.

Coleman, J. S. (1982). *The asymmetric society*. Syracuse, NY: Syracuse University Press.

Coleman, J. S. (1990). *Foundations of social theory*. Cambridge, MA: Harvard University Press.

Coleman, J. S. (1993). "The rational reconstruction of society": 1992 presidential address. *American Sociological Review* 58(1), 1–15.

Collins, R. (1979). *The credential society: An historical sociology of education and stratification.* New York: Academic Press.

Colyvas, J. A. (2012). "Performance metrics as formal structures and through the lens of social mechanisms: When do they work and how do they influence?" *American Journal of Education* 118(2), 167–97.

Colyvas, J. A., and Powell, W. W. (2006). "Roads to institutionalization: The remaking of boundaries between public and private science". *Research in Organizational Behavior* 27, 305–53.

Coursera website. (2015). Retrieved on 1/27/2015 from <https://www.coursera.org/>.

Creighton, A. L. (1990). *The emergence of incorporation as a legal form for organizations.* Doctoral dissertation. Stanford University: Stanford, CA.

Crosby, B. C., and Bryson, J. M. (2005). *Leadership for the common good: Tackling public problems in a shared-power world,* 2nd edn. San Francisco, CA: John Wiley and Sons.

Cyert, R. M., and March, J. G. (1963). *A behavioral theory of the firm.* Englewood Cliffs, NJ: Prentice-Hall.

Cyranoski, D., Gilbert, N., Ledford, H., Nayar, A., and M. Yahia. 2011. "Education: The PhD Factory". *Nature* 472: 276–9. Retrieved 1/28/2015 at: <http://www.nature.com/news/2011/110420/full/472276a/box/1.html>.

Czarniawska, B., and Sevón, G. (Eds). (1996). *Translating organizational change.* Berlin: Walter de Gruyter.

Czarniawska, B., and Wolff, R. (1998). "Constructing new identities in established organization fields: Young universities in old Europe". *International Studies of Management and Organization* 28(3), 32–56.

Dahl, R. A. (1957). "The concept of power". *Behavioral Science* 2(3): 201–15.

David, R. J., and Han, S. K. (2004). "A systematic assessment of the empirical support for transaction cost economics". *Strategic Management Journal* 25(1), 39–58.

Davidson, A. (1997). *From subject to citizen: Australian citizenship in the twentieth century.* Cambridge: Cambridge University Press.

Davis, P. (1998). "The burgeoning of benchmarking in British local government: The value of 'learning by looking' in the public services". *Benchmarking for Quality Management and Technology* 5(4), 260–70.

Davis, G. F. (2009). *Managed by the markets: How finance re-shaped America.* Oxford: Oxford University Press.

Davis, G. F., and Marquis, C. (2005). "Prospects for organization theory in the early twenty-first century: Institutional fields and mechanisms". *Organization Science* 16(4), 332–43.

Davis, G. F., and C. White. 2012. "Want to be an Intrapreneur? Learn from Social Movements". Forbes.com. Retrieved 1/28/2015 at: <http://www.forbes.com/sites/ashoka/2012/12/18/want-to-be-an-intrapreneur-learn-from-social-movements/>.

Dees, J. G. (1998). *The meaning of social entrepreneurship.* Stanford University: Draft Report for the Kauffman Center for Entrepreneurial Leadership. Accessed 6/29/2015 at: <https://csistg.gsb.stanford.edu/sites/csi.gsb.stanford.edu/files/TheMeaningofsocialEntrepreneurship.pdf>.

Dehon, C., McCathie, A., and Verardi, V. (2010). "Uncovering excellence in academic rankings: A closer look at the Shanghai ranking". *Scientometrics* 83(2), 515–24.

Democratic People's Republic of Korea's Socialist Constitution. 1995. Retrieved 1/28/2015 at: <http://www1.korea-np.co.jp/pk/061st_issue/98091708.htm#Chapter%205:Fundamental%20Rights%20and%20Duties%20of%20Citizens>.

Demsetz, H. (1988). *The organization of economic activity.* Oxford: Blackwell.

Dimaggio, P. J., and Anheier, H. K. (1990). "The sociology of nonprofit organizations and sectors". *Annual Review of Sociology* 16, 137–59.

DiMaggio, P., and Powell, W. W. (1983). "The iron cage revisited: Collective rationality and institutional isomorphism in organizational fields". *American Sociological Review* 48(2), 147–60.

Djelic, M. L., and Quack, S. (Eds). (2003). *Globalization and institutions: Redefining the rules of the economic game.* Cheltenham, UK: Edward Elgar Publishing.

Djelic, M. L., and Sahlin-Andersson, K. (Eds). (2006). *Transnational governance: Institutional dynamics of regulation.* Cambridge: Cambridge University Press.

Dobbin, F. (1994). "Cultural models of organization: The social construction of rational organizing principles". *The Sociology of Culture: Emerging Theoretical Perspectives*, 118. Available at SSRN: <http://ssrn.com/abstract=2417452>.

Dobbin, F. (2004). *The new economic sociology: A reader.* Princeton, NJ: Princeton University Press.

Dobbin, F., and Sutton, J. R. (1998). "The strength of a weak state: The rights revolution and the rise of human resources management divisions". *American Journal of Sociology* 104(2), 441–76.

Dobbin, F., Sutton, J. R., Meyer, J. W., and Scott, W. R. (1993). "Equal opportunity law and the construction of internal labor markets". *American Journal of Sociology* 99(2), 396–427.

Dobbin, F., and Kelly, E. (2007). "How to stop harassment: Professional construction of legal compliance in organizations". *American Journal of Sociology* 112(4), 1203–43.

Dobbin, F. (2009). *Inventing equal opportunity.* Princeton, NJ: Princeton University Press.

Drori, G. S., Delmestri, G., and Oberg, A. (2013). "Branding the university: Relational strategy of identity construction in a competitive field". In L. Engwall and P. Scott (Eds), *Trust in Higher Education Institutions*, London, UK: Portland Press, pp. 134–47.

Drori, G., Höllerer, M., and Walgenbach, P. (Eds). (2014). *Global themes and local variations in organization and management.* New York, NY: Routledge.

Drori, G. S., Meyer, J. W., and Hwang, H. (2006). *Globalization and organization: world society and organizational change.* Oxford: Oxford University Press.

Drori, G. S., Meyer, J.W., Ramirez, F.O., and Schofer, E. (2003). *Science in the modern world polity: Institutionalization and globalization.* Stanford, CA: Stanford University Press.

Drori, G. S., and Moon, H. (2006). "The Changing Nature of Tertiary Education: Neo-Institutional Perspectives on Cross-National Trends in Disciplinary Enrollment, 1965–1995". In D. P. Baker, and A. W. Wiseman (Eds), *The Impact of Comparative Education Research on Institutional Theory.* Bingley, UK: Emerald Group, pp. 157–85.

Drucker, P. (1992). "The society of organizations". *Harvard Business Review*, Sept–Oct.: 95–104.

Durkheim, E. (2012). *The elementary forms of the religious life.* New York, NY: Courier Dover Publications.

Dutton, J. E., and Dukerich, J. M. (1991). "Keeping an eye on the mirror: Image and identity in organizational adaptation." *Academy of Management Journal* 34(3), 517–54.

Dwivedi, O. P. (1967). "Bureaucratic corruption in developing countries". *Asian Survey* 245–53.

Ebrahim, A. (2003a). "Making sense of accountability: Conceptual perspectives for northern and southern nonprofits". *Nonprofit Management and Leadership* 14(2), 191–212.

Ebrahim, A. (2003b). *NGOs and organizational change: Discourse, reporting, and learning.* Cambridge: Cambridge University Press.

Edelman, L. B. (1992). "Legal ambiguity and symbolic structures: Organizational mediation of civil rights law". *American Journal of Sociology* 97(6), 1531–76.

Edelman, L. B., and Suchman, M. C. (1997). "The legal environments of organizations". *Annual Review of Sociology* 23, 479–515.

Edelman, L. B., Fuller, S. R., and Mara-Drita, I. (2001). "Diversity rhetoric and the managerialization of law". *American Journal of Sociology* 106(6), 1589–641.

Edelman, L. B., Krieger, L. H., Eliason, S. R., Albiston, C. R., and Mellema, V. (2011). "When organizations rule: Judicial deference to institutionalized employment structures". *American Journal of Sociology* 117(3), 888–954.

Edelman, L. B., Uggen, C., and Erlanger, H. S. (1999). "The endogeneity of legal regulation: Grievance procedures as rational myth". *American Journal of Sociology* 105(2), 406–54.

Eikenberry, A. M., and Kluver, J. D. (2004). "The marketization of the nonprofit sector: Civil society at risk?" *Public Administration Review* 64, 2: 132–40.

Elliott, M. (2007). "Human rights and the triumph of the individual in world culture". *Cultural Sociology* 1(3), 353–63.

Elsbach, K. D., and Kramer, R. M. (1996). "Members' responses to organizational identity threats: Encountering and countering the Business Week rankings". *Administrative Science Quarterly* 41(3), 442–76.

Ernst, B., and Kieser, A. (2002). "Consultants as agents of anxiety and providers of managerial control." *Academy of Management Proceedings*, 1, pp. C1-C6. Accessed 6/29/2015 at: <http://proceedings.aom.org/content/2002/1/C1.9.short>.

Espeland, W. N., and Sauder, M. (2007). "Rankings and reactivity: How public measures recreate social worlds". *American Journal of Sociology* 113(1), 1–40.

Espeland, W. N., and Stevens, M. L. (1998). "Commensuration as a social process". *Annual Review of Sociology* 24, 313–43.

Evers, A. (2005). "Mixed welfare systems and hybrid organizations: Changes in the governance and provision of social services". *International Journal of Public Administration* 28(9–10), 737–48.

Evetts, J. (2003). "The sociological analysis of professionalism: Occupational change in the modern world". *International Sociology* 18(2), 395–415.

Fair Trade Federation website. (2013). History of Fair Trade in the United States. Retrieved on July 23, 2013 from <http://www.fairtradefederation.org/history-of-fair-trade-in-the-united-states/>.

Fair Trade International. (2012). Fair Trade by the Numbers: Key Data for 2009-2011. Retrieved on 1/28/2015 from <http://www.fairtrade.net/fileadmin/user_upload/content/2009/resources/2012-02_Fairtrade_ByTheNumbers_2009-11.pdf>.

Fair Trade USA. (2012). Certification Manual. Retrieved on 1/28/2015 from <http://www.fairtradeusa.org/sites/all/files/wysiwyg/filemanager/standards/FTUSA_MAN_Ce rtificationManual.pdf>.

Fair Trade USA. (2013). Farm Workers Standard Version 1.1. Retrieved on 1/28/2015 from <http://www.scsglobalservices.com/files/standards/ftusa_stn_fws_criteria_v1-1_012213.pdf>.

Fairtrade International website. (2015). Retrieved on 1/28/2015 from <http://www.fairtrade.net/>.

Fairtlough, G. (2008). Post-bureaucratic organizations. In S. Clegg, and J. Bailey (Eds), *International Encyclopedia of Organization Studies*. Thousand Oaks, CA: Sage, pp. 1274–6.

Fama, E. F. (1980). "Agency Problems and the Theory of the Firm". *The Journal of Political Economy* 88(2), 288–307.

Farneti, F., and Guthrie, J. (2009). "Sustainability reporting by Australian public sector organisations: Why they report". *Accounting Forum* 33, 2, 89–98.

Faulconbridge, J. R., and Muzio, D. (2012). "Professions in a globalizing world: Towards a transnational sociology of the professions". *International Sociology 27*(1), 136–52.

Feldman, M. S., and March, J. G. (1981). "Information in organizations as signal and symbol". *Administrative Science Quarterly* 26(2), 171–86.

Ferguson, J. (1990). *The anti-politics machine: "Development," depoliticization, and bureaucratic power in Lesotho*. Cambridge: Cambridge University Press.

Fine, A. H., Thayer, C. E., and Coghlan, A. (2000). "Program evaluation practice in the nonprofit sector". *Nonprofit Management and Leadership* 10(3), 331–9.

Finkelstein, S., Hambrick, D. C., and Cannella, A. A. (2009). *Strategic leadership: Theory and research on executives, top management teams, and boards*. New York, NY: Oxford University Press.

Finnemore, M. (2014). "Dynamics of global governance: Building on what we know". *International Studies Quarterly* 58(1), 221–4.

Finnemore, M. (1993). "International organizations as teachers of norms: The United Nations Educational, Scientific, and Cultural Organization and science policy". *International Organization* 47(4), 565–97.

Fisman, R., and Sullivan, T. (2013). *The org: The underlying logic of the office*. Princeton, NJ: Princeton University Press.

Fligstein, N. (1985). "The spread of the multidivisional form among large firms, 1919-1979". *Advances in Strategic Management* 17, 55–78.

Fligstein, N. (1990). *The transformation of corporate control*. Cambridge, MA: Harvard University Press.

Fligstein, N. (1997). "Social skill and institutional theory". *American Behavioral Scientist* 40(4), 397–405.

Fombrun, C. J. (2007). "List of lists: A compilation of international corporate reputation ratings". *Corporate Reputation Review* 10(2), 144–53.

Foucault, M. (1978). "Governmentality" (lecture at the Collège de France, 1 February). In G. Burchell, C. Gordon and P. Miller (Eds), *The Foucault Effect: Studies in Governmentality*. Hemel Hempstead: Harvester Wheatsheaf, 1991, pp. 87–104.

Fourcade, M. (2011). "Cents and Sensibility: Economic Valuation and the Nature of 'Nature'". *American Journal of Sociology 116*(6), 1721–77.

Frank, D. J. (1999). "The social bases of environmental treaty ratification, 1900–1990". *Sociological Inquiry 69*(4), 523–50.

Frank, D. J., and Gabler, J. (2006). *Reconstructing the university: Worldwide shifts in academia in the 20th century*. Stanford, CA: Stanford University Press.

Frank, D. J., Hironaka, A., and Schofer, E. (2000). "The nation-state and the natural environment over the twentieth century". *American Sociological Review* 65(1): 96–116.

Frank, D. J., and Meyer, J. W. (2002). "The profusion of individual roles and identities in the postwar period". *Sociological Theory* 20(1), 86–105.

Frank, D. J., and Meyer, J. W. (2007). "University expansion and the knowledge society". *Theory and Society 36*(4), 287–311.

Frank, D. J., Camp, B. J., and Boutcher, S. A. (2010). "Worldwide trends in the criminal regulation of sex, 1945 to 2005". *American Sociological Review* 75(6), 867–93.

Freeman, R. E. (1984). *Strategic management: A stakeholder approach.* Boston: Pitman.

Freeman, R. E., Harrison, J. S., Wicks, A. C., Parmar, B. L., and De Colle, S. (2010). *Stakeholder theory: The state of the art.* Cambridge: Cambridge University Press.

Freeland, R. F. (1996). "The myth of the M-form? Governance, consent, and organizational change". *American Journal of Sociology* 102(2): 483–526.

Freidson, E. (1994). *Professionalism reborn: Theory, prophecy, and policy.* Chicago, IL: University of Chicago Press.

Fridman, D. (2010). "A new mentality for a new economy: Performing the homo economicus in Argentina" (1976–83). *Economy and Society* 39(2), 271–302.

Friedland, R., and Alford, R. R. (1991). "Bringing society back in: Symbols, practices and institutional contradictions". In W. W. Powell and P. J. DiMaggio (Eds). *The New Institutionalism in Organizational Analysis* Chicago, IL: University of Chicago Press, pp. 232–66.

Friedman, L. J., and McGarvie, M. D. (Eds). (2003). *Charity, philanthropy, and civility in American history.* Cambridge: Cambridge University Press.

Frumkin, P. (2002). *On being nonprofit: A conceptual and policy primer.* Cambridge MA: Harvard University Press.

Fukuyama, F. (1995). "Social capital and the global economy: A redrawn map of the world". *Foreign Affairs* 74(5), 89–103.

Fukuyama, F. (2001). "Social capital, civil society and development". *Third World Quarterly* 22(1), 7–20.

Gabel, M., and Bruner, H. (2003). *Global inc: An atlas of the multinational corporation.* New York: New Press.

Galbraith, J. R. (1973). *Designing complex organizations.* Reading, MA: Addison-Wesley Longman Publishing.

Ganzeboom, H. B., De Graaf, P. M., and Treiman, D. J. (1992). "A standard international socio-economic index of occupational status". *Social Science Research* 21(1), 1–56.

Ganzeboom, H. B., and Treiman, D. J. (1996). "Internationally comparable measures of occupational status for the 1988 International Standard Classification of Occupations". *Social Science Research* 25(3), 201–39.

Garfinkel, H. (1967). *Studies in ethnomethodology.* Englewood Cliffs, NJ: Prentice Hall.

Garud, R., Hardy, C., and Maguire, S. (2007). "Institutional entrepreneurship as embedded agency: An introduction to the special issue". *Organization Studies* 28(7), 957–67.

Gaventa, J. (1980). *Power and powerlessness: Quiescence and rebellion in an Appalachian valley.* Urbana IL: University of Illinois Press.

Gavetti, G., D. Levinthal, W. Ocasio. (2007). "Neo-Carnegie: The Carnegie School's past, present, and reconstructing for the future". *Organization Science* 18(3), 523–36.

Gee, J. P., Hull, G., and Lankshear, C. (1996). *The new work order.* Sydney: Allen and Unwin.

Ghemawat, P., and Pisani, N. (2013). "Are multinationals becoming less global?" *Harvard Business Review Online Edition* (October 28).

Ghoshal, S., and Moran, P. (1996). "Bad for practice: A critique of the transaction cost theory". *Academy of Management Review* 21(1), 13–47.

Gioia, D. A., Price, K. N., Hamilton, A. L., and Thomas, J. B. (2010). "Forging an identity: An insider-outsider study of processes involved in the formation of organizational identity". *Administrative Science Quarterly* 55(1), 1–46.

Gioia, D. A., Schultz, M., and Corley, K. G. (2000). "Organizational identity, image, and adaptive instability". *Academy of Management Review* 25(1), 63–81.

Gittell, R., and Vidal, A. (1998). *Community organizing: Building social capital as a development strategy*. London, UK: Sage Publications.

Gittleson, K. (2012). "Can a company live forever" BBC. Retrieved October 1, 2013 at: <http://www.bbc.co.uk/news/business-16611040>.

Global Exchange website. (2013). Frequently Asked Questions. Retrieved on July 23, 2013 from <http://www.globalexchange.org/fairtrade/coffee/faq>.

Global Initiative to End All Corporal Punishment of Children website. (2015a) Countdown to Universal Prohibition. Retrieved on 1/28/2015 from <http://www.endcorporalpunishment. org>.

Global Initiative to End All Corporal Punishment of Children website. (2015b) Introduction: A Human Rights Issue. Retrieved on 1/28/2015 from <http://www.endcorporalpunishment. org>.

Global Reporting Initiative. (2010/11). "GRI Year in Review 2010/11". Retrieved 1/28/2015: <https://www.globalreporting.org/resourcelibrary/GRI-Year-In-Review-2010-2011.pdf>.

Global Reporting Initiative. (2013). "Guiding Principles and Standard Disclosures." Amsterdam, Netherlands. Retrieved 1/28/2015 at: <https://www.globalreporting.org/resourcelibrary/ GRIG4-Part1-Reporting-Principles-and-Standard-Disclosures.pdf>.

Global Reporting Initiative website. (2013). "About GRI." Retrieved 8/29/2013 at: <https://www. globalreporting.org/information/about-gri/Pages/default.aspx>.

Global Reporting Initiative website. (2014). "GRI Organizations Search." Retrieved 12/2/2014 at: <https://www.globalreporting.org/Pages/GRIOrganizationsSearchPage.aspx>.

Glynn, M. A. (2000). "When cymbals become symbols: Conflict over organizational identity within a symphony orchestra". *Organization Science* 11(3): 285–98.

Godfrey, B. J., and Zhou, Y. (1999). "Ranking world cities: Multinational corporations and the global urban hierarchy". *Urban Geography* 20(3), 268–81.

Goffman, E. (1959). *The presentation of self in everyday life*. Garden City, NY: Doubleday.

Goldsmith, S., and Eggers, W. D. (2004). *Governing by network: The new shape of the public sector*. Washington, DC: Brookings Institution Press.

Goldstein, A. (2012). "Revenge of the managers: Labor cost-cutting and the paradoxical resurgence of managerialism in the shareholder value era, 1984 to 2001". *American Sociological Review* 77(2), 268–94.

Goodstein, D. (1994). "The Big Crunch." NCAR 48 Symposium. Portland, OR: California Institute of Technology. Accessed on 6/22/2015 at: <http://www.its.caltech.edu/~dg/crunch_ art.html>.

Google website. (2014). "Diversity at Google." Accessed 6/22/2015 at: <http://www.google.com/ diversity/at-google.html>.

Gould, D. J., and Amaro-Reyes, J. A. (1983). "The effects of corruption on administrative performance". *World Bank Staff Working Paper* 580, 2514.

Granovetter, M. (1985). "Economic action and social structure: The problem of embeddedness". *American Journal of Sociology* 91(3), 481–510.

Gray, G. C., and Silbey, S. S. (2014). "Governing inside the organization: Interpreting regulation and compliance". *American Journal of Sociology* 120(1), 96–145.

Greenwood, R., Oliver, C., Suddaby, R., and Sahlin-Andersson, K. (Eds). (2008).*The Sage handbook of organizational institutionalism.* Thousand Oaks, CA: Sage.

Greenwood, R., Raynard, M., Kodeih, F., Micelotta, E. R., and Lounsbury, M. (2011). "Institutional complexity and organizational responses". *The Academy of Management Annals* 5(1), 317–71.

Greer, J., and Singh, K. (2000). "A brief history of transnational corporations". *Global Policy Forum.* New York.

Grey, C. and Garsten, C. (2001). "Trust, control and post-bureaucracy". *Organization Studies* 22 (2), 229–50.

Grimm, C. M., and Smith, K. G. (1991). "Research notes and communications management and organizational change: A note on the railroad industry". *Strategic Management Journal* 12(7), 557–62.

Gugerty, Mary Kay. (2010). "The emergence of nonprofit self-regulation in Africa". *Nonprofit and Voluntary Sector Quarterly* 39(6), 1087–112.

Gugerty, M. K., and Prakash, A. (Eds). (2010). *Voluntary regulation of NGOs and nonprofits: An accountability club framework.* New York: Cambridge University Press.

Guthrie, J. P. (2001). "High-involvement work practices, turnover, and productivity: Evidence from New Zealand". *Academy of Management Journal* 44(1), 180–90.

Habermas, J. (1984). *The theory of communicative action,* Vol. 1. Boston: Beacon.

Habermas, J. (1987). *The theory of communicative action: Lifeworld and system: A critique of functionalist reason* (Vol. 2). Boston: Beacon.

Hafner-Burton, E. M., Tsutsui, K., and Meyer, J. W. (2008). "International human rights law and the politics of legitimation: Repressive states and human rights treaties". *International Sociology* 23(1), 115–41.

Hafner-Burton, E. M., and Tsutsui, K. (2005). "Human rights in a globalizing world: The paradox of empty promises". *American Journal of Sociology* 110(5), 1373–411.

Hales, C. P. (1986). "What do managers do? A critical review of the evidence". *Journal of Management Studies* 23(1), 88–115.

Hall, P. D. (2006). "A historical overview of philanthropy, voluntary associations, and nonprofit organizations in the United States, 1600–2000". In Powell, W. W. & Steinberg, R. (Eds.). *The nonprofit sector: A research handbook.* New Haven, CT: Yale University Press, pp. 32–65.

Hallett, T. (2010). "The myth incarnate: Recoupling processes, turmoil, and inhabited institutions in an urban elementary school". *American Sociological Review* 75(1), 52–74.

Hallström, K. T. (2004). *Organizing international standardization: ISO and the IASC in quest of authority.* Cheltenham: Edward Elgar Publishing.

Hannan, M. T., Baron, J. N., Hsu, G., and Koçak, Ö. (2006). "Organizational identities and the hazard of change". *Industrial and Corporate Change* 15(5), 755–84.

Hannan, M. T., and Freeman, J. (1977). "The population ecology of organizations". *American Journal of Sociology* 82(5), 929–64.

Hannan, M. T., and Freeman, J. (1993). *Organizational ecology.* Cambridge, MA: Harvard University Press.

Hannum, E., and Buchmann, C. (2003). *The consequences of global educational expansion.* Cambridge, MA: American Academy of Arts and Sciences.

Hansmann, H. (1987). "Economic theories of nonprofit organization". *The Nonprofit Sector: A Research Handbook* 1, 27–42.

Hansmann, H., and Kraakman, R. (2000). "The essential role of organizational law". *Yale Law Journal* 110(3), 387–440.

Hartog, J. (2000). "Over-education and earnings: Where are we, where should we go?" *Economics of Education Review* 19(2), 131–47.

Harvard Business School website. (2015). "History." Accessed 6/22/2015 at: <http://www.hbs.edu/about/facts-and-figures/Pages/history.aspx>.

Healy, D. (2010). *The dynamics of desistance: Charting pathways through change.* Portland, OR: Willan Publishing.

Heath, C., and S. B. Sitkin. (2001). "Big-B versus big-O: What is organizational about organizational behavior?" *Journal of Organizational Behavior* 22(1), 43–58.

Heckscher, C. (1994), "Defining the Post-Bureaucratic Type," in C. Heckscher and A. Donnellon (Eds.), The Post-Bureaucratic Organization: New Perspectives on Organizational Change, Thousand Oaks, CA: Sage, pp. 14–62.

Heckscher, C., and Donnellon, A. (Eds). (1994). *The post-bureaucratic organization: New perspectives on organizational change.* Thousand Oaks, CA: Sage Publications.

Hedström, P., and Swedberg, R. (Eds). (1998). *Social mechanisms: An analytical approach to social theory.* Cambridge: Cambridge University Press.

Heinrich, C. J. (2002). "Outcomes–based performance management in the public sector: implications for government accountability and effectiveness". *Public Administration Review* 62(6), 712–25.

Held, D. (2006). *Models of democracy.* Stanford, CA: Stanford University Press.

Higgins, W., and Hallström, K. T. (2007). "Standardization, globalization and rationalities of government". *Organization* 14(5), 685–704.

Hilgartner, S., and Bosk, C. L. (1988). "The rise and fall of social problems: A public arenas model". *American Journal of Sociology* 94(1), 53–78.

Hirsch, P. M., and M. Lounsbury. (1997a). "Ending the family quarrel: Toward a reconciliation of 'Old' and 'New' Institutionalisms". *American Behavioral Science* 40(4), 406–418.

Hirsch, P. M., and M. Lounsbury. (1997b). "Putting the organization back into organizational theory: Action, change, and the 'new' institutionalism". *J. Management Inquiry* 6(1), 79–88.

Hirschhorn, L. (1997). *Re-working authority: Leading and authority in the post-modern organization.* Cambridge, MA: MIT Press.

Hood, C. (1995). "Contemporary public management: A new global paradigm?" *Public Policy and Administration* 10(2), 104–17.

Hsu, G., and Hannan, M. T. (2005). "Identities, genres, and organizational forms". *Organization Science* 16(5), 474–90.

Huber, G. P. (1984). "The nature and design of post-industrial organizations". *Management Science* 30(8), 928–51.

Huselid, M. A. (1995). "The impact of human resource management practices on turnover, productivity, and corporate financial performance". *The Academy of Management Journal* 38(3), 635–72.

Hwang, H., and Colyvas, J. A. (2011). "Problematizing actors and institutions in institutional work". *Journal of Management Inquiry* 20(1), 62–6.

Hwang, H., and Colyvas, J. (2013). "Actors, actors! actors? The proliferation of the actor and its consequences". *European Group for Organization Studies Annual Meetings, 4 (July).* Montreal, Canada.

Hwang, H., and Powell, W. W. (2009). "The rationalization of charity: The influences of professionalism in the nonprofit sector". *Administrative Science Quarterly* 54(2), 268–98.

Ichniowski, C., Shaw, K., and Prennushi, G. (1997). "The effects of human resource management practices on productivity: A study of steel finishing lines". *American Economic Review* 87(3), 291–313.

Iedema, R. (2003). *Discourses of post-bureaucratic organization*. Philadelphia, PA: John Benjamins Publishing.

IFC website. (2014). <www.ifc2014.org>.

Indira Gandhi National Open University website. (2014). "Profile." Accessed 6/22/2015 at: <http://ignou.ac.in/ignou/aboutignou/profile/2>.

Ingram, P., and Clay, K. (2000). "The choice-within-constraints new institutionalism and implications for sociology". *Annual Review of Sociology* 26, 525–46.

ISO. (2013). Number of International Organization for Standardization (ISO) publications per year, 1955–2012. Geneva, Switzerland: International Organization for Standardization.

Iversen, T., and Cusack, T.R. (2000). "The causes of welfare state expansion: Deindustrialization or globalization?" *World Politics* 52(3), 313–49.

Jackson, M. O. (2010). *Social and economic networks*. Princeton, NJ: Princeton University Press.

Jamali, D., and Mirshak, R. (2007). "Corporate social responsibility (CSR): Theory and practice in a developing country context". *Journal of Business Ethics* 72(3), 243–62.

Jana, R. (2013). "Inside facebook's internal innovation culture". *Harvard Business Review*. Retrieved on 1/27/2015 from <https://hbr.org/2013/03/inside-facebooks-internal-inno/>.

Jang, Y. S. (2000). "The worldwide founding of ministries of science and technology, 1950–1990". *Sociological Perspectives*, 43(2), 247–70.

Jay, J. (2013). "Navigating paradox as a mechanism of change and innovation in hybrid organizations". *Academy of Management Journal* 56(1), 137–59.

Jensen, M. C., and Meckling, W. H. (1976). "Agency costs and the theory of the firm". *Journal of Financial Economics* 3(4), 305–60.

Jepperson, R. L. (2002). "The development and application of sociological neoinstitutionalism". In J. Berger and M. Zelditch, (Eds), *New Directions in Contemporary Sociological Theory*. Lanham, MD: Rowman and Littlefield Publishers, pp. 229–66.

Johnson, G., Prashantham, S., Floyd, S. W., and Bourque, N. (2010). "The ritualization of strategy workshops". *Organization Studies* 31(12), 1–30.

Jones, C., Hesterly, W. S., and Borgatti, S. P. (1997). "A general theory of network governance: Exchange conditions and social mechanisms". *Academy of Management Review* 22(4), 911–45.

Josserand, E., Teo, S., and Clegg, S. (2006). "From bureaucratic to post-bureaucratic: The difficulties of transition". *Journal of Organizational Change Management* 19(1), 54–64.

Kalev, A., Dobbin, F., and Kelly, E. (2006). "Best practices or best guesses? Assessing the efficacy of corporate affirmative action and diversity policies". *American Sociological Review* 71(4), 589–617.

Kaplan, D. (2011). "Fair trade has growing influence". *Houston Chronicle*. Retrieved on 1/28/2015 from <http://www.chron.com/business/article/Q-A-Fair-Trade-USA-has-growing-influence-1609310.php>.

Kaufman, J. (2008). "Epidemiologic analysis of racial/ethnic disparities: Some fundamental issues and a cautionary example". *Social Science and Medicine* 66(8), 1659–69.

Kellogg, K. C. (2009). "Operating room: Relational spaces and microinstitutional change in surgery". *American Journal of Sociology* 115(3), 657–711.

Kelly, E. L. (2006). "Work-family policies: The United States in international perspective". In M. Pitt-Catsouphes, E. E. Kossek, and S. Sweet, (Eds). (2006). *The Work and Family Handbook: Multi-disciplinary Perspectives, Methods, and Approaches*. Mahwah, NJ: Lawrence Erlbaum Associates Publishers, pp. 99–123.

Kelly, E., and Dobbin, F. (1998). "How affirmative action became diversity management: Employer response to antidiscrimination law, 1961 to 1996". *American Behavioral Scientist* 41(7), 960–84.

Kelly, E., and Dobbin, F. (1999). "Civil rights law at work: Sex discrimination and the rise of maternity leave policies". *American Journal of Sociology* 105(2), 455–92.

Kernaghan, K. (2003). "Integrating values into public service: The values statement as centerpiece". *Public Administration Review* 63(6), 711–19.

Khurana, R. (2007). *From higher aims to hired hands: The social transformation of American business schools and the unfulfilled promise of management as a profession*. Princeton, NJ: Princeton University Press.

Kim, Y. S., Jang, Y. S., and Hwang, H. (2002). "Structural expansion and the cost of global isomorphism: A cross-national study of ministerial structure, 1950–1990". *International Sociology*, 17(4), 481–503.

Kim, E. H., and Lu, Y. (2013). "Corporate governance reforms around the world and cross-border acquisitions". *Journal of Corporate Finance* 22, 236–53.

Kimberly, J. R., and Evanisko, M. J. (1981). "Organizational innovation: The influence of individual, organizational, and contextual factors on hospital adoption of technological and administrative innovations". *Academy of Management Journal* 24(4), 689–713.

King, B. G., Felin, T., and Whetten, D. A. (2010). "Perspective-finding the organization in organizational theory: A meta-theory of the organization as a social actor". *Organization Science 21*(1), 290–305.

King, B. G., and Soule, S. A. (2007). "Social movements as extra-institutional entrepreneurs: The effect of protests on stock price returns". *Administrative Science Quarterly 52*(3), 413–42.

Knowlton, L. W., and Phillips, C. C. (2012). *The logic model guidebook: Better strategies for great results*. Thousand Oaks, CA: Sage.

Koo, J. W., and Ramirez, F. O. (2009). "National incorporation of global human rights: Worldwide expansion of national human rights institutions, 1966–2004". *Social Forces* 87(3), 1321–53.

KPMG International Survey of Corporate Responsibility Reporting 2011. Retrieved August 29, 2013 at: <http://www.kpmg.com/Global/en/IssuesAndInsights/ArticlesPublications/corporate-responsibility/Documents/2011-survey.pdf>.

Kraatz, M. S., and Block, E. S. (2008). "Organizational implications of institutional pluralism". In R. Greenwood, et al., (Eds), *The Sage Handbook of Organizational Institutionalism*. Thousand Oaks, CA: Sage, pp. 243–76.

Krippner, G. R. (2005). "The financialization of the American economy". *Socio-Economic Review* 3(2), 173–208.

Krücken, G., Blümel, A., and Kloke, K. (2013). "The managerial turn in higher education? On the interplay of organizational and occupational change in German academia". *Minerva* 51(4), 417–42.

Krücken, G., and Drori, G. S. (Eds). (2009). *World society: The writings of John W. Meyer*. Oxford: Oxford University Press.

Krücken, G., and Meier, F. (2006). "Turning the university into an organizational actor". In G. Drori, J. Meyer, and H. Hwang, (Eds), *Globalization and Organization: World Society and Organizational Change.* Oxford: Oxford University Press, pp. 241–57.

Kumar, K. (2009). *From post-industrial to post-modern society: New theories of the contemporary world.* New York: John Wiley and Sons.

Kurke, L. B., and Aldrich, H. E. (1983). "Note—Mintzberg was right! A replication and extension of the nature of managerial work". *Management Science* 29(8); 975–84.

Kushnir, K., Mirmulstein, M. L., and Ramalho, R. (2010). "Micro, small, and medium enterprises around the world: How many are there, and what affects the count?" Washington, DC: The World Bank.

Lamberti, L., and Lettieri, E. (2009). "CSR practices and corporate strategy: Evidence from a longitudinal case study". *Journal of Business Ethics* 87(2), 153–68.

Larson, M. S. (1977). *The rise of the professionalism: A sociological analysis.* Berkeley, CA: University of California Press.

Lauren, P. G. (2011). *The evolution of international human rights: Visions seen.* Philadelphia, PA: University of Pennsylvania Press.

Lawrence, T. B., and Suddaby, R. (2006). "Institutions and institutional work". In S. Clegg, et al., (Eds), *The SAGE Handbook of Organization Studies, 2nd Edn.* London: Sage, pp. 215–54.

Lawrence, T. B., Suddaby, R., and Leca, B. (Eds). (2009). *Institutional work: Actors and agency in institutional studies of organizations.* Cambridge: Cambridge University Press.

Lawrence, T., Suddaby, R., and Leca, B. (2011). "Institutional work: Refocusing institutional studies of organization". *Journal of Management Inquiry* 20(1), 52–8.

Lazonick, W., and O'Sullivan, M. (2000). "Maximizing shareholder value: A new ideology for corporate governance". *Economy and Society* 29(1), 13–35.

Lee, C. K., & Strang, D. (2006). "The international diffusion of public-sector downsizing: Network emulation and theory-driven learning." *International Organization, 60*(4), 883–909.

Lester M. Salamon, S. Wojciech Sokolowski, and Associates. (2004). *Global Civil Society: Dimensions of the Nonprofit Sector, Volume Two.* Bloomfield, CT: Kumarian Press.

Lewis, B. W., Walls, J. L., and Dowell, G. W. (2014). "Difference in degrees: CEO characteristics and firm environmental disclosure". *Strategic Management Journal* 35(5), 712–22.

Lindenmeyr, A. (1990a). "Voluntary associations and the Russian autocracy: The case of private charity". *The Carl Beck Papers in Russian and East European Studies* 807, 1–66.

Lindenmeyr, A. (1990b). "The ethos of charity in imperial Russia". *Journal of Social History* 23 (4): 679–94.

Lipsky, M. (2010). *Street-level bureaucracy: Dilemmas of the individual in public service*, 30th ann. ed. New York, NY: Russell Sage Foundation.

Locke, R. (2002). The Promise and Perils of Globalization: The Case of Nike. MIT Working Paper IPC-002-07. Boston, MA: *MIT* Sloan School of Management. Retrieved 1/30/2015 at <https://ipc.mit.edu/sites/default/files/documents/02-007.pdf>.

Lounsbury, M. (2001). "Institutional sources of practice variation: Staffing college and university recycling programs". *Administrative Science Quarterly* 46(1), 29–56.

Lounsbury, M. (2008). "Institutional rationality and practice variation: New directions in the institutional analysis of practice". *Accounting, Organizations and Society* 33(4), 349–61.

Luca, M. (2011). *Reviews, reputation, and revenue: The case of Yelp.com.* Cambridge, MA: Harvard Business School.

Luhmann, N. (translated by Holmes and Larmore) (1982). *The differentiation of society*. New York, NY: Columbia University Press.

Luhmann, N. (1993). *Communication and social order: Risk: A sociological theory*. London: Transaction Publishers.

Luhmann, N. (2005). "The paradox of decision making". *Advances in Organization Studies 14*, 85–196.

Lukes, S. (1974). *Power: A radical view*. London: Macmillan.

Lynch-Cerullo, K., and Cooney, K. (2011). "Moving from outputs to outcomes: An overview of the evolution of performance measurement in the human service nonprofit sector". *Administration in Social Work 35*, 364–88.

MacIndoe, H., and Barman, E. (2012). "How organizational stakeholders shape performance measurement in nonprofits: exploring a multidimensional measure". *Nonprofit and Voluntary Sector Quarterly 42*(4), 716–38.

MacKenzie, D. A. (2006). *An engine, not a camera: How financial models shape markets*. Cambridge, MA: MIT Press.

MacKenzie, D. A., Muniesa, F., and Siu, L. (Eds.). (2007). *Do economists make markets? On the performativity of economics*. Princeton, NJ: Princeton University Press.

Madison, J. (1787). *The Federalist no. 10*.

Mair, J., and Marti, I. (2006). "Social entrepreneurship research: A source of explanation, prediction, and delight". *Journal of World Business 41*(1), 36–44.

March, J. G. (1966). "The power of power". In D. Easton, Ed., *Varieties of Political Theory*. Englewood Cliffs, NJ: Prentice-Hall, pp. 39–70.

March, J. G. (1978). "Bounded rationality, ambiguity, and the engineering of choice". *The Bell Journal of Economics 9*(2), 587–608.

March, J. G. (1982). "Theories of choice and making decisions". *Society 20*(1), 29–39.

March, J. G. (1987). "Ambiguity and accounting: The elusive link between information and decision making". *Accounting, Organizations and Society 12*(2), 153–68.

March, J. G. (1994). *Primer on decision making: How decisions happen*. New York, NY: Simon and Schuster.

March, J. G., and Olsen, J. P. (1975). "The uncertainty of the past: Organizational learning under ambiguity". *European Journal of Political Research 3*(2), 147–71.

March, J. G., and Olsen, J. P. (1976). *Ambiguity and choice in organizations*. Bergen: Universitetsforlaget.

Markle, K., and Shackelford, D. A. (2013). *The impact of headquarter and subsidiary locations on multinationals' effective tax rates*. NBER Working Paper No. w19621. Cambridge MA: NBER.

Marrée, J., and Groenewegen, P. P. (1997). *Back to Bismarck: Eastern Europe health care systems in transition*. Amsterdam: The Netherlands Institute for Health Services Research.

Marshall, T. H. (1950). *Citizenship and social class*. Cambridge: Cambridge University Press.

Marshall, J. H. and Suárez, D. (2014). "The flow of management practices". *Nonprofit and Voluntary Sector Quarterly 43*(6), 1033–51.

Matten, D., and Moon, J. (2008). "'Implicit' and 'explicit' CSR: A conceptual framework for a comparative understanding of corporate social responsibility". *Academy of Management Review 33*(2), 404–24.

Mattli, W., and Büthe, T. (2003). "Setting international standards: Technological rationality or primacy of power?" *World Politics 56*(1), 1–42.

Masuda, Y. (1980). *The information society as post-industrial society.* Washington DC: World Future Society.

Mbaku, J. M. (1996). "Bureaucratic corruption in Africa: The futility of cleanups". *The Cato Journal.* 16(1), 99–116.

McCarthy, J. D., and Zald, M. D. (1973). *The trend of social movements in America: Professionalization and resource mobilization.* Morristown, NJ: General Learning Press.

McClay, W. M. (1994). *The masterless: Self and society in modern America.* Chapel Hill, NC: University of North Carolina Press.

McCourt, W. (2008). "Public management in developing countries: From downsizing to governance". *Public Management Review* 10(4), 467–79.

McDonnell, M. H., and King, B. (2013). "Keeping up appearances: Reputational threat and impression management after social movement boycotts". *Administrative Science Quarterly* 58(3), 387–419.

McKinsey website. (2014a). "McKinsey and Company—Global LGBT Inclusion." Accessed 8/26/2014 at: <http://www.catalyst.org/knowledge/mckinsey-company%E2%80%94global-lgbt-inclusion>.

McKinsey website. (2014b). "LGBT colleagues at McKinsey." Accessed 8/26/2014 at: <http://www.mckinsey.com/careers/our_people_and_values/diversity_and_inclusion_networks/lgbt_at_mckinsey>.

Mclaughlin, K., Osborne, S. P., and Ferlie, E. (2002). *New Public Management: Current trends and future prospects.* London: Routledge.

McSweeney, B. (2006). "Is a post-bureaucratic age possible?" *Journal of Organizational Change Management* 19(1), 22–37.

McWilliams, A., and Siegel, D. (2000). "Corporate social responsibility and financial performance: Correlation or misspecification?" *Strategic Management Journal* 21(5), 603–9.

Mead, G. H. (1934). *Mind, self and society.* Chicago, IL: University of Chicago Press.

Melucci, A. (1996). *Challenging codes: Collective action in the information age.* Cambridge: Cambridge University Press.

Mendel, P. (2006). "The making and expansion of international management standards". In G. Drori, J. Meyer, and H. Hwang, (Eds), *Globalization and Organization.* Oxford: Oxford University Press, pp. 137–66.

Metz, M. H. (1989). "Real school: A universal drama amid disparate experience". *Politics of Education Association Yearbook* 4(5), 75–91.

Meyer, H. D., and Benavot, A. (Eds). (2013). *PISA, power, and policy: The emergence of global educational governance.* Oxford: Symposium books.

Meyer, J. W. (1986). "Social environments and organizational accounting". *Accounting, Organizations and Society* 11(4), 345–56.

Meyer, J. W. (1996). "Otherhood: The promulgation and transmission of ideas in the modern organizational environment". In B. Czarniawska and G. Sevon, (Eds), *Translating Organizational Change.* Berlin: De Gruyter, pp. 241–52.

Meyer, J. W. (2010). "World society, institutional theories, and the actor". *Annual Review of Sociology* 36, 1–20.

Meyer, J. W., and Bromley, P. (2013). "The worldwide expansion of 'organization'". *Sociological Theory* 31(4), 366–89.

Meyer, J. W., Frank, D. J., Hironaka, A., Schofer, E., and Tuma, N. B. (1997a). "The structuring of a world environmental regime, 1870–1990". *International Organization* 51(04), 623–51.

Meyer, J. W., and Jepperson, R. L. (2000). "The 'actors' of modern society: The cultural construction of social agency". *Sociological Theory* 18(1), 100–20.

Meyer, J. W., Kamens, D., Benavot, A., Cha, Y. K., and Wong, S. Y. (1992a). *School knowledge for the masses: World models and national curricula in the Twentieth Century.* London: Falmer.

Meyer, J. W., Pope, S., and Isaacson, A. (2015). "Legitimating the transnational corporation in a stateless world society". In K. Tsutsui and A. Kim, (Eds), *Corporate Social Responsibility in a Globalizing World.* Cambridge: Cambridge University Press, pp. 27–72.

Meyer, J. W., and Rowan, B. (1977). "Institutionalized organizations: Formal structure as myth and ceremony". *American Journal of Sociology* 83(2), 340–63.

Meyer, J. W., Boli, J., Thomas, G. M., and Ramirez, F. O. (1997). "World society and the nation-state". *American Journal of Sociology* 103(1), 144–81.

Meyer, J., Drori, G., and Hwang, H. (2006). "World society and the organizational actor". In G. Drori, J. Meyer and H. Hwang, (Eds). *Globalization and Organization.* Oxford: Oxford University Press, pp. 25–49.

Meyer, J. W., Ramirez, F. O., and Soysal, Y. N. (1992). "World expansion of mass education, 1870–1980". *Sociology of Education* 65(2), 128–49.

Meyer, J. W., and B. Rowan. (1978). "The structure of educational organizations". In M. Meyer et al., *Environments and Organizations.* San Francisco, CA: Jossey-Bass, pp. 78–109.

Meyerson, D. (2001). *Tempered radicals: How people use difference to inspire change at work.* Cambridge, MA: Harvard Business Press.

Middleton, J. (2005). "The cry for useless knowledge: Fear of over-education in late nineteenth-century England". *History of Education Researcher* 76, 91.

Miller, P., and Rose, N. (1990). "Governing economic life". *Economy and Society* 19(1): 1–31.

Minkoff, D. C. (1993). "The organization of survival: Women's and racial-ethnic voluntarist and activist organizations, 1955–1985". *Social Forces* 71(4), 887–908.

Minow, M. (2007). "Living up to rules: Holding soldiers responsible for abusive conduct and the dilemma of the superior orders defence". *McGill Law Journal* 52(1): 1–54.

Mintzberg, H. (1973). *The nature of managerial work.* New York: HarperCollins.

Mintzberg, H. (1975). "The manager's job: Folklore and fact". *Harvard Business Review*, July–August: 49–61.

Mintzberg, H. (1994). "The fall and rise of strategic planning". *Harvard Business Review* 72(1): 107–14.

Mitlin, D. (2007). "Finance for low-income housing and community development". *Environment and Urbanization* 19(2), 331.

Moeran, B., and Strandgaard Pederson, J. (Eds). (2011). *Negotiating values in the creative industries: Fairs, festivals and competitive events.* Cambridge: Cambridge University Press.

Moon, H., and Wotipka, C. M. (2006). "The worldwide diffusion of business education, 1881–1999". In G. Drori, J., Meyer, and H. Hwang, (Eds), *Globalization and Organization.* Oxford: Oxford University Press, pp. 121–36.

Morgan, G., Kristensen, P. H., and Whitley, R. (Eds). (2001). *The multinational firm: Organizing across institutional and national divides.* Oxford: Oxford University Press.

Mörth, U. (2004). *Soft law in governance and regulation: An interdisciplinary analysis.* Cheltenham: Edward Elgar.

Mullis, I. V., Martin, M. O., Foy, P., and Arora, A. (2012). *TIMSS 2011 international results in mathematics*. The Netherlands: International Association for the Evaluation of Educational Achievement.

Murray, C. J., and Frenk, J. (2010). "Ranking 37th—measuring the performance of the US health care system". *New England Journal of Medicine 362*(2), 98–9.

National Center for Educational Statistics website. (2013a). Bachelor's Enrollment accessed 12/3/2013 at: (Bachelor's) <http://nces.ed.gov/programs/digest/d11/tables/dt11_286.asp>.

National Center for Educational Statistics website. (2013b). MBA Enrollment accessed 12/3/2013 at: <http://nces.ed.gov/programs/digest/d12/tables/dt12_314.asp>.

National Research Council. (1998). Trends in the Early Careers of Life Scientists, Report by the Committee on Dimensions, Causes, and Implications of Recent Trends in the Careers of Life Scientists. Washington DC: National Research Council.

National Science Foundation. (2006). *Doctorate recipients from US universities*. Accessed 6/22/2015 at: <http://www.nsf.gov/statistics/doctorates/pdf/sed2006.pdf>.

Neal, R. (2002). *Caffeine nation*. CBS News. Retrieved on 1/28/2015 from <http://www.cbsnews.com/news/caffeine-nation/>.

Neumark, D. and Cappelli, P. (1999). "Do 'high performance' work practices improve establishment-level outcomes?" *ILR Review 54*(4), 737–75.

Newcomer, K. E. (1997). "Using performance measurement to improve programs". *New Directions for Evaluation 75*, 5–14.

Ng, I. C., and Tseng, L. M. (2008). "Learning to be sociable: the evolution of homo economicus". *American Journal of Economics and Sociology 67*(2), 265–86.

Nike Website (2013). "*Labor.*" Retrieved on 6/28/2013 at: <http://www.nikeresponsibility.com/report/content/chapter/labor#topic-progress-and-performance2>.

Nixon, R. (2011, April 14). "U.S. Groups Helped Nurture Arab Uprisings." *New York Times*. Accessed on 6/22/2015 at: <http://www.nytimes.com/2011/04/15/world/15aid.html?_r=4andpagewanted=1andemc=eta1>.

OECD. 2014. *Tax transparency 2014: Report on progress*. Accessed on 6/22/2015 at: <http://www.oecd.org/tax/transparency/GFannualreport2014.pdf>.

Olson, O., Guthrie, J., and Humphrey, C. (Eds). (1998). *Global warning: Debating international developments in new public financial management*. Oslo: Cappelen.

Orton, J. D., and Weick, K. E. (1990). "Loosely coupled systems: A reconceptualization". *Academy of Management Review 15*(2), 203–23.

Osborne, D. (1993). "Reinventing government". *Public Productivity & Management Review 16* (4): 349–56.

Osborne, S. (2006). "The New Public Governance?" *Public Management Review 8*(3), 377–87.

Osborne, S. P. (Ed.). (2010). *The new public governance? Emerging perspectives on the theory and practice of public governance*. London: Routledge.

Osborne, D., and Gaebler, T. (1992). *Reinventing government: How the entrepreneurial spirit is transforming government*. Reading, MA: Adison Wesley Public Comp.

Pache, A. C., and Santos, F. (2010). When worlds collide: The internal dynamics of organizational responses to conflicting institutional demands. *Academy of Management Review, 35*(3), 455–76.

Pache, A. C., and Santos, F. (2010a). "Inside the hybrid organization: An organizational level view of responses to conflicting institutional demands". *Academy of Management Journal* 56 (3), 971–1001.

Pache, A. C., and Santos, F. (2010b). "When worlds collide: The internal dynamics of organizational responses to conflicting institutional demands". *Academy of Management Review* 35(3), 455–76.

Packard, T. (1995). "TQM and organizational change and development". In B. Bummer and P. McCallion, (Eds), *Total Quality Management in the Social Services.* Albany, NY: Rockefeller College Press.

Palmer, D. A., Jennings, P. D., and Zhou, X. (1993). "Late adoption of the multidivisional form by large US corporations: Institutional, political, and economic accounts". *Administrative Science Quarterly*, 38(1), 100–31.

Parigi, P. (2012). *The rationalization of miracles.* Cambridge: Cambridge University Press.

Parker, M. (1992). "Post-modern organizations or postmodern organization theory?" *Organization Studies 13*(1), 1–17.

Perrow, C. (1991). "A society of organizations". *Theory and Society* 20(6), 725–62.

Perrow, C. (1999). "Organizing to reduce the vulnerabilities of complexity". *Journal of Contingencies and Crisis Management* 7(3), 150–5.

Perrow, C. (2002). *Organizing America: Wealth, power, and the origins of American capitalism.* Princeton, NJ: Princeton University Press.

Perutz, M. F. (1999). "Will biomedicine outgrow support?" *Nature* 399, 299–301.

Peters, B. G., and Pierre, J. (1998). "Governance without government? Rethinking public administration". *Journal of Public Administration Research and Theory* 8(2), 223–43.

Pierson, P. (2000). "Increasing returns, path dependence, and the study of politics". *American Political Science Review 94*(02), 251–67.

Poister, T. H. (2008). *Measuring performance in public and nonprofit organizations.* New York: John Wiley and Sons.

Porter, B. D. (2002). *War and the rise of the state.* New York, NY: Simon and Schuster.

Posnikoff, J. F. (1997). "Disinvestment from South Africa: They did well by doing good". *Contemporary Economic Policy 15*(1), 76–86.

Powell, W. W., and Bromley, P. 2015. "New institutionalism and the analysis of complex organizations." In James D. Wright (editor-in-chief), *International Encyclopedia of Social and Behavioral Sciences, 2nd Edn.* Vol 16. Oxford: Elsevier, pp. 764–9.

Power, M. (1997). *The audit society: Rituals of verification.* Oxford: Oxford University Press.

Power, M. (2004). "The risk management of everything". *The Journal of Risk Finance 5*(3), 58–65.

Power, M. (2007). *Organized uncertainty: Designing a world of risk management.* Oxford: Oxford University Press.

Prakash, A., and Gugerty, M. K. (2010a). "Trust but verify? Voluntary regulation programs in the nonprofit sector". *Regulation and Governance* 4(1), 22–47.

Prakash, A., and Gugerty, M. K. (Eds). (2010b). *Advocacy organizations and collective action.* New York, NY: Cambridge University Press.

Presthus, R. (1962). *The organizational society: An analysis and a theory.* New York: Knopf.

Preuss, L., Haunschild, A., and Matten, D. (2009). "The rise of CSR: Implications for HRM and employee representation". *The International Journal of Human Resource Management* 20(4), 953–73.

Price, D. J. (1961). *Science since Babylon*. New Haven, CT: Yale University Press.

Provan, K. G., and Kenis, P. (2008). "Modes of network governance: Structure, management, and effectiveness". *Journal of Public Administration Research and Theory 18*(2), 229–52.

Putnam, R. D. (1995). "Bowling alone: America's declining social capital". *Journal of Democracy 6*(1), 65–78.

Putnam, R. D. (2000). *Bowling alone. The collapse and revival of American society*. New York: Simon and Schuster.

Putnam, R. D. (Ed.). (2002). *Democracies in flux: The evolution of social capital in contemporary society*. Oxford: Oxford University Press.

Putnam, R. D., and Campbell, D. E. (2012). *American grace: How religion divides and unites us*. New York: Simon and Schuster.

Putnam, R. D., Leonardi, R., and Nanetti, R. Y. (1994). *Making democracy work: Civic traditions in modern Italy*. Princeton, NJ: Princeton University Press.

Ramirez, F. O. (2009). "World society and the socially embedded university" *Social Science Review* 40, 1–30 2009.

Ramirez, F. O., and Christensen, T. (2013). "The formalization of the university: Rules, roots, and routes". *Higher Education* 65(6), 695–708.

Read, J. (2009). "A genealogy of homo-economicus: Neoliberalism and the production of subjectivity". *Foucault Studies* 6, 25–36.

Red Cross website. (2013). *Leadership*. Retrieved on July 25, 2013 from <http://www.redcross.org/about-us/governance/leadership>.

Reus-Smit, Christian. (2011). "Human rights in a global ecumene". *International Affairs 87*(5), 1205–18.

Rhodes, R. A. (1997). "From marketization to diplomacy: It's the mix that matters". *Public Policy and Administration 12*(2), 31–50.

Rhodes, R. A. (1997). *Understanding governance: Policy networks, governance, reflexivity and accountability*. Buckinghamshire: Open University Press.

Rhodes, R. A. (2007). "Understanding governance: Ten years on". *Organization Studies 28*(8), 1243–64.

Rivera, L. A. (2012). "Hiring as cultural matching: The case of elite professional service firms". *American Sociological Review* 77(6), 999–1022.

Rodrigues, S., and Child, J. (2008). "The development of corporate identity: A political perspective". *Journal of Management Studies* 45(5), 885–911.

Roach, B. (2007). "Corporate power in a global economy: A GDAE teaching module on social and environmental issues in economics". Medford, MA: Global Development and Environment Institute. Tufts University. Retrieved on 1/27/2015 from http://www.ase.tufts.edu/gdae/education_materials/modules/Corporate_Power_in_a_Global_Economy.pdf.

Rose, N., O'Malley, P., and Valverde, M. (2006). "Governmentality". *Annual Review of Law and Social Science* 2, 83–104.

Ruef, M. (2002). "At the interstices of organizations: The expansion of the management consulting profession, 1933–97". In K. Sahlin Andersson and L. Engwall, (Eds), *The Expansion of Management Knowledge*. Stanford, CA: Stanford University Press, pp. 74–97.

Ruef, M. and Scott, W. R. (1998). "A multidimensional model of organizational legitimacy: Hospital survival in changing institutional environments". *Administrative Science Quarterly* 43(4), 877–904.

Sahlin-Andersson, K., and Engwall, L. (Eds). (2002). *The expansion of management knowledge: Carriers, flows, and sources*. Stanford, CA: Stanford University Press.

Sahlin, K., and Wedlin, L. (2008). "Circulating ideas: Imitation, translation and editing". In R. Greenwood, et al., (Eds), *The Sage Handbook of Organizational Institutionalism*. Thousand Oaks, CA: Sage, pp. 218–42.

Salaman, G. (2005). "Bureaucracy and beyond: Managers and leaders in the 'post-bureaucratic' organization". In P. Du Gay, ed., *The Values of Bureaucracy*. Oxford: Oxford University Press, pp. 141–64.

Salamon, L. M. (1981). "Rethinking public management: Third-party government and the changing forms of government action". *Public Policy* 29(3), 255–75.

Salamon, L. M. (1987). "Of market failure, voluntary failure, and third-party government: Toward a theory of government-nonprofit relations in the modern welfare state". *Nonprofit and Voluntary Sector Quarterly* 16(1–2), 29–49.

Salamon, L. M., and Anheier, H. K. (1997). "The civil society sector". *Society* 34(2), 60–5.

Salamon, L. M., and Anheier, H. K. (1992). "In search of the non-profit sector II: The problem of classification". *Voluntas* 3(3), 267–309.

Salmi, J. (2009). *The challenge of establishing world-class universities*. Washington, DC: World Bank Publications.

Saltman, R. B., and Figueras, J. (1997). "European health care reform: Analysis of current strategies". *WHO regional publications European series*. Copenhagen: World Health Organization.

Santos, M. (2011). "CSR in SMEs: Strategies, practices, motivations and obstacles". *Social Responsibility Journal* 7(3), 490–508.

Sassen, S. (2006). *Territory, authority, rights: From medieval to global assemblages*. Princeton, NJ: Princeton University Press.

Satow, R. L. (1975). "Value-rational authority and professional organizations: Weber's missing type". *Administrative Science Quarterly* 20(4), 526–31.

Sauder, M., and Espeland, W. N. (2009). "The discipline of rankings: Tight coupling and organizational change". *American Sociological Review* 74(1), 63–82.

Schanberg, Sydney H. (1996) "On the playgrounds of America, every kid's goal is to score: In Pakistan, Where children stitch soccer balls for six cents an hour, the goal is to survive." *Life Magazine* (June), 38–48.

Scharpf, F. W. (1997). "Economic integration, democracy and the welfare state". *Journal of European Public Policy* 4(1), 18–36.

Schmidt, W. H., McKnight, C. C., Houang, R. T., Wang, H., Wiley, D. E., Cogan, L. S., and Wolfe, R. G. (2001). *Why schools matter: A cross-national comparison of curriculum and learning*. San Francisco, CA: Jossey-Bass.

Schneiberg, M., and Bartley, T. (2008). "Organizations, regulation, and economic behavior: Regulatory dynamics and forms from the nineteenth to twenty-first century". *Annual Review of Law and Social Science*, 4, 31–61.

Schofer, E., and Hironaka, A. (2005). "The effects of world society on environmental protection outcomes". *Social Forces* 84(1), 25–47.

Schofer, E., and Longhofer, W. (2011). "The structural sources of association". *American Journal of Sociology* 117(2), 539–85.

Schofer, E., and Meyer, J. W. (2005). "The worldwide expansion of higher education in the twentieth century". *American Sociological Review* 70(6), 898–920.

Scott, W. R. (2013). *Institutions and organizations: Ideas, interests, and identities.* Thousand Oaks, CA: Sage Publications.

Scott, W. R., Ruef, M., Mendel, P. J., and C. Caronna. (2000). *Institutional change and healthcare organizations: From professional dominance to managed care.* Chicago: University of Chicago Press.

Schumpeter, J. A. (1942). *Capitalism, socialism and democracy.* New York: Harper and Row.

Sealander, J. (2003). *The failed century of the child: Governing America's young in the twentieth century.* Cambridge: Cambridge University Press.

Seeman, M. (1959). "On the meaning of alienation". *American Sociological Review* 24(6), 783–91.

Seligman, A. (1992). *Idea of civil society.* New York: Simon and Schuster.

Shankland, A., and Cornwall, A. (2007). "Realizing health rights in Brazil: The micropolitics of sustaining health system reform". In A. Bebbington and W. McCourt, (Eds), *Development Success: Statecraft in the South.* Basingstoke: Palgrave Macmillan.

Shapiro, J. (2013). "The Business Habits of Effective Terrorists: Why Terror Masterminds Rely on Micro-Management." *Foreign Affairs.* Accessed 10/6/2015 at <https://www.foreignaffairs.com/articles/middle-east/2013-08-14/business-habits-highly-effective-terrorists>.

Sharkey, A. J. (2014). "Categories and organizational status: The role of industry status in the response to organizational deviance". *American Journal of Sociology,* 119(5), 1380–433.

Sharkey, A. J., and Bromley, P. (2015). "Can ratings have indirect effects? Evidence from the organizational response to peers' environmental ratings". *American Sociological Review* 80(1): 63–91.

Shin, J. C., and Kehm, B. M., (Eds). (2013). *Institutionalization of world-class university in global competition.* Netherlands: Springer.

Shor, I. (1992). *Empowering education: Critical teaching for social change.* Chicago, IL: University of Chicago Press.

Sicherman, N. (1991). "'Overeducation' in the labor market". *Journal of Labor Economics* 9, 2: 101–22.

Simmel, G. (1903). "The metropolis and mental life". In Gary Bridge and Sophie Watson, (Eds), *The Blackwell City Reader.* Oxford and Malden, MA: Wiley-Blackwell, 2002, pp. 324–39.

Simola, H. (2005). "The Finnish miracle of PISA: Historical and sociological remarks on teaching and teacher education". *Comparative Education* 41(4), 455–70.

Simon, H. A. (1972). "Theories of bounded rationality". *Decision and Organization* 1, 161–76.

Simon, H. A. (1982). *Models of bounded rationality: Empirically grounded economic reason.* Cambridge, MA: MIT Press.

Simon, H. A. (1991). "Bounded rationality and organizational learning". *Organization Science* 2 (1), 125–34.

Skocpol, T. (2013). *Diminished democracy: From membership to management in American civic life.* Norman, OK: University of Oklahoma Press.

Skowronek, S. (1982). *Building a new American state: The expansion of national administrative capacities, 1877–1920.* Cambridge: Cambridge University Press.

Skvortsov, N., Moskaleva, O., and Dmitrieva, J. (2013). "World-Class Universities: Experience and practices of Russian Universities". In Q. Wang, Y. Cheng, and N. C. Liu, (Eds), *Building World-Class Universities.* Rotterdam: SensePublishers, pp. 55–69.

Smelser, N. J., and Swedberg, R. (Eds). (2010). *The Handbook of Economic Sociology.* Princeton, NJ: Princeton University Press.

Sneddon, C., and Fox, C. (2007). "Power, development, and institutional change: Participatory governance in the lower Mekong basin". *World Development* 35(12), 2161–81.

Sørensen, E., and Torfing, J. (2005). "The democratic anchorage of governance networks". *Scandinavian Political Studies* 28(3), 195–218.

Sorensen, J. E., and Sorensen, T. L. (1974). "The conflict of professionals in bureaucratic organizations". *Administrative Science Quarterly* 19(1), 98–106.

Sorensen, J. N. (2002). "Safety culture: A survey of the state-of-the-art". *Reliability Engineering and System Safety* 76(2), 189–204.

Soule, S. A., and Olzak, S. (2004). "When do movements matter? The politics of contingency and the equal rights amendment". *American Sociological Review* 69(4), 473–97.

Soule, S. A., and Zylan, Y. (1997). "Runaway train? The diffusion of state-level reform in ADC/AFDC eligibility requirements, 1950–1967". *American Journal of Sociology* 103(3), 733–62.

Spector, M., and Kitsuse, J. (1987). *Constructing social problems.* Menlo Park, CA: The Benjamin Cummings Publishing Company.

Speer, P. W., and Hughey, J. (1995). "Community organizing: An ecological route to empowerment and power". *American Journal of Community Psychology* 23(5), 729–48.

Stacy, H. (2009). *Human rights for the 21st century: Sovereignty, civil society, culture.* Stanford, CA: Stanford University Press.

Starbucks website. (2013). Starbucks Ethical Coffee Sourcing and Farmer Support. Retrieved on July 23, 2013 <http://globalassets.starbucks.com/assets/6e52b26a7602471dbff32c9e66e685e3.pdf>.

Stark, D. (2011). *The sense of dissonance: Accounts of worth in economic life.* Princeton, NJ: Princeton University Press.

Starr, P. (1982). *The social transformation of American medicine: The rise of a sovereign profession and the making of a vast industry.* New York, NY: Basic Books.

Staw, B. M., and Epstein, L. D. (2000). "What bandwagons bring: Effects of popular management techniques on corporate performance, reputation, and CEO pay". *Administrative Science Quarterly* 45(3), 523–56.

Steinberg, P. E. (2006). "Calculating similitude and difference: John Seller and the 'placing' of English subjects in a global community of nations". *Social and Cultural Geography* 7, 687–707.

Stinchcombe, A. L. (1965). "Social structure and organizations". In J. March, (Ed.), *Handbook of Organizations.* Chicago, Il: Rand McNally, pp. 142–93.

Strang, D., and Meyer, J. W. (1993). "Institutional conditions for diffusion". *Theory and Society* 22(4), 487–511.

Strang, D., David, R. J., and Akhlaghpour, S. (2014). "Coevolution in management fashion: An agent-based model of consultant-driven innovation". *American Journal of Sociology* 120(1), 1–39.

Strange, S. (1996). *The retreat of the state: The diffusion of power in the world economy.* Cambridge: Cambridge University Press.

Strathern, M. (Ed.). (2000). *Audit cultures: Anthropological studies in accountability, ethics, and the academy.* London: Routledge.

Suarez, D., and Bromley, P. (2012). "Institutionalizing a global social movement: Human rights as university knowledge". *American Journal of Education* 118(3), 253–80.

Suddaby, R., Elsbach, K. D., Greenwood, R., Meyer, J. W., and Zilber, T. B. (2010). "Organizations and their institutional environments—Bringing meaning, values, and culture back in: Introduction to the special research forum". *Academy of Management Journal* 53(6), 1234–40.

Sullivan, W. M. (1995). *Work and integrity: The crisis and promise of professionalism in America.* San Francisco, CA: Jossey-Bass.

Sutton, J. R., and Dobbin, F. (1996). "The two faces of governance: Responses to legal uncertainty in US firms, 1955 to 1985". *American Sociological Review* 61(5), 794–811.

Sutton, J. R., Dobbin, F., Meyer, J. W., and Scott, W. R. (1994). "The legalization of the workplace". *American Journal of Sociology* 99(4): 944–71.

Swift, M. (2011). "At Google, groups are the key to the company's culture." *San Jose Mercury News.* Retrieved 1/30/2015 at <http://www.mercurynews.com/breaking-news/ci_18335726>.

Tabulawa, R. (2003). "International aid agencies, learner-centred pedagogy and political democratisation: A critique". *Comparative Education* 39(1), 7–26.

Taylor, Frederick, W. (1911). *The principles of scientific management.* New York and London: Harper Brothers.

Ten Thousand Villages website. (2013). History. Retrieved on July 23, 2013 from <http://www.tenthousandvillages.com/about-history>.

Thomas, G. M., and Meyer, J. W. (1984). "The expansion of the state". *Annual Review of Sociology* 10, 461–82.

Thornton, A. (2013). Reading history sideways: *The fallacy and enduring impact of the developmental paradigm on family life.* Chicago, IL: University of Chicago Press.

Thornton, P. H., and Ocasio, W. (2008). "Institutional logics". In Greenwood, R., Oliver, C., Suddaby, R., and Sahlin-Andersson, K. (Eds) *The Sage Handbook of Organizational Institutionalism.* Thousand Oaks, CA: Sage, pp. 99–129.

Thornton, P. H., Ocasio, W., and Lounsbury, M. (2012). *The institutional logics perspective: A new approach to culture, structure, and process.* Oxford: Oxford University Press.

Thrane, S. and Hald, K. S. (2006). "The emergence of boundaries and accounting in supply fields: The dynamics of integration and fragmentation". *Management Accounting Research* 17(3), 288–314.

Thurgood, L., Golladay, M. J., and Hill, S. T. (2006). *U.S. doctorates in the 20th century*, NSF 06-319. Arlington, VA: National Science Foundation, Division of Science Resources Statistics. Retrieved from <http://www.nsf.gov/statistics/nsf06319/pdf/nsf06319.pdf>.

Tilly, Charles. (1993). *Coercion, capital and European states, A.D. 990–1990.* New York: Wiley/Blackwell.

Tilly, Charles, (Ed.) (1975). *The formation of national states in Western Europe.* Princeton, NJ: Princeton University Press.

Tocqueville, A. de ([1890]1972). *Democracy in America.* New York, NY: Washington Square Press.

Tosi, H. L., Werner, S., Katz, J. P., and Gomez-Mejia, L. R. (2000). "How much does performance matter? A meta-analysis of CEO pay studies". *Journal of Management* 26(2), 301–39.

Touraine, A. (1971). *The post-industrial society: Tomorrow's social history: classes, conflicts and culture in the programmed society.* New York: Random House.

UNESCO Institute for Statistics. (2011). "Global Education Digest 2011: Comparing Education Statistics Across the World." Retrieved on 12/2/2013 at: <http://www.uis.UNESCO.org/Education/Documents/ged-2011-en.pdf>.

UNESCO Institute of Statistics. (2014). Retrieved at: <http://stats.uis.UNESCO.org/UNESCO/TableViewer/tableView.aspx?ReportId=3349andIF_Language=eng>.

Union of International Associations website. (2015). Retrieved on 1/27/2015 from <www.uia.org>.

US Department of Transportation website. (2013). Key Officials. Retrieved on July 25, 2013 from <http://www.dot.gov/key-officials>.

Van Buren III, H. J., and Greenwood, M. (2011). "Bringing stakeholder theory to industrial relations". *Employee Relations* 33 (1): 5–21.

Van Dooren, W. (2005). "What makes organisations measure? Hypotheses on the causes and conditions for performance measurement". *Financial Accountability and Management* 21(3), 363.

Van Reenen, J., Bloom, N., Draca, M., Kretschmer, T., Sadun, R., Overman, H., and Schankerman, M. (2010). *The economic impact of ICT. Final report to the European Commission.* London: Center for Economic Performance, London School of Economics.

Veblen, T. (1978). *The theory of business enterprise.* Piscataway, NJ: Transaction Publishers.

Verhoest, K., van Theil, S., Bouckaert, G., and Lægreid, P. (2012). *Government agencies: Practices and lessons from 30 countries.* London: Palgrave Macmillan.

Waddock, S. A., and Graves, S. B. (1997). "The corporate social performance". *Strategic Management Journal* 8(4), 303–19.

Wagenhofer, A. (2009). "Global accounting standards: Reality and ambitions". *Accounting Research Journal* 22(1), 68–80.

Walmart website. (2013). Executive Management. Retrieved on July 25, 2013 from <http://corporate.walmart.com/our-story/leadership/executive-management>.

Wampler, B. (2010). *Participatory budgeting in Brazil: Contestation, cooperation, and accountability.* University Park, PA: Pennsylvania State University Press.

Weber, E. (1976). *Peasants into Frenchmen: The modernization of rural France, 1870–1914.* Stanford, CA: Stanford University Press.

Weber, M. (1921). *Die rationalen und soziologischen Grundlagen der Musik.* Munich: Drei Masken Verlag.

Weber, M. (1958). *The Protestant ethic and the spirit of capitalism,* trans. Talcott Parsons. New York: Charles Scribner's Sons.

Weber, M. (1964). "The fundamental concepts of sociology". In M Weber, *The theory of social and economic organization.* New York: The Free Press, pp. 105–24.

Weber, M. (1968). *Economy and society.* New York: Bedminster.

Weick, K. E. (1976). "Educational organizations as loosely coupled systems". *Administrative Science Quarterly* 21(1), 1–19.

Weick, K. E. (1995). *Sensemaking in organizations.* Thousand Oaks, CA: Sage.

Weick, K. E. (1998). "Introductory essay—Improvisation as a mindset for organizational analysis". *Organization Science* 9(5), 543–55.

Weisbrod, B. A. (2000). *To profit or not to profit: The commercial transformation of the nonprofit sector.* New York: Cambridge University Press.

Weiss, T. G., and Wilkinson, R. (2014). "Rethinking global governance? Complexity, authority, power, change". *International Studies Quarterly* 58(1), 207–15.

Westphal, J. D., and Zajac, E. J. (2001). "Decoupling policy from practice: The case of stock repurchase programs". *Administrative Science Quarterly* 46(2), 202–28.

Westphal, J. D., and Zajac, E. J. (2013). "A behavioral theory of corporate governance: Explicating the mechanisms of socially situated and socially constituted agency". *The Academy of Management Annals* 7(1), 607–61.

Whetten, D. A. (2006). "Albert and Whetten revisited: Strengthening the concept of organizational identity". *Journal of Management Inquiry* 15(3), 219–34.

Whetten, D. A., and Mackey, A. (2002). "A social actor conception of organizational identity and its implications for the study of organizational reputation". *Business and Society* 41(4), 393–414.

Wilensky, H. L. (1964). "The professionalization of everyone?" *American Journal of Sociology* 7(2), 137–58.

Williamson, O. E. (1973). "Markets and hierarchies: Some elementary considerations". *The American Economic Review* 62(2): 316–25.

Williamson, O. E. (1981). "The economics of organization: The transaction cost approach". *American Journal of Sociology* 87(3): 548–77.

Woodward, J. (1958). *Management and technology*. London: HMSO.

Woolf, S. H., Chan, E. C., Harris, R., Sheridan, S. L., Braddock, C. H., Kaplan, R. M., Krist, A., O'Connor, A. M., and Tunis, S. (2005). "Promoting informed choice: Transforming health care to dispense knowledge for decision making". *Annals of internal medicine* 143(4), 293–300.

World Development Indicators Online (2013). Washington, DC: The World Bank.

World Fair Trade Organization. (2009) Charter of Fair Trade Principles. Retrieved on 1/28/2015 from <http://www.wfto.com/index.php?option=com_contentandtask=viewandid=1082andItemid=334andlimit=1andlimitstart=2>.

World Public Opinion. (2011). "Poll finds strong international consensus on human rights." Accessed 6/22/2015 at: <http://www.worldpublicopinion.org/pipa/articles/btjusticehuman_rightsra/701.php?lb=bthrandpnt=701andnid=andid=>.

Wotipka, C. M., and Ramirez, F. O. (2008). "World society and human rights". In B. Simmons, F. Dobbin, and G. Garrett (Eds), *The Global Diffusion of Markets and Democracy*. Cambridge: Cambridge University Press, pp. 303–43.

Wright, P., and Ferris, S. P. (1997). "Agency conflict and corporate strategy: The effect of divestment on corporate value". *Strategic Management Journal* 18(1), 77–83.

Yaziji, M., and Doh, J. (2009). *NGOs and corporations: Conflict and collaboration*. Cambridge: Cambridge University Press.

Zajac, E. J., and Westphal, J. D. (2004). "The social construction of market value: Institutionalization and learning perspectives on stock market reactions". *American Sociological Review* 69 (3), 433–57.

Zald, M. N., and McCarthy, J. D. (Eds). (1987). *Social movements in an organizational society: Collected essays*. Piscataway, NJ: Transaction Publishers.

Zelizer, V. A. (1981). "The price and value of children: The case of children's insurance". *American Journal of Sociology* 86(5), 1036–56.

Zelizer, V. A. (1985). *Pricing the priceless child: The changing social value of children*. Princeton, NJ: Princeton University Press.

Zorn, D. M. (2004). "Here a chief, there a chief: The rise of the CFO in the American firm". *American Sociological Review*, 69(3), 345–64.

Zuckerman, Ezra W. (1999). "The categorical imperative: Securities analysts and the illegitimacy discount". *American Journal of Sociology* 104(5): 1398–438.

▓ INDEX

Diagrams drawings etc are given in italics.